SOFTBALL

Steps to Success

Second Edition

Diane L. Potter, EdD
Gretchen A. Brockmeyer, EdD
Springfield College
Springfield, Massachusetts

Human Kinetics

Library of Congress Cataloging-in-Publication Data

Potter, Diane L., 1935-
Softball: steps to success / Diane L. Potter, Gretchen A. Brockmeyer. -- 2nd ed.
p. cm. -- (Steps to success activity series)
ISBN 0-87322-794-8
1. Softball--Training. 2. Slow pitch softball--Training.
I. Brockmeyer, Gretchen A., 1943- . II. Title. III. Series.
GV881.4.T72P68 1999
796.357'8--dc21 99-17942
CIP

ISBN: 0-87322-794-8

Acquisitions Editor: Jeff Riley; **Developmental Editor:** Julie A. Marx; **Assistant Editor:** Laura Ward Majersky; **Copyeditor:** Jacqueline Eaton Blakley; **Proofreader:** Myla Smith; **Graphic Designer:** Keith Blomberg; **Graphic Artist:** Nancy Loch; **Cover Designer:** Jack Davis; **Cover Photographer:** Tom Roberts; **Illustrators:** Keith Blomberg (line drawings) and Sharon Smith (diagrams); **Printer:** United Graphics

Human Kinetics books are available at special discounts for bulk purchase. Special editions or book excerpts can also be created to specification. For details, contact the Special Sales Manager at Human Kinetics.

Printed in the United States of America 10 9 8 7 6 5 4

Human Kinetics
Web site: www.HumanKinetics.com

United States: Human Kinetics, P.O. Box 5076, Champaign, IL 61825-5076
800-747-4457
e-mail: humank@hkusa.com

Canada: Human Kinetics, 475 Devonshire Road, Unit 100, Windsor, ON N8Y 2L5
800-465-7301 (in Canada only)
e-mail: orders@hkcanada.com

Europe: Human Kinetics, 107 Bradford Road, Stanningley
Leeds LS28 6AT, United Kingdom
+44 (0) 113 255 5665
e-mail: hk@hkeurope.com

Australia: Human Kinetics, 57A Price Avenue, Lower Mitcham, South Australia 5062
08 8277 1555
e-mail: liaw@hkaustralia.com

New Zealand: Human Kinetics, Division of Sports Distributors NZ Ltd.
P.O. Box 300 226 Albany, North Shore City, Auckland
0064 9 448 1207
e-mail: blairc@hknewz.com

CONTENTS

Preface	v
The Steps to Success Staircase	vii
The Game of Softball	1
Step 1 Catching and Throwing	**9**
Step 2 Fielding	**24**
Step 3 Pitching	**33**
Step 4 Hitting	**49**
Step 5 Baserunning	**69**
Step 6 Position Play	**85**
Step 7 Offensive Situational Play	**98**
Step 8 Defensive Situational Play	**111**
Step 9 Modified Games	**151**
Step 10 Coed Slow-Pitch Game	**168**
Rating Your Progress	170
Glossary	172
About the Authors	175

PREFACE

Over the years, it has been our observation that softball is an activity appearing in physical education curricula and in youth sports that typically is played, but not taught. Softball can be a wonderful game for participants of all ages. However, it is a wonderful game only when one has developed an understanding of, an appreciation for, and an ability to master the game concepts, as well as the physical skills needed. The teacher or coach who asks an unskilled player to apply yet-undeveloped skills and knowledge in a complex game setting is placing the participant in a no-win situation. The student or player who is placed in that kind of situation is likely destined for frustration, failure, and a dislike of the game.

This book is designed to take players through a progression of skill-development practice. You will move from practicing individual skills to combining two, three, and four skills in gamelike drill settings, and then apply them in modified games. Finally, you will be given the opportunity to display and demonstrate your skills and knowledge in regulation game play.

The major focus of this book is on skill development applicable to both the slow-pitch and fast-pitch games. In this second edition, sections on fast-pitch softball skills and offensive and defensive concepts have been added, since fast-pitch softball in school athletics and youth sport programs is becoming increasingly popular.

The practice drills described in this book are designed so that they can be practiced inside on a gymnasium floor or outside on any grass area, as well as on a regulation softball diamond. You will find that you do not need a fully lined softball field, 9- or 10-player teams, coaches, and uniforms to practice many of the fundamental skills. A wall, lines on a gymnasium floor, a rebound net, or a blanket hung over a clothesline can all be used by individuals, pairs, or groups of various sizes for practicing softball skills.

The preparation of this book was made possible through the assistance of many people, not all of whom can be mentioned by name. Over the years, many Springfield College students and players we have taught and coached have challenged our views of softball and how it should be taught. Coaching 7- to 10-year-olds in the Brimfield Youth Sports softball program over the past eight years has done much to enhance our perspective on the importance of developing fundamental skills and game concepts. Young players who have successfully mastered the fundamental skills and concepts of the game have been encouraged to continue to play as members of school varsity teams and recreational teams. We have learned from all of our students and players, and thus have developed the approach presented in this book. To all of you, we are forever indebted.

Once again our sincere thanks go to four Springfield College students who were responsible for the pictures provided to the illustrator for the first edition of this book: to David Blizard for his excellent photography, and to Jody Dobkowski, Shelly Quirk, and Christopher Mayhew, who were the models for the pictures. Many of these illustrations continue to be used in this second edition. Thanks to Bruce Oldershaw, former director of the audio-visual aids

(AVA) department at Springfield College, for his assistance with film developing. Thanks also to Kenneth Dawley, formerly of the AVA department, and to Tammy Oswell, a former player and student, who developed all of the film and printed the photographs used by the illustrator of the first edition. A special thanks goes to colleague Lynn Johnson from the University of Vermont for her continued encouragement and for her photographs of Erin Barney, one of her student-athletes who was the model for several new fast-pitch technique photographs used by the illustrator for this second edition. We especially thank colleague Diane Schumacher, Softball Hall of Famer and former Springfield College player, for her consultation and suggestions used in Step 3 regarding pitching.

One learns much as a player of the sport. Diane Potter wishes to especially acknowledge the influence of Ralph Raymond, coach of the 1996 U.S. gold-medal–winning Olympic team, as the inspiration for and essence of this book. Her passion for the game, emphasis on fundamentals, and pride in the execution of quality play are a direct result of his coaching years ago when she was a player on his Cochituate Corvettes team. Hopefully players, teachers, and coaches of all ages who use this book will be fortunate enough to have a comparable experience with the sport of softball.

We are indebted to Dr. Judy Patterson Wright, series editor; Jeff Riley, acquisitions editor; and Julie Marx, developmental editor of this second edition, for their encouragement, for serving as sounding boards for ideas, and for support throughout the preparation of the manuscript.

THE STEPS TO SUCCESS STAIRCASE

Get ready to climb a staircase—one that will lead you to be a great softball player. You cannot leap to the top; you get there by climbing one step at a time.

Each of the 10 steps you are about to take is an easy transition from the one before. The first few steps of the staircase provide a solid foundation of basic skills and concepts. As you progress, you will combine the single skills together in ways they are typically used in game situations. As you refine your physical skills, you will also learn game-play concepts as you apply the skills and combinations in modified games. Being able to anticipate, being ready, and becoming proficient at reading and reacting to game situations enable you to more fully and actively participate in the game of softball. You will learn to anticipate in batting, running, fielding, and throwing so that you make the proper plays and fulfill your various offensive and defensive positions. As you near the top of the staircase, the climb will ease, and you'll find that you have developed a sense of confidence in your softball-playing ability that makes further progress a real joy.

Familiarize yourself with this section, as well as the section "The Game of Softball," for an orientation and an understanding of how to set up your practice sessions around the steps.

Follow the same sequence each step (chapter) of the way:

1. Read the explanations of what is covered in the step, why the step is important, and how to execute or perform the step's focus, which may be a basic skill, concept, tactic, or a combination of them.
2. Follow the numbered illustrations in the Keys to Success showing exactly how to position your body to execute each basic skill successfully. There are three phases in each skill: preparation (getting into a starting position), execution (performing the skill that is the focus of the step), and follow-through (recovering to the starting position).
3. Look over the common errors that may occur and the recommendations of how to correct them.
4. Read the directions and the Success Goal for each drill. The drills help you improve your skills through repetition and purposeful practice, so practice accordingly and record your score. Compare your score with the Success Goal for the drill. You need to meet the Success Goal of each drill before moving on to practice the next one because the drills are arranged in an easy-to-difficult progression to help you achieve continued success. Pace yourself by adjusting the drills to increase or decrease difficulty.
5. Have a qualified observer—such as your teacher, coach, or trained partner—evaluate your basic skill technique as soon as you can reach all of the Success Goals for one step. Your observer should use the Keys to Success found at the beginning of most steps. This is a qualitative, or subjective, evaluation of your basic technique or form.
6. Repeat these procedures for each of the 10 Steps to Success. Then rate yourself according to the directions for "Rating Your Progress."

Good luck on your step-by-step journey to enhancing your softball skills, building confidence, experiencing success, and having fun!

THE GAME OF SOFTBALL

The history of softball is rich with stories of the exploits of individuals and teams. For example, there is the story of Kathy Arendsen, the current head softball coach at Mississippi State University who owns a 338-26 career pitching record, striking out Reggie Jackson, at that time the "Mr. October" of the New York Yankees and now a Baseball Hall of Famer, each of his three times at bat during a celebrity game. Another true story occurred in 1962 and is especially meaningful to one of your authors, because I was there as a member of the Cochituate Corvettes to play an exhibition benefit game against the Raybestos Brakettes. Prior to the game, Joan Joyce, considered by many to be the greatest women's fast-pitch pitcher of all time, pitched to Ted Williams, considered by most to be the greatest hitter of all time. From a pitching distance of 38 feet (the legal distance then), Joan threw pitches clocked at over 100 miles per hour. Unlike the other celebrities who missed every pitch they swung at, Ted fouled off one pitch and connected for one base hit during his batting stint. As a final example of one team's "game of a lifetime," prior to the institution of rules governing home runs in slow-pitch games, Steel's Silver Bullets of Grafton, Ohio scored 75 runs and hit 56 homers in a super-slow–pitch championship game in 1989.

The game we know today as softball was invented by George Hancock in 1887 at the Farragut Boat Club in Chicago. Hancock intended softball to be a game the rich members of the boat club could play indoors. Later, however, an outdoor version of the game called *kittenball* was developed by Lewis Rober, who introduced it to his fellow Minneapolis firemen. Today, *softball* (as it was finally named at a 1926 YMCA convention) is played all over the world by millions of people from all walks of life. The skills needed to play the game are few; very simply, one must be able to catch, throw, hit, and run bases with a moderate degree of skill.

The game of softball has several variations, each with unique rules that set it apart. There are official rules for coed slow-pitch softball and for men's and women's games of fast-pitch, modified-pitch, slow-pitch; boys and girls (youth) fast- and slow-pitch; 16-inch pitch; and a new addition—super-slow–pitch. The rules of men's and women's games vary only slightly; however, the rules for fast-pitch and slow-pitch make the games distinct from each other. Instruction in fast-pitch has been added to this second edition of *Softball: Steps to Success* because of the many requests from players, teachers, and coaches involved in the fast-pitch game.

Playing a Game

Official games of softball are played on a field like that depicted in figure 1. The *playing field* is the area within which the ball may be legally played and fielded. The playing field usually has as its boundaries an outfield fence, as well as two side fences extending from the ends of the backstop to the outfield fence and running parallel to and 25 to 30 feet from the foul lines. The area outside the playing field is the *out-of-play/dead-ball territory*. The playing field is made up of *fair territory*, which is that part of the playing field between and including the first- and third-base foul lines and the outfield fence, including the airspace above; and *foul territory*, that part of the playing field between the first- and third-base foul lines and the out-of-play/dead-ball territory. The playing field is further divided into *infield*, that portion of fair territory that includes areas normally covered by infielders; and *outfield*, that portion of fair territory that is outside the diamond formed by the base lines, or the area not normally covered by an infielder between first and third bases and the outfield fence. Most softball playing fields have a dirt infield (see the shaded area in figure 1) and a grass outfield.

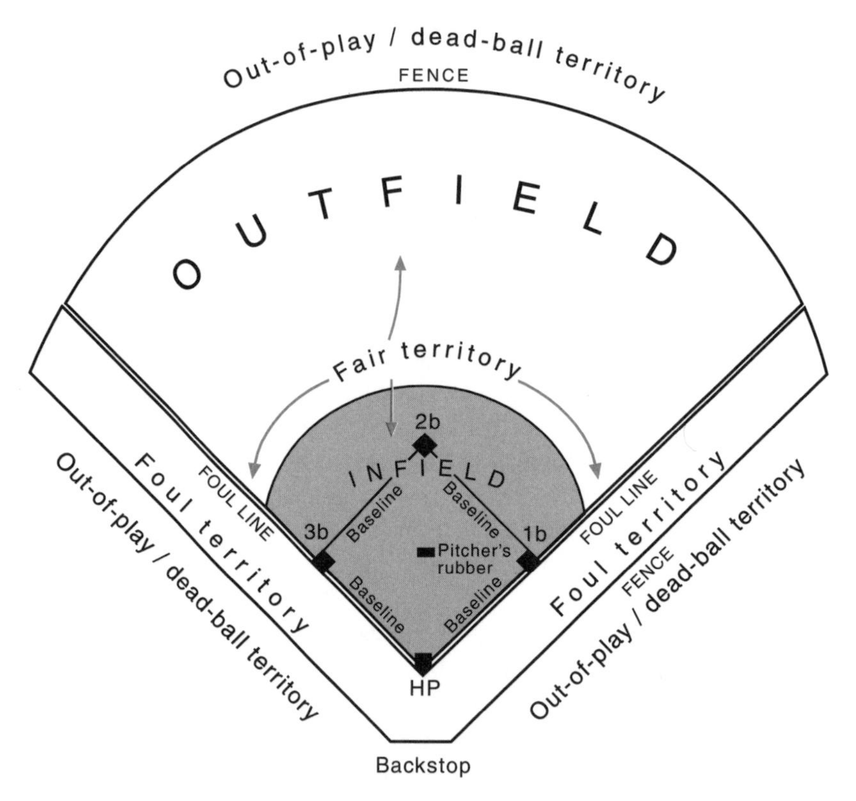

Figure 1 Softball playing field.

Distances between bases, pitching distances, and distances from home plate to the outfield fence vary, depending on the game being played. Unofficial games are played on all kinds of fields that have at least a home plate and three bases set out in a diamond figure.

Any variety of softball involves two teams alternately playing offense and defense. A team is on offense when it is *at bat*, attempting to score runs. The defensive team is the team *in the field*, attempting to prevent the team at bat from scoring runs. Fast-pitch and modified-pitch teams have 9 players in the field on defense, whereas all slow-pitch teams have 10 defensive players, although some allow extra players to bat. Defensive positions are identified by the numbers 1 through 10 as follows: pitcher (1), catcher (2), first baseman (3), second baseman (4), third baseman (5), shortstop (6), left fielder (7), center fielder (8), right fielder (9), and (in slow-pitch only) short fielder (10). (See figure 2.) The left fielder, center fielder, right fielder, and short fielder are called *outfielders. Infielders* are the first baseman, second baseman, third baseman, and shortstop. The pitcher and catcher, though playing in the infield and having some of the same kinds of responsibilities as infielders, are usually called the *battery*, rather than infielders.

Games are played in *innings;* an inning is completed when each team has had a time at bat, making three outs, and has played defense in the field for the three outs of the other team. (An *out* occurs when an offensive player does not reach a base safely). A *regulation game* consists of seven innings. In competitive play, the choice of first or last at bat in an inning is decided by a coin toss, unless stated differently in the rules of the organization governing the game. The *visiting team* is up to bat first in an inning; the *home team* bats last. Typically, in any kind of league play, the team upon whose field the game is being played is the home team.

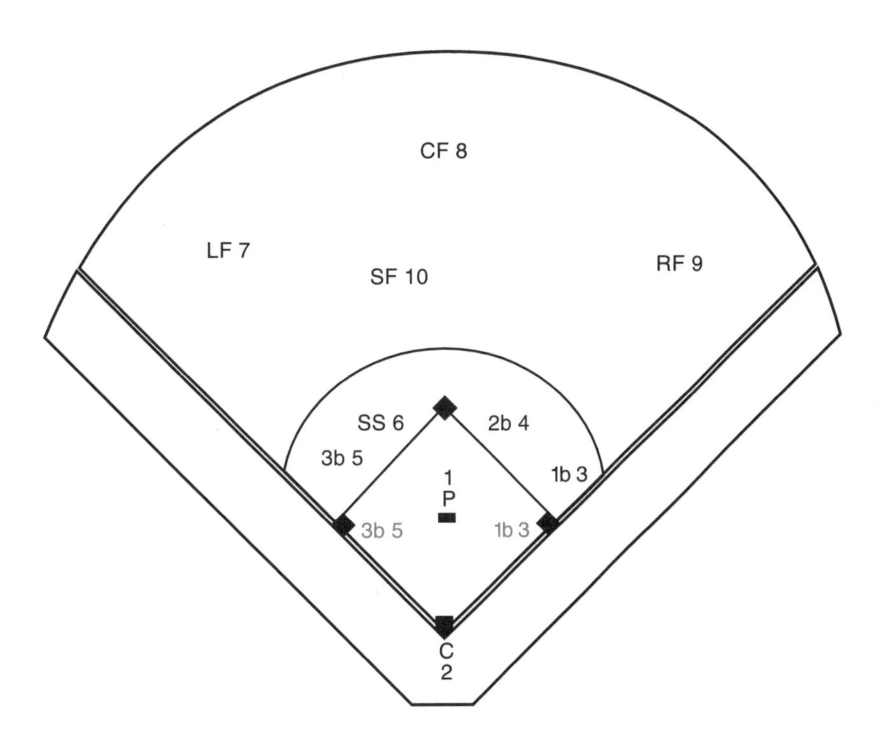

Figure 2 Starting positions (first- and third-base starting positions for fast-pitch are shown in color).

A *run* is scored each time a baserunner legally touches first base, second base, third base, and home plate before the defensive team makes the third out of the inning. The winner of a game is the team that scores the greater number of runs.

In addition to the preceding basic rules of play, other rules are introduced and explained as they apply to specific skills and concepts taught in this book. Reference is made throughout the book to official and modified rules of play. *Official* rules are those used in an official game between two high school, college, summer league, or Olympic teams. High schools play under the rules of either the National Federation of State High Schools Association (NFHS) or the National Association of Girls and Women in Sport (NAGWS). College women play under the rules of either the National Collegiate Athletic Association (NCAA) or NAGWS. Recreational teams play under the rules of the Amateur Softball Association (ASA). The United States Specialty Sports Association (USSSA) governs the play in some slow-pitch leagues. International play is governed by the rules of the International Softball Federation (ISF). The majority of the official fast-pitch softball rules for high schools, colleges, and for the ASA are the same because they follow the rules made by the International Softball Federation. However, the aforementioned organizations do have a few rules that apply only to their own competitions. For the purposes of this book, discussion of rules as they occur in the learning progressions is based on the ASA's *Official Rules of Softball.*

Modified rules, on the other hand, are rules that the teacher or coach makes up, usually to encourage students to focus on a particular skill or combination of skills. The player rotation rules used in the modified game called Scrub (Step 9), for example, are designed to ensure that every player experiences playing all the defensive field positions. Those rules are not official and would not be used during any official game.

A glossary is provided at the end of this book. Turn to that section and become familiar with the definitions of softball terms *before* you begin your climb up the Steps to Success staircase. This glossary does not include *all* the terms used in softball, however. If you are interested in looking at a complete set of rules and definitions, check out an official rulebook at your local library or a sports store where softball equipment and clothing are sold.

Equipment Selection and Safety Concerns

In order to play softball safely, you need to have reliable equipment and practice facilities free from danger. Here are some suggestions for selecting personal equipment and for safety checks prior to practicing softball skills.

When selecting personal equipment for softball, consider the following:

1. Fielder's glove
   - All leather, including laces and bound edges of hand opening (be especially wary of plastic or synthetic materials in laces and edges)
   - Easily adjustable strap over back of hand (Velcro is nice)
   - Size large, but manageable; shorter finger length for second baseman, third baseman, and shortstop; longer for outfielder, first baseman, and catcher (if a fielder's glove is used instead of a mitt at first-base or catcher positions)
2. Bat
   - Length and weight enabling you to swing the barrel of the bat into the contact zone easily
   - Grip size that feels comfortable in your hands and composition that ensures a secure grip for your hands on the handle (a safety grip is required on all bats)
   - Composition: hardwood, metal, plastic, graphite, carbon, magnesium, fiberglass, and ceramic. Most bats used in softball today are made from an aluminum alloy. Your selection of a bat may be governed more by price than by the material the bat is made from, although those two factors are closely related. It is quite possible to

spend hundreds of dollars for a softball bat! Aluminum bats have two advantages: the ball comes off the bat faster and travels a greater distance, and the bats do not break during normal use and therefore last a long time. Metal bats can be dented as a result of hitting rocks, but not as a result of hitting a softball.

3. Batting glove
   - The batting glove, initially worn only on the hand holding the bottom end of the bat, was first used in baseball to ensure a more secure grip on the wooden bat. Unlike wooden softball bats that by rule must have a composition grip attached to the handle area, the wooden baseball bat by rule had to be made from one solid piece of wood with the grip area free from any foreign substance. Very often sweaty bare hands on bare wood resulted in the bat flying out of the hands of the batter during a swing. The metal softball bat used most often today typically has a replaceable rubber-type grip that offers a secure handhold on the bat for the batter. Although the safety need for the batting glove in softball is not the same as for baseball, the trend is for players to mimic the major league player and wear not one but two batting gloves! For defensive players, especially the catcher and the first baseman, wearing a batting glove under the fielding glove offers added protection for the hand catching the ball.
4. Footwear
   - Shoes with soft or hard rubber cleats are the footwear of choice for most youth and recreational softball programs. Metal sole or heel plates are allowed in some levels of play if the cleat on the plate is not longer than three-quarters of an inch. Round or track-type spikes are not allowed. Before selecting your footwear for softball, be sure to check the rules governing your specific level of play.

All equipment must be in compliance with the rules governing play. For example, if play is governed by ASA rules, the bat must be marked "Official Softball" by the manufacturer. A bat marked "Little League"—even if it complies with the ASA requirements of length, weight, maximum barrel size, and so on—could not be used by a player in a game being played under ASA rules.

For safety's sake, do the following before practicing or playing softball:

1. Periodically check your own personal equipment:
   - Glove—for broken laces, especially in the web area
   - Footwear—well fitting, no holes, strong arch support, soles that provide good traction (especially on wet or damp ground)
   - Shirt—loose fitting so that it does not restrict your movements, especially for throwing
   - Pants or shorts—loose fitting for free movement
   - Sunglasses—if used, should have nonbreakable safety lenses
2. Check the playing field for these:
   - Glass and other sharp objects
   - Holes in the field
   - Dangerous obstructions, such as football blocking sleds, lacrosse or field hockey goals, and so on
   - Loose equipment lying around, especially balls and bats
3. When practicing skills, remember these tips:
   - When working with a partner on throwing, fielding, and so on, line up so neither player looks directly into the sun.

- When inside, or outside near a building, be aware of windows, lights, and people; do not practice with a window in the line of flight of the ball.
- Be sympathetic to the skill ability of partners.
- Do not throw the bat!
- Do not hit rocks with the bat!

Softball Today

Participation opportunities abound for softball enthusiasts of all ages and abilities. The Amateur Softball Association (ASA) is the governing body for softball in the United States. Under the sponsorship of the ASA, 270,000 teams participate each year in a wide variety of classifications of fast-pitch and slow-pitch programs. There is also a full ASA program for youth teams and a Junior Olympic program that has 73,500 participating teams. Softball is played by millions of people in over 100 countries of the world. International competition opportunities are growing every year. The World Championship and the Pan American Games are well established. However, it was not always so.

The women's fast-pitch game is the game currently gaining the most attention. The Women's NCAA National Collegiate Softball Championships can be seen on television, and women's fast-pitch softball finally became an Olympic sport at the 1996 Atlanta Games. The road to that historic event was a long and arduous one, starting in 1965 with the first International Softball Federation (ISF) World Championships held in Melbourne, Australia. Australia defeated the highly favored United States team to become the first world champions. The second world championship was held in Japan in 1970, and the host Japanese team defeated the United States to become the new world champions. Finally, in 1974, at the world championship held in Stratford, Connecticut, the United States, represented by the Raybestos Brakettes, won the third world championship. Softball was first played at the Pan American Games in 1979, and that event continues to provide strong international competition for the United States national team as it prepares for the world championships and now the Olympics. The United States national team won the gold medal in Atlanta, and now young girls and women have their own female role models in Olympic stars Lisa Fernandez, Dot Richardson, Laura Berg, and Sheila Cornell Douty. The increased exposure from the Olympics has caused a trickle-down effect to school and local recreation programs, in which more and more girls are participating in fast-pitch softball. With the inclusion of softball in the National Sports Festival (now the United States Olympic Festival), the development of Olympic-level competitors is an ongoing process.

Should you not aspire to Olympic-level competition, there are still hundreds of thousands of recreational teams providing opportunities for participation at every level of ability. Softball truly is a sport for everyone:

- It can be played and enjoyed by all ages and abilities from "10-and-under" to "50-and-over" leagues.
- It is an excellent coed activity with special coed rules.
- It can be played on the local sandlot as well as in an Olympic stadium.
- It requires you to participate mentally as well as physically.
- It provides a "social occasion" for you to enjoy old friends and make new ones.

Now grab a ball and take the field!

Warm-up and Cool-down

Prior to practicing, you need a 5- to 10-minute warm-up period to increase your heart rate and flexibility. After finishing your practice, end with a five-minute cool-down period. If you follow this sequence, you will not only help prepare your body and mind to play softball—you'll also help prevent injuries.

Your first goal is to "get your blood moving." Starting at home plate, jog around the perimeter of the field and return to home plate. Next, select and complete one of the aerobic exercises below. Both selections will increase your heart rate and utilize some movements used in the game.

1. Stand at first base, facing home plate with your left foot against the inside edge of the base, knees bent, hands on knees. Staying low, pivot to your right and sprint to second base, taking your first step with your left foot (this is a *crossover step start*). Stop at second base (do not overrun the base). Immediately assume the same position at this base and, using the crossover step start, sprint to third (again, do not overrun). Repeat from third going to home plate (you *may* overrun home plate). Stand in a *track-start* position at home plate (crouch position facing first base, feet in forward stride with one foot on the plate). Sprint to first base, overrunning the base. Turn *to the left*, return to the base quickly, and assume the *rocker-start* position (stand over the base, one foot on the front edge, the other foot on the ground behind the base). Take your first step with the foot behind the base and sprint to second (do not overrun as before). Continue as in the first round, this time using the rocker start at each base until crossing home plate. These two complete laps complete the exercise. Run at top speed between bases. Set up and start to sprint to the next base quickly. Little time should elapse between sprints.
2. Place two gloves 10 feet apart on the ground (or use some other appropriate flat markers—*do not use balls or bats!*). Run around the gloves in a figure-eight pattern, crossing in the center between the gloves. Do 10 repetitions starting around the first glove in a clockwise direction, then 10 traveling in the opposite direction (you need to unwind!).

Now that you have the blood flowing to your muscles, you need to spend a few minutes stretching the muscles you will be using so you don't pull or injure them. The shoulders, arms, torso, back, and legs will typically be used in any softball practice or game. Do your exercises in a relaxed state of mind and body. Move slowly into the stretch position and hold it for 8 to 10 seconds. *Do not bounce in the stretch position.* During the 8- to 10-second stretch, relax and at the end of 10 seconds try to gently increase the range of the stretch. Be sure to do at least one exercise for each body part listed above. There are several books on stretching that can give you specific exercises if you need ideas.

At the end of each practice session or game, take a few minutes to cool down by stretching out those muscles used the most and relaxing so that your heart rate returns to a resting rate. Concentrate on your body as you properly stretch each part. A properly stretched muscle is a relaxed muscle. This is the best time to stretch, because your muscles are warm. It takes only five minutes to repeat at least one each of the shoulder, arm, torso, back, and leg warm-up exercises. Spending a few minutes in this cool-down period will help prevent soreness and stiffness after a hard practice or game.

National and International Organizations

Use the following resources and organizations to learn more about softball rules and programs in your area.

The NAGWS Softball Guide can be purchased from
The American Alliance for Health, Physical Education, Recreation and Dance
1900 Association Drive
Reston, VA 20191
Phone: 1-800-213-7193
ISBN: 0-88314-389-5

The National Governing Body for softball is
The Amateur Softball Association of America
2801 N.E. 50th Street
Oklahoma City, OK 73111-7203
Phone: 405-424-5266
Web site: **http://www.softball.org/**

United States Specialty Sports Association
3935 South Crater Road
Petersburg, VA 23805
Phone: 804-732-4099
Web site: **http://www.usssa.com/**

International Softball Federation
4141 N.W. Expressway, Suite 340
Oklahoma City, OK 73116
Phone: 405-879-9801
Web site: **http://www.worldsport.com/sports/softball/home.html**

Legend for diagrams

P	Pitcher	CF	Center fielder	(wavy arrow)	Rolled ball
C	Catcher	RF	Right fielder	(long-dash arrow)	Hit ball
1b	First baseman	SF	Short fielder	(short-dash arrow)	Thrown ball
2b	Second baseman	B	Batter	(solid arrow)	Player movement
3b	Third baseman	BBR	Batter baserunner		
SS	Shortstop	H	Hitter		
LF	Left fielder	F	Fielder		

STEP 1 CATCHING AND THROWING

Softball is a game of *catching* and *throwing*. Imagine yourself in the following situations: A hard line drive is hit to you at shortstop. In one fluid motion, you catch the ball and throw it to the first baseman, doubling up the runner who left too soon. Or imagine that as the left fielder, you race to your right to catch a fly ball, stop, and, stepping in the direction of your throw, throw the ball to second base to prevent the runner on first from advancing. The fundamental defensive skills of *catching* and *throwing* are keys to your success as a softball player. Every softball player, regardless of position played, must master these skills. The term *catching* also describes the unique way the catcher receives the ball from the pitcher. Another related skill is *fielding*, which is a term used for catching ground balls and fly balls. These skills will be dealt with later in the book. Right now you are going to learn how to catch, move the ball and your body into the throwing position, and throw the ball—all in one continuous, fluid motion.

There are three general types of throws used in softball: *overhand*, *sidearm*, and *underhand*. The full, hard underhand throw is commonly used only by the fast-pitch pitcher (see Step 3). However, various underhand *tosses*, including the slow-pitch pitch and the short *feed* to second base to start the double play, might technically be called underhand throws. The sidearm throw (see Step 8) is used for relatively short throws where the ball must travel with speed, parallel to the ground. The highly skilled infielder will occasionally use the sidearm throw when, after fielding a ground ball, a quick-release throw is necessary because of lack of time. It is the least accurate of the throws and should be used sparingly.

The overhand throw is the one most often used in the game of softball. It is especially useful when the ball must travel a significant distance and when accuracy is a factor. Because of the major role the overhand throw plays in softball, it is the first throw to learn if you are a less experienced player, or to review if you are more experienced. The overhand throw is your ticket to being a successful defensive player, and therefore receives the most attention in this section.

Why Are Catching and Throwing the Ball Important?

Can you imagine someone throwing you the ball and your not knowing what to do to protect yourself? Or imagine yourself playing center field, catching a fly ball, and not being able to get the ball to second base—never mind all the way to home plate. In a game, your ability to catch and quickly throw the ball helps you make a play on a baserunner attempting to advance to the next base, and outfielders *must* use the overhand throw because of the great distance the ball must travel.

How to Execute the Catch

Initially, catching a ball involves *tracking* the ball—watching it and determining the path it is taking—then moving your body, glove, and throwing hand into that path in order to catch the ball. As a fielder, you have no control over the flight of the ball. Therefore, in order to catch a ball, you must visually pick up the flight of the ball by focusing on it while it is coming toward you and move your body in line with the oncoming ball. Once you are in line with the ball, stand squarely, facing the ball with your glove-side foot slightly ahead. Reach your hands out in front of your body to make contact with the ball, and simultaneously shift your weight onto your front foot.

Catching a ball also involves *anticipation* and a certain amount of *decision-making* on your part. If the ball is arriving above your waist, point the fingers

FIGURE 1.1 **KEYS TO SUCCESS**

TRACKING AND ANTICIPATION

Above Waist

1. Point fingers up ___
2. Focus on ball ___
3. Line up body to ball ___

Below Waist

1. Point fingers down ___
2. Focus on ball ___
3. Line up body to ball ___

At Waist

1. Point fingers horizontally ___
2. Focus on ball ___
3. Line up body to ball ___

of your glove and of your throwing hand up, as shown in figure 1.1a. If the ball is below your waist, your fingers point down (see figure 1.1b). A ball coming directly at your waist is often the hardest to catch; to catch it, position your glove hand palm-down, fingers parallel to the ground with thumb down, and place your throwing hand palm-up under your glove hand, as shown in figure 1.1c. Correct positioning of the hands is crucial to effective catching.

After making the tracking and anticipation decisions about the ball coming toward you, you are now ready to catch the ball. As the ball comes into your glove, squeeze the ball with the thumb and ring finger of your glove hand and at the same time cover the ball with your throwing hand. "Give" with the ball (also called using "soft hands"), cushioning its impact, by drawing the ball and glove toward your throwing-side shoulder. As you move the ball and glove to the throwing position, take a two-finger grip on the ball by placing your index and middle fingers on one seam and your thumb on a seam on the side of the ball opposite your fingers (see figure 1.2).

At the same time, shift your weight onto your back foot and turn your body so that your glove side is toward the throwing target. With your weight on your back foot, separate your hands and bring the ball in

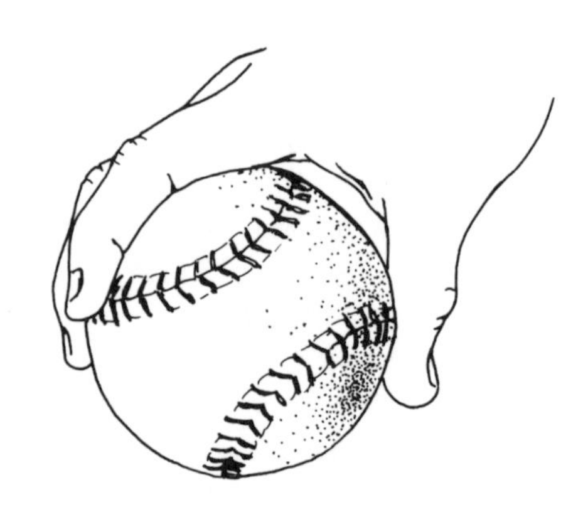

Figure 1.2 Two-finger grip.

your throwing hand to the throwing position. Your glove-side elbow should point at the throwing target. This follow-through position for catching a ball is the beginning of the preparatory phase for the overhand throw. This action makes it possible for you to make the transition from the catch to the throw one continuous motion. Figure 1.3a-c shows the catch-to-throw transition leading into the preparation phase for the throw when the ball arrives above your waist.

Using two hands to catch the ball not only makes for a surer catch, but also makes it easier for you to throw the ball quickly, because you already have the ball in your throwing hand as soon as you catch the ball. Catching the ball one-handed with the glove only makes for a more time-consuming transition from catch to throw and results in a much slower release time. One-handed catches should be used only when the ball is out of your two-hand reach.

FIGURE 1.3 **KEYS TO SUCCESS**

CATCHING

a

b

c

Preparation

1. Feet in forward stride, glove-side foot ahead ___
2. Focus on ball ___
3. Adjust glove to ball height ___
   - ball above waist, fingers up
   - ball below waist, fingers down
   - ball at waist, fingers parallel to ground
4. Shift weight forward ___
5. Meet ball out front ___

Execution

1. Use two hands, squeeze ball ___
2. Start shifting weight back, begin pivot ___
3. Give with the ball ___
4. Two-finger grip on ball in glove ___

Follow-Through

1. Continue to shift weight back ___
2. Glove side toward target ___
3. Glove elbow points to target ___
4. Weight on back foot ___
5. Arms extend, move ball to throwing position ___
6. Throwing wrist extends ___

How to Execute the Overhand Throw

To initiate the overhand throw, continue from the position described in the follow-through phase of the catch (figure 1.3c). As you take the ball out of your glove, be sure to grip the ball across the seams with the first two fingers and thumb of your throwing hand as shown in figure 1.2. Now say to yourself, "Turn, step, and throw." These cues will remind you to *turn* your glove side toward the target while extending your throwing hand back; to *step* in the direction of the target with your glove-side foot, shifting your weight onto that foot while keeping your hips square to the target; and to *throw* the ball by bringing your arm forward and snapping your wrist, leading with the elbow. Keep your elbow high and your upper arm parallel to the ground. Rotate your forearm through the vertical, keeping the ball high as it goes by your head. After you release the ball, your weight will be forward, your knees will be bent, your throwing shoulder forward, your throwing hand low and to the outside of your glove-side knee, and your throwing-side foot will come forward to put you in a balanced position. Figure 1.4a-c shows the three phases of the overhand throw, which is the completion of the catch-and-throw combination skill.

FIGURE 1.4 **KEYS TO SUCCESS**

OVERHAND THROW

Preparation

1. Weight on back foot ___
2. Glove side to target ___
3. Arms extended, glove to target ___
4. Wrist cocked, ball to rear ___

Execution

1. Step toward target ___
2. Push off rear foot ___
3. Elbow leads throw, hand trails ___
4. Weight on front foot ___
5. Hips square ___
6. Forearm rotates through vertical ___
7. Ball high ___
8. Glove hand low ___
9. Snap wrist ___

Follow-Through

1. Wrist snapped ___
2. Weight forward ___
3. Knees bent ___
4. Throwing hand low ___
5. Throwing shoulder forward ___
6. Assume balanced position ___

How to Apply Catching and Throwing in Game Situations

Playing catch with a partner will help you anticipate how a teammate will work with you as you catch and throw in a game. In a game, the ball is seldom hit or thrown directly at you, so it's difficult to use your basic catching and throwing technique in a stationary position. You must be able to *adapt* the basic techniques of catching and throwing for various circumstances that arise when playing the game.

You should always try to get your entire body in front of the ball when catching. Catching the ball outside of the midline of the body should be attempted only when it is impossible to get the body in front of the ball. For most people, the glove-side catch (either two-hand or one-hand) is easier than the catch on the throwing side, because the glove hand is on the same side of the body as the ball. To glove the ball one-handed, merely extend your arm and body toward the ball, making sure the pocket of your glove is open to receive the ball (see figure 1.5a). Catching the ball on the throwing side involves *backhanding* the ball (see figure 1.5b). This means moving your glove hand across your body to the throwing side and turning the glove over, its thumb side toward the ground, the fingers parallel to the ground, and

FIGURE 1.5 **KEYS TO SUCCESS**

CATCHING OUTSIDE THE MIDLINE OF THE BODY

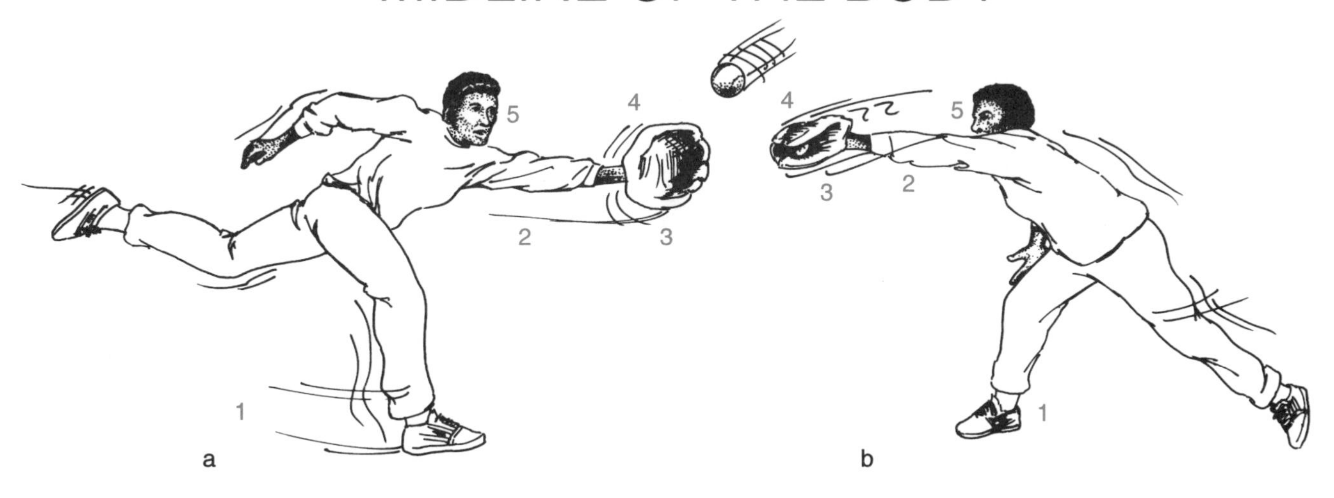

Glove-Side (Forehand) Catch

1. Move to the ball ___
2. Reach out to catch ball ___
3. Glove pocket open to ball ___
4. Thumb up, little finger down ___
5. Focus on the ball ___

Throwing-Side (Backhand) Catch

1. Move to the ball ___
2. Glove hand across body ___
3. Turn glove over, thumb toward the ground ___
4. Glove pocket open to ball ___
5. Focus on the ball ___

the open pocket facing the line of direction of the throw. Because you must reach across your body to make this catch, you cannot extend as far as when going to the glove side. If necessary, you can increase your reach by turning your back on the ball's origin and stepping toward the ball with your glove-side foot. However, in order to make this catch, you have probably sacrificed the smooth transition into the throw. Thus, whenever you can, get your body in front of the ball; then you will be in a good position to follow up with a throw. Even if the ball is outside the midline of the body, if you can reach the ball with two hands, catch it with two hands.

How to Catch and Throw in One Continuous Motion

In a game situation, catching and throwing are typically combined into one skill. The continuous motion from one skill (catching) to the other (throwing) saves time and makes it more likely that you will execute the play successfully. To make the catch and throw continuous, remember that the follow-through phase of the catch becomes the preparation phase for the throw. Figure 1.6a-c shows the continuous motion of the catch-to-throw transition.

FIGURE 1.6 KEYS TO SUCCESS

COMBINED CATCH AND THROW

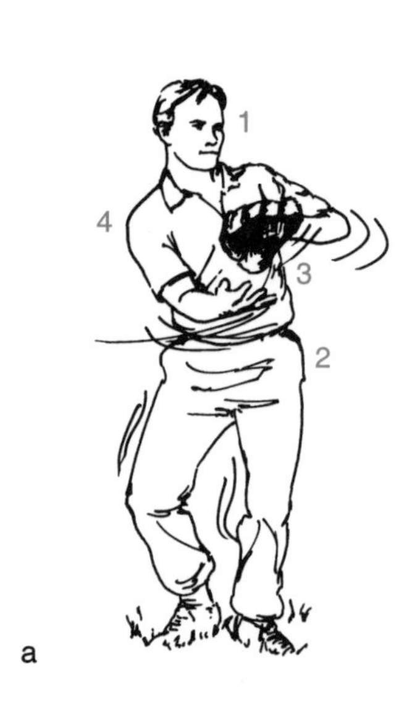

Catch

1. Focus on ball ___
2. Body lined up with ball ___
3. Use two hands ___
4. Give with the ball ___

Turn

1. Weight back ___
2. Glove side to target ___
3. Two-finger grip ___
4. Ball to rear shoulder ___

Throw

1. Step to target ___
2. Elbow leads ___
3. Ball high ___
4. Snap wrist ___

CATCHING AND THROWING SUCCESS STOPPERS

Catching and throwing problems are usually caused by failure to watch the ball go into the glove and by improper release of the ball. Catching the ball with one hand and "short-arming" the throw or failing to go through the full range of motion are also common mistakes in catching and throwing.

Error	Correction
Catching	
1. You miss the ball or the ball drops out of your glove.	1. Watch the ball. Use two hands. Cover the ball with your throwing hand as soon as the ball enters your glove.
2. The ball stings your hand when you catch it.	2. Give with the ball as you make contact; reach out in front to meet the ball, and draw the glove and ball to your throwing shoulder.
Overhand Throwing	
1. The ball doesn't go very far.	1. You may be "pushing" the ball. Extend your arm fully to the rear to initiate the throw. Lead with your elbow as you bring the ball forward.
2. The ball's trajectory is too high.	2. Snap your wrist as you release the ball, or release the ball later.
3. The ball curves when you make a long throw, or goes to the right or left of the target.	3. Check that you are throwing overhand, not sidearm. Be sure your elbow is up and your forearm passes your head vertically. Step toward the target as you throw. Imagine that you are throwing your hand toward the target as you release the ball.
Combined Catch and Throw	
1. The ball transfer from glove to throwing hand is slow.	1. Catch the ball with two hands, then immediately take the two-finger grip.
2. Your catch and release is slow.	2. Move into position to catch the ball in front of your throwing side, and make the catch and throw one continuous motion.

CATCHING AND THROWING DRILLS

1. Self-Toss

Without using a glove, gently toss a ball up into the air in front of your body so that it goes just above head height. Using both hands, reach up and out to catch the ball, draw it into your throwing shoulder, and then drop your hands and toss it again. Now, toss the ball onto a high, slanted surface, such as the roof of a shed or garage, so that it will roll off for you to catch. As you concentrate on the catching action, focus on the cue "reach and give" in the self-toss and the roof practice.

Success Goal = 20 catches without dropping the ball:
10 from a self-toss ___
10 from a roof toss ___

Success Check

- Reach up to meet the ball, and watch it go into your hands ___
- Give with the ball as it comes into your hands ___
- Bring the ball and hands to the throwing position ___

To Increase Difficulty

- Increase the distance you toss the ball so you have to move farther to catch it.
- Increase the height you toss the ball so you can work on more difficult tracking skills.

To Decrease Difficulty

- Use a Nerf or Wiffle ball.
- Use a lower toss.

2. Partner Toss

With a partner, stand 10 feet apart, facing one another. Using your gloves, one ball, and underhand tosses, toss and catch back and forth for 15 catches each. Be sure to stand in a forward-stride position, your glove-side foot ahead, when catching. As part of the catch, focus on bringing the ball to the throwing position. Remember to focus on "reach, give, and prepare to throw."

Success Goal = 30 catches without dropping the ball ___

Success Check

- Feet in forward stride, glove-side foot ahead ___
- Reach to meet the ball in front of your body ___
- Use two hands, squeeze the ball in your glove ___
- Take a two-finger grip, bring the ball to the throwing position ___

To Increase Difficulty

- Catch at three different levels: above the waist, below the waist, and at the waist.
- Tosser may vary the height and distance of the toss to each side of the receiver's body.

To Decrease Difficulty

- Use a softer ball.
- Tosser may use a softer toss.
- Use a larger ball.

3. Fence Throw

Stand 20 feet away from an unobstructed high fence, such as the backstop (decrease the distance if using a shorter fence). Throw the ball directly against the fence 10 times. Repeat the phrase "turn, step, and throw" to yourself as you go through the complete throwing action. Be sure that your arm goes through the full range of motion, and make the entire motion smooth.

Success Goal = 10 throws with correct form as shown in figure 1.4 ___

Success Check

- Turn so your glove side is toward the fence with throwing arm extended fully to the rear ___
- Step toward the fence with glove-side foot ___
- Throw with your hand and elbow high as the ball passes forward by the head ___
- Follow through to your glove-side knee ___

To Increase Difficulty

- Make the target smaller.
- Increase the distance of the throw.

To Decrease Difficulty

- From a standing position, "turn, step, and throw" the ball as far as you can and run after it. Throw it back as far as you can and run to get it. Focus on "turn, step, and throw" each time you throw.

4. Target Accuracy

When you play softball, it is crucial to be able to throw the ball where you want. If you cannot throw the ball to the proper place, you will not be fully doing your part to help your team get baserunners out.

Mark a target about chest-high on a fence or a wall. Make the target a rectangle that is big enough for you to hit with a throw from 20 feet (if you have little experience, make the target at least 8 feet wide; if you are more experienced, make the target narrower).

a. Stand 20 feet from the target. Using the overhand throwing motion, throw 10 balls at the target. As you throw, say to yourself "turn, step, and throw." Remember, you want to use the *full range* of the throwing motion. Even though this drill uses a target, you should focus on the "turn, step, and throw" actions of the overhand motion.
b. Throw 10 more balls at the same target. This time, concentrate on the target throughout the throwing action.

Success Goal =

a. At least 5 throws hitting the target ___
b. 8 overhand throws hitting the target out of 10 attempts ___

Success Check

- Point your glove at the target ___
- Step toward the target with your glove-side foot ___
- Forcefully rotate your forearm forward ___
- Shift your body weight forward as you follow through ___

To Increase Difficulty

- Decrease the size of the target.
- Lengthen the throwing distance.

To Decrease Difficulty

- Increase the size of the target.
- Shorten the distance of the throw.

5. Increase the Distance

You need to be accurate when throwing the ball different distances. You sometimes have to throw the ball a long distance (from the outfield), and other times your throw will be shorter (from the infield).

On the floor (or field) in front of the target used in the last drill, mark off distances of 20, 30, 40, 50, and 60 feet.

a. Stand on the 20-foot mark. Using the overhand throw, deliver 10 consecutive balls toward the target. Count the number of on-target hits. Each time you meet the Success Goal, move back to the next mark and repeat the drill. You may not move back to a greater distance until you meet the goal for each target. See whether you can work your way back to a distance of 60 feet (the distance from home plate to first base).

Success Goal = 8 on-target throws out of 10 attempts at each distance ___

Success Check

- Focus on the target ___
- Force your body weight forward by driving off the back foot ___
- At the point of release, your fingers are directly behind the ball ___
- As you release the ball, snap your wrist toward the target ___

b. The players to whom you throw the ball in a softball game are much smaller than the target you have been throwing at. In fact, the target for a game throw is the glove of the person catching the ball. Make your drill target narrower and repeat the drill. Deliver 10 overhand throws from each distance and count the number of on-target hits. Remember, you cannot move back to the next distance until you meet the appropriate Success Goal.

Success Goal = 8 on-target throws out of 10 attempts at each distance ___

Success Check

- As you release the ball, have your fingers directly behind the ball, and snap your wrist ___
- As you follow through, drive your throwing-side shoulder forward and down ___
- Bring your throwing-side foot forward and assume a balanced position ___

To Increase Difficulty

- Increase the throwing distance.
- Increase the number of on-target hits.
- Make the target smaller.

To Decrease Difficulty

- Shorten the throwing distance.
- Decrease the number of on-target hits.
- Begin the throw with the glove side toward the target (appropriate at shorter distances only).

6. Partner Throw-and-Catch for Accuracy

a. You and a partner stand 20 feet apart. The catching partner holds the glove chest-high as a target, and the thrower aims for the glove target. The receiver should catch the ball and move it immediately to the throwing position, then throw it back. Do 20 throws and catches with the last 5 short in front so the receiver has to move forward to catch the ball.

b. Next, challenge each other by setting the glove target chest-high in three different positions: the receiver's glove side, throwing side, and directly in front of the body. Make 10 throws and catches at each glove target position and then switch roles.

Success Goal =

a. 15 combined on-target throws for the thrower and successful catches for the receiver out of 20 attempts ___

b. 8 combined on-target throws for the thrower and successful catches for the receiver out of 10 attempts when the ball is thrown chest-high:

directly at the receiver ___
to the receiver's glove side ___
to the receiver's throwing side ___

Success Check

- Thrower, look for the target and step directly toward it ___
- Move your arm through the full range of motion for the throw ___
- Snap your wrist and follow through as you release the ball ___
- Catcher, give a big, open-glove target and watch the ball go into the glove ___
- Squeeze the ball in your glove with the thumb and ring finger of your glove hand ___
- Cover the ball with the throwing hand on all catches except those out of "two-hand catch" range ___

To Increase Difficulty

- Continuously catch and throw the ball to the target area rather than stopping after catching and then preparing to throw.
- Receiver extends the possible target positions beyond just chest-high and randomly varies the target setup for each throw.
- Receiver moves the target before the throw is started.

To Decrease Difficulty

- Shorten the throwing distance.
- Make the targets only slightly to the side and in front of the receiver.
- Throw back and forth to chest height using only the amount of force your partner is able to handle when catching.

7. Challenge of Game-Situation Accuracy

a. Use the same basic practice setup as in the previous drill. This time, however, imagine yourselves making throws and catches in real game situations such as tag plays, force plays, and backhand plays. As you begin this drill, take turns selecting a play to work on. The receiver should set an appropriate glove target for the selected play—for example, just below the knees for making a tag play—and the thrower should make the throw to that target. Continue until each partner has attempted 10 throws and 10 catches for the selected game-play situation, and then change the simulated game situation.

b. Once you have had consistent success at making throws and catches for the various game situations selected, practice making the plays in random order, changing the selected target after each attempt. The practice opportunity in the (a) portion of this drill is designed to help you develop a patterned throwing response to a variety of game-situation targets. In a real game, you get only one chance to make an accurate throw and a successful catch on each play. In order to be successful in this portion of the drill, you must make accurate throws and successful catches on the first attempt.

Success Goal =

a. 8 successful throws and catches out of 10 attempts on throws:

	Throws	Catches
Just below your knees, as in making a tag play	___	___
High and out front with a stretch, as on a force play	___	___
Head-high to your glove side with a stretch, as on a force play	___	___
Knee-high to your throwing side for a backhand catch	___	___

b. 8 successful throws and catches out of 10 attempts on random targets ___

Success Check

- Focus on the glove target throughout the throw ___
- Use full range of motion for the throw ___
- Step in the direction of the throw with the glove-side foot ___
- Give a big, open-glove target and watch the ball go into your glove ___

To Increase Difficulty

- When in the role of thrower, receive the return throw from the catcher and make your throw to the target all in one continuous motion.
- After returning the ball to the thrower, the catcher quickly moves several steps to one side or the other and sets the glove target. When making the throw, the thrower must step toward the new position of the catcher.

To Decrease Difficulty

- Shorten the distance of the throw.
- Decrease the number of targets.
- Catcher sets the target before you begin your throw.

8. Line Drives

One of the hardest-hit balls to catch is the line drive, because it is batted sharply and comes at you hard and fast. It is difficult to get in front of it in time to catch it, and you need to be sure to "give" with the catch to cushion the force.

With a partner, stand 40 to 60 feet apart, facing one another, and play catch. Snap your wrist forcefully as you release the ball so that it travels with considerable speed in a horizontal path, as would a line-drive hit. Set targets for your partner both above and below your waist and to your glove- and throwing-arm sides. (Use the backhand catching technique on all line drives to your throwing-arm side). When you catch the ball, move it directly into the throwing position, but do not immediately throw it.

Success Goal = 6 successful throws and catches out of 8 attempts above and below the waist, in front, to glove side, and to throwing side:

	Throws: above	Throws: below	Catches: above	Catches: below
in front	___	___	___	___
to the glove side	___	___	___	___
to the throwing side	___	___	___	___

Success Check

- Whenever possible, get in front of the ball and use two hands ___
- Turn your glove to the backhand position for line drives to your throwing-arm side ___
- Snap your wrist on the throw ___

To Increase Difficulty

- Increase the distance the ball is thrown to the side of the receiver.
- Increase the force of the throw.

To Decrease Difficulty

- Use less force on the throw and take more time between throws.
- Reduce the distance of the throw.

9. Leaping Line Drives

This is the same as the previous drill, except you now throw your line drive above your partner's head so that a leaping catch must be attempted. The receiver comes down with the ball in the throwing position and immediately throws it back to you.

Repeat this sequence for 15 leaping line drives. Count the number of successful line-drive catches and throws back.

Success Goal = 8 successful combined leaping line-drive catches and throws out of 15 attempts ___

Success Check

- Aim your throw at a point about a foot above your partner's head ___
- Throw a catchable line drive ___
- Shift your body weight forward and step toward your partner to increase your force ___
- Time your jump to receive the ball above and in front of your head ___
- Lead with the ball in the throwing position ___
- Immediately step toward your partner and return throw ___

To Increase Difficulty

- Throw the line drive to the glove side and to the throwing side above your partner's head.
- Throw the line drive higher above your partner's head.

To Decrease Difficulty

- Throw the ball directly at your partner and only slightly above the head.

10. Continuous Line-Drive Catches and Throws

You and your partner stand 60 feet apart. Throw a line drive to your partner, who catches it and immediately throws a line drive back to you. You catch the line drive and, in one motion, throw a line drive back to your partner. Continue this line-drive catching and throwing for five minutes. Count the number of consecutive catches you make together. If the ball is dropped by either partner, you must begin counting again at 1. In this drill, the footwork of turning and throwing is essential. Work on it.

Success Goal = 25 or more consecutive line-drive catches between partners ___

Success Check

- Make accurate throws ___
- Initiate your turn as you are catching the ball ___
- Have the ball back to the throwing position as the turn is completed ___

To Increase Difficulty

- Extend the range in all directions for your partner to catch the ball.
- Increase the force of the throw.
- Decrease the time between throws.

To Decrease Difficulty

- Throw the ball directly at your partner.
- Decrease the force of your throw.

11. Quick-Release Game

This is a combination of drill 6 and drill 8, except each partner starts the drill with a softball in hand. Each partner throws a ball to the other partner at the same time. Catch and immediately release (throw) the ball to your partner. Try to keep the two balls going continuously without a drop or bad throw. Be sure to use correct form, especially the footwork of turning and stepping when throwing.

Success Goal = 20 successful sequences of the combination of catching and quick-release throwing, neither partner making an error ___

Success Check

- Use two hands to catch ___
- Bring the ball to the throwing position as you turn and step to throw ___
- Make the catch and quick-release throw one continuous movement ___

To Increase Difficulty

- Move partners farther apart and make the receiver move farther to catch the accurate throw.
- Speed up the rhythm of the catch-and-throw patterns.
- Work on throwing line drives.

To Decrease Difficulty

- Move partners closer together.
- Slow down the rhythm of the catch-and-throw patterns.
- Use a softer ball.
- Throw the ball with less force.

CATCHING AND THROWING SUCCESS SUMMARY

The skill foundation of a good defensive player is strength in catching and throwing. Softball games are won on solid defensive play. Keep the other team from scoring, get one run, and your team is a winner. The player who can catch the ball and make strong, accurate overhand throws is going to make significant contributions to the team's success, so work hard to develop these skills.

Remember, make the catch and throw one smooth, continuous motion. Track the ball early and move your body into position in line with the ball. Reach out to catch the ball in front of your body with two hands if possible, and as you draw it to the throwing position, remember "turn, step, and throw." Step in the direction of your throw with the glove-side foot. Use a two-finger grip, move the ball high and forward past your head, and snap your wrist on the release.

Before you move on to fielding ground balls and fly balls, ask a partner or instructor to rate your success with the catching and throwing Keys to Success checklists (see figures 1.3 and 1.4).

STEP 2 FIELDING

Whatever the situation, whether you're the center fielder who needs to catch a deep fly ball when the other team has the bases loaded and you need one more out to end the inning, or you're handling a routine ground ball at second base to make the first play of the game, you need to know how to handle balls hit your way. Defense wins ball games, and a major part of defense is fielding. When the batter hits a ball in a game, it comes to you—the fielder—as a ground ball, a line drive, or a fly ball. As indicated in the preceding chapter, the specialized technique you use to catch such a ball is called *fielding*. In this step, you'll first learn how to field balls that come to you on the ground, then we'll cover how to field fly balls coming to you in the air.

Why Is Fielding Important?

When the batter hits a grounder or a fly, a defensive player must field the ball before making the throw for a putout (in the case of the grounder) or in order to make the out (in the case of the fly ball). The play most often made by an infielder on a hit ball is fielding a grounder. If the ground ball is not fielded properly, the ball will likely go into the outfield, thus allowing the batter to reach first base safely. Because baserunners must reach bases safely to be in a position to score runs, it is vital that infielders field ground balls and throw to appropriate bases with consistency and accuracy. Outfielders are the last line of defense—therefore, fielding ground balls is as important for them as it is for infielders. Ground balls misplayed by the outfielders allow the baserunners to advance, putting them in scoring position and increasing the pressure on the defense.

The batter in slow-pitch softball has a tendency to hit the ball high (and sometimes far) into the air for two reasons. The trajectory of the slow-pitch pitch is high to low; therefore, the batter tends to swing up at the ball, causing the ball to go up into the air. Second, the pitch travels toward the batter rather slowly; therefore, the batter has time to see the ball and make good contact. In fast-pitch softball, the ball is also often hit into the air as a fly ball. Pitching is very fast, so the batter is not always able to make good contact. Hitting the ball just off-center on the lower part of the ball will cause it to go into the air as a fly ball or pop-up. A caught fly ball puts the batter out and requires baserunners to tag up before advancing once the catch is made. All fielders playing any form of softball need to know how to field fly balls correctly. Outfielders catch long fly balls; infielders catch pop-ups (fly balls hit in or near the infield).

How to Field Ground Balls

Whenever possible, you, the fielder, should move to a position directly in front of the ground ball before attempting to field it. Fielding the ball on the run makes both catching and throwing the ball very difficult. Being in a stationary position as you field the ball makes it very easy to get down low and watch the ball go directly into your glove, as shown in figure 2.1a-c. When fielding a ground ball and making a throw to put a baserunner out, try to make the fielding and the throw one continuous motion. Remember the key points from catching and throwing: watch the ball go into your glove, use two hands, turn your glove side toward the target, and step in the direction of the target as you throw. When fielding, getting rid of the ball quickly is important in order to put the baserunner out, but don't forget that your first priority is to field the ball. You cannot throw anyone out without first having the ball in your possession.

FIGURE 2.1 **KEYS TO SUCCESS**

FIELDING GROUND BALLS

a

b

c

Preparation

1. Stagger stride ___
2. Knees bent, weight on balls of feet ___
3. Back flat ___
4. Focus on ball ___

Execution

1. Hands low, glove open to ball ___
2. Meet ball out front ___
3. Use two hands ___
4. Watch ball go into glove ___
5. Throwing hand on ball ___

Follow-Through

1. Shift weight back ___
2. Glove side to target ___
3. Ball to overhand throwing position ___
4. Glove-side elbow to target ___

Game-Play Fielding

During a game, you are often required to get into position to field ground balls that are not coming directly toward you. You need to be able to move to balls coming to your right and your left when fielding grounders, because that's where hitters are trying to place their hits in game play. The hitter's job is to try to make it as difficult as possible for you to field the ball coming your way.

You should move laterally into position to field a ball only a short distance away by using a *slide step* (see figure 2.2). From your ready ground ball fielding position (see figure 2.1a), take a sideways step with the foot on the ball side, then close with the other foot. Repeat these sliding steps until you are directly in front of the ball, keeping your hands low and glove open to the ball as you watch it go into your glove.

For a ball rebounding at too great a distance to reach using the slide step, use the *crossover* approach (see figure 2.3). From a ready position (knees bent and hands at knees), pivot the ball-side foot toward the ball and cross over that foot with the other foot, taking a first step running to the ball. If possible, run into position directly behind the ball and field the ball with two hands. If the ball must be fielded in the air on the run, use the glove-side or backhand glove stop as shown in figure 1.5a-b. If the ball is on the ground to the throwing side, use the crossover step.

How to Field Fly Balls

Fielding a fly ball is, for most players, more difficult than fielding a ground ball. The tracking skill you worked on in Step 1 is very important when fielding fly balls. Tracking the ball through the air is difficult, because you have little against which to judge the changing position of the ball. Clouds or treetops in your field of vision can help you make the judgment as to where you must move your body in order

Figure 2.2 Slide step.

Figure 2.3 Crossover step.

to intercept the flight of the ball. Again, many of the principles you learned when working on catching and fielding ground balls will also be applied as you learn to catch a fly ball.

Field the fly ball above and in front of your head. As you learned in simple catching, your fingers point up. Just as when fielding a ground ball, you want to get in front of the fly ball. However, if you're an outfielder who must immediately throw the caught ball a great distance, it is helpful to be moving slightly in the direction of the throw as you catch the ball. Fielding the ball in front of your throwing shoulder allows you to more easily blend the catch and ensuing throw into one continuous motion (see figure 2.4a-c).

FIGURE 2.4 KEYS TO SUCCESS

FIELDING FLY BALLS

Preparation

1. Stagger stride, glove-side foot ahead ___
2. Knees slightly bent ___
3. Focus on ball ___
4. Hands chest-high, fingers up ___

Execution

1. Watch ball go into glove ___
2. Meet ball high out front ___
3. Use two hands ___
4. Two-finger grip ___

Follow-Through

1. Shift weight onto throwing-side foot ___
2. Glove side toward target ___
3. Ball to throwing position ___
4. Glove elbow toward target ___

FIELDING SUCCESS STOPPERS

Fielding errors usually occur because the fielder does not get in front of the ball, fails to track the ball off the bat, or takes her eyes off the ball as it approaches. The most common errors committed when fielding ground balls and fly balls are listed below, along with suggestions on how to correct them.

Error	Correction
1. You are late getting into position to field the ball.	1. Start to move into position as soon as the ball starts coming your way.
2. The ball goes "through" you, under your glove.	2. Remember the catching skills for a ball coming below your waist: Keep your glove fingers pointed down; don't squash the ball like a bug with your glove. Bend your knees, keep your head down, and get down to the ball.
3. The ball bounces out of your glove.	3. Watch the ball go into the pocket of your glove and cover it at once with your throwing hand.
4. On a fly ball, you have trouble judging where the ball will come down.	4. Track the ball using clouds, treetops, and buildings to help with depth perception.
5. You catch the fly ball as if in a basket below your waist.	5. *Don't!* Get your body under the ball so you can catch the ball above and in front of your head.

FIELDING GROUND BALLS AND FLY BALLS DRILLS

1. Wall/Rebound Net Fielding

Stand 15 feet away from a wall, or a rebound net if you are practicing outside. When using the rebound net, tip the top of the net frame slightly forward to work on ground balls and slightly back to work on fly balls. Throw the ball against the wall (1 to 2 feet above the ground to work on grounders, well above your head to work on fly balls) so that it rebounds back to you. Get into a fielding position directly in front of the ball. Field the ball and, in one continuous motion, come into the throwing position and throw to the wall for a repeat grounder or fly ball.

Success Goal = 10 consecutive fielding plays with correct form as shown in figures 2.1 and 2.4 ___

Success Check

- Get in front of the ball ___
- Watch the ball go into your glove ___
- Use two hands ___

To Increase Difficulty

- Throw the ball to the wall with more force.
- Increase the speed of fielding and throwing to the wall.

To Decrease Difficulty

- Use a softer ball.
- Stand farther away from the wall to increase the time to see and react to the ball.
- Use a softer throw to the wall.

2. Fancy Footwork

Using a wall or rebound net as in the previous drill, direct your throw at a slight angle to the wall or net so that the rebound goes away from your starting position. Throwing the ball slightly off-center to the right causes the rebound to go to your right. Throwing the ball to the left of center causes the ball to go to your left.

Start by directing your throws just off-center. Gradually increase the angle of the throws in order to increase the distance you must move to the ball. Use the appropriate footwork (such as a slide step or crossover step) for the distance you must move to the ball. As the angle of the throw increases, move back away from the wall or net to allow yourself time to reach the ball. Vary your throws so that you practice going both to your right and to your left for the ball. Fielding the ball to your throwing-hand side is more difficult because you must travel farther to get into fielding position in front of the ball.

Success Goal = 7 successful glove-side and throwing-side fielding plays out of 10 attempts ___

Success Check

- Use appropriate footwork for the distance traveled to the ball ___
- Whenever possible, get in front of the ball ___

To Increase Difficulty

- Angle the throw more in order to increase the distance traveled.
- Move closer to the wall to lessen the time to react.

To Decrease Difficulty

- Focus the practice on moving to the glove side.
- Decrease the angle of rebound to lessen the distance traveled.

3. Ground Ball Catch

You and a partner stand 30 feet apart. The person with the ball throws a ground ball to the fielding partner so that the ball travels *on the ground* at least two-thirds of the distance. The other person fields the ball and returns it with an overhand throw, as if throwing out a baserunner. Practice 10 plays before switching fielder and thrower roles. Field the ball as it is thrown on the ground: directly at you, short in front of you (you must move forward to field the ball), to your glove side, and to your throwing side.

Success Goal = 7 successful fielding plays out of 10 attempts:

on direct ground balls ___
on short ground balls ___
on glove-side ground balls ___
on throwing-side ground balls ___

Success Check

- Use appropriate footwork and move quickly into position to field the ball ___
- Reach forward to field the ball ahead of your feet ___
- Make the fielding action and the throw all one continuous motion ___
- Look for your target and step toward the target to throw ___

To Increase Difficulty

- Increase the force of the grounder.
- Increase the distance of lateral grounders.
- Vary the speed of the grounders from slow to fast.
- Vary the direction and speed of the grounders randomly.

To Decrease Difficulty

- Reduce the force of the grounder.
- Use a softer ball.
- Increase the distance between partners.
- Reduce the distance of lateral grounders.

4. Partner Fly Ball Throws

Stand 60 feet away from your partner, positioned so that neither of you is looking into the sun. The thrower delivers a high throw simulating a fly ball to the fielder: directly in front, to the glove side, to the throwing side, and slightly behind. The fielder moves under the ball and catches it using proper technique. In a continuous motion, the fielder throws the ball overhand back to the thrower as if throwing out a baserunner attempting to advance after the catch. You can add increased force to your throw by using a crow-hop step: while in throwing position with your glove side facing the target, step toward the target with the glove-side foot, hop onto the throwing-side foot to close it to the glove-side foot, then take another step toward the target with the glove-side foot as you throw the ball. The footwork rhythm is step-together-step or step-close-step. Your partner should not have to move more than one step to catch your throw.

Success Goal = 7 catches and on-target throws out of 10 attempts:

	Catches	On-target throws
in front	___	___
to the glove side	___	___
to the throwing side	___	___
slightly behind	___	___

Success Check

- Move as soon as you see the ball released by the thrower ___
- Field the ball in front of your throwing-side shoulder ___
- Get behind the ball, move toward the target as you field the ball ___
- Use the crow-hop step as you make an overhand throw ___

To Increase Difficulty

- Vary the height, lateral distance, and depth to which the ball is thrown.
- Vary the distance and direction of the throw after the catch by adding a third partner who will change positions to receive the thrown ball from the fielder.
- Increase the speed of the drill by using two balls. As soon as the first ball is caught, the thrower throws the second ball in a different direction.

To Decrease Difficulty

- Throw the ball higher so there is a longer tracking time.
- Use a softer ball.
- Decrease the lateral distance the fielder moves to get under the ball.
- Have the thrower, when throwing randomly, cue the fielder as to the direction the throw will go.

5. React to the Bouncing Ground Ball

Softball fields are never perfectly level, so ground balls may not roll smoothly. You therefore must be ready to field ground balls that bounce, sometimes quite erratically, as they approach you. Such grounders can be very difficult to field. As in drill 3 (Ground Ball Catch), you and your partner stand 30 feet apart. Your partner now throws bouncing ground balls for you to field. Each throw should be directed hard at the ground and at least half the distance to you so that the ball bounces to you.

First, the thrower sends 10 bouncing grounders directly at you. Switch roles. Then the thrower sends 10 bouncing grounders to your glove side. Switch roles. Then you'll field 10 bouncing grounders to your throwing side. Switch roles. Finally, the thrower sends 10 bouncing ground balls randomly to all directions.

In fielding all these bouncing grounders, predict the location and height at which the ball will arrive. Get into position and field the ball with both hands. Make the overhand throw back to your partner.

Success Goal = 8 bouncing grounders fielded out of 10 attempts:

directly in front ___
on the glove side ___
on the throwing side ___
in random directions ___

Success Check

- Watch the bouncing ball go into your glove ___
- Get in front of the ball ___
- Use two hands ___

To Increase Difficulty

- Vary the distances of the first bounce from the fielder, beginning far away from the fielder and moving progressively closer.
- Vary the lateral distance, direction, or the force of the bouncing grounder.
- Have the fielder face away from the thrower; when the thrower says "turn" (at the time of release of the ball), the fielder turns, locates the ball, reads its direction, moves into position, fields the ball, and throws it back using an overhand throw.

To Decrease Difficulty

- Decrease the number of bounces of the grounder.
- Use a softer ball.
- Decrease the lateral distance of the bouncing grounder.
- Set an order to the varying directions of the grounder (directly at the fielder, to her glove side, to her throwing side, then repeat).

6. Catcher's Pop-Up

The pop-up—a hit ball that the batter undercuts, sending it high into the air (often near the catcher)—is one of the more difficult fly balls to catch. Ask a partner to be a tosser for you. The tosser should stand slightly behind and to your throwing side. As the fielder, you assume a crouched stance like that of a catcher receiving a pitch.

The tosser throws the ball into the air well over the catcher's head and verbally signals the catcher to look up and field the pop-up. Infielders typically assist the catcher in locating pop-ups by calling "up," "up-back," "up-right," and "up-left." Using this terminology in this drill will carry over well for later game-situation practice and play.

The tosser throws 10 pop-ups of varying heights and distances according to the sequences in the Success Goal. Switch roles after each set of 10 throws.

Success Goal = 7 catches out of 10 attempts:

directly overhead ___
to the glove side ___
to the throwing side ___
behind ___
in random directions ___

Success Check

- Immediately look up for the ball in the direction called ___
- Use appropriate footwork (slide step, crossover, and so on) ___
- Use two hands to catch the ball ___

To Increase Difficulty

- Randomly toss the ball in various directions, distances, and heights.
- Have the catcher wear a mask that must be flipped off as he stands up.
- Toss lower pop-ups so there is less tracking time.

To Decrease Difficulty

- Use a softer ball.
- Have the catcher begin from a standing position.
- Toss the ball higher so the catcher has more time to get under it.
- Before tossing the ball, cue the catcher as to the direction of the toss.

7. Drop Step

You and a partner stand 10 feet apart. One of you is a tosser, the other is a fielder. The tosser holds a ball in the throwing hand. The fielder stands in a square stance facing the tosser with the feet shoulder-width apart and the toes of each foot even (equidistant from the tosser).

The tosser fakes a throw to the right or left of the fielder. On this signal, the fielder starts to run back for a fly ball coming to that side, taking the first step back (a *drop step*) with the foot on the side of the indicated throw—all while maintaining visual contact with the ball, which is still in the tosser's hand.

Now the tosser throws a fly ball to the side originally signaled. It should be deep and high enough to force the fielder to continue running to catch the ball. Change roles after each sequence listed below. The direction of the signal and ensuing throw should sometimes vary, as should the throw's distance, as follows:

a. Fake and throw right two times, no variance.
b. Fake and throw left two times, no variance.
c. Fake and throw right two times, vary distance.
d. Fake and throw left three times, vary distance.
e. Fake and throw random direction five times, random distance.

Success Goal = 9 catches out of 15 attempts ___

Success Check

- Focus on the ball in the thrower's hand ___
- Use the correct foot on the drop step ___

To Increase Difficulty

- Vary the height and distance of the throw.
- Reduce the arc of the ball flight so there is less time to track it.

To Decrease Difficulty

- Do not vary the distance of the throws.
- Use a softer ball.
- Make the arc on the ball higher so there is more tracking time.
- Shorten the distance the fielder has to run.

8. Continuous Grounder Fielding

You and your partner stand 30 feet apart. Now you both field and throw ground balls to each other continuously—you throw a ground ball to your partner, and your partner, in one motion, fields the ground ball and throws a ground ball back for you to field.

Mix up the directions, the speeds, and the types of ground balls (rolling or bouncing) you throw to one another. The object is to make each other work hard so that you both will become solid, consistent fielders. However, *do not* try to throw the ball past your partner.

Repeat two sets of 30 throws (15 per partner). Count the number of successful fielding plays you and your partner make in a row. Each time one of you misses a ground ball, begin counting again at 1.

Success Goal = 24 consecutive grounders fielded out of two sets of 30 grounders ___

Success Check

- Read and react ___
- Get a jump on the ball position ___
- Be a vacuum cleaner—pick up everything! ___
- Relax, be loose ___

To Increase Difficulty

- Decrease the distance between partners.
- Randomly vary the direction, speed, and type of ground ball (rolling or bouncing).

To Decrease Difficulty

- Reduce the variety of throws.
- Set a pattern of throws—for example, five rolling throws alternating with five bouncing throws.

FIELDING SUCCESS SUMMARY

Besides pitching (especially in fast-pitch), fielding ground balls and fielding fly balls are the two most important defensive skills in softball. When your team is in the field, every player (including the pitcher) must be able to successfully field the ball and make appropriate, accurate throws to put out members of the team at bat. Softball, unlike many other team sports, is very much like an individual sport. You, and you alone, have the chance to make the play on the batter who has hit the ball to you. You are just like the tennis player who must return the serve from the opponent across the net. On the other hand, in basketball, the forward driving past a guard will in all likelihood be picked up by another defensive player and be guarded as he attempts a shot at the basket. In softball, the fly ball or ground ball that you miss will seldom be playable by another fielder to put the batter out. Good fielding and throwing are critical for becoming a complete softball player.

Although a fly ball is usually considered a sure out, you know from your practice that catching it is easier said than done! Ask a skilled observer to watch you field ground balls and fly balls. Ask the person to pay particular attention to your movement to the ball. Do you react quickly to the ball off the bat? Do you get in front of the ball, watch it go into your glove, field it with two hands, and make the field and throw all one continuous motion?

To become a skilled fielder, you must field and throw literally hundreds and hundreds of ground balls and fly balls that come to you from all directions, at varying speeds, distances, and heights. You must practice fielding a ball in every way a batter could possibly hit it to you. Your success as a fielder depends on your ability to read and react to the ball off the bat, move into position, and field and throw the ball in one continuous motion.

STEP 3 PITCHING

The *pitch* is the skill used by the defense to put the ball into play in a regulation game. The softball pitch is delivered with an underhand motion. Pitching technique varies with the type of softball game being played. The *windmill* and the *slingshot* are the two most common deliveries used by the pitcher in fast-pitch softball. The revolutions of the arm (one or one and a half) in the windmill pitch make it possible for the pitcher to throw the ball very fast. In addition, the experienced fast-pitch pitcher can throw a pitch that will "break" sharply up (called a *rise ball*) or sharply down (called a *drop ball*).

The game of modified-pitch softball employs most of the same game rules as fast-pitch softball except for the pitching regulations. The modified pitch is a pendulum-type delivery in which the arm swings down and backward behind the body. As the arm swings forward, the ball must be released to the batter. The elbow in the modified pitch must be locked as the pitch is released. The modified pitch is very easy to learn.

The slow-pitch game requires a pitch delivered with an arc and without excessive speed. Pitching in slow-pitch is a skill that most players can master in a relatively short time. The arced pitch in slow-pitch is a finesse skill. It is not a power- or strength-related skill as is the windmill or slingshot. In fact, the modified pitch may be easier to execute than the slow pitch because the ball is delivered with a flat trajectory; thus, the pitcher does not need to master the technique of making the path of the ball conform to the required arc.

Why Is Pitching Important?

Can you imagine the games of tennis, volleyball, or racquetball without the serve? The serve begins the game. Likewise, in softball you cannot start or continue the game without the pitch; the batter would never get to hit without the pitch! Pitching usually dominates the fast-pitch game, especially in elite-level play. If you want to become an effective fast-pitch pitcher, you must be willing to spend many hours developing your technique so that you can have both speed and movement on the ball. Pitching in slow-pitch and modified-pitch softball is not as overpowering a factor in the game as it is in fast-pitch; however, it is still an important skill, and the pitcher is a vital player on every team.

As the pitcher in games of slow-pitch and modified-pitch, you should work on getting the pitch over the corners of the plate as consistently as possible. The slow-pitch and modified-pitch games are designed as hitting games. The pitching regulations ensure that, as the pitcher, you give the hitters a good chance to hit the ball. This makes it possible for your teammates to catch or field the ball and make the necessary plays to get the baserunners out. Again, your job is to put the ball into play so that the game can continue. In all pitching, however, it is important to make a pitch that challenges the batter. This is done by consistently pitching the ball over the inside or outside corners of the plate. You never want to pitch a "fat" ball over the plate's center.

How to Execute the Slow Pitch

Slow-pitch pitching requires an underhand delivery. Hold the ball using a three-finger grip. Place the index, middle, and ring fingers on one long seam and your thumb on a seam on the opposite side of the ball. Prior to your delivery, your pivot foot (throwing-side foot) must be in contact with the pitching rubber, and you must face the batter squarely and come to a complete stop with the ball in front of your body for a minimum of one second (see figure 3.1a). Start your delivery by swinging your arm down, back to the rear, and then forward in the same path in an underhand, pendulum motion. Take a step toward the batter with your non-pivot foot as you release the ball, as shown in figure 3.1b. (The rules also allow this step to be taken backward or to the side. At the elite level of play, the step backward or to the side protects you more when a ball is hit right back at you.) Your pivot foot must be in contact with the pitching rubber as you release the ball. The pitched ball must follow the path of an arc between 6 and 12 feet high while traveling the distance to home plate (official pitching distances vary according to age and gender). After releasing the ball, assume your fielding position and be ready for any ball hit back toward you (see figure 3.1c).

Although the expectation in the slow-pitch game is for a lot of hitting, the pitcher can make hitting more difficult by putting the pitch over the corners of the plate and by putting different spins on the ball as it is released. The hitter will have difficulty making solid contact on a pitch that is spinning, and the tendency will be for the hitter to pop the ball up or hit it on the ground. The ball can be made to spin clockwise, counterclockwise, forward, or backward by either the movement of your hand on the release or the manner in which the ball comes off your fingers. For a forward or backward spin, hold the ball across a seam with the two long seams parallel to the ground and perpendicular to the line of direction of the pitch. For a

FIGURE 3.1 **KEYS TO SUCCESS**

THE SLOW PITCH

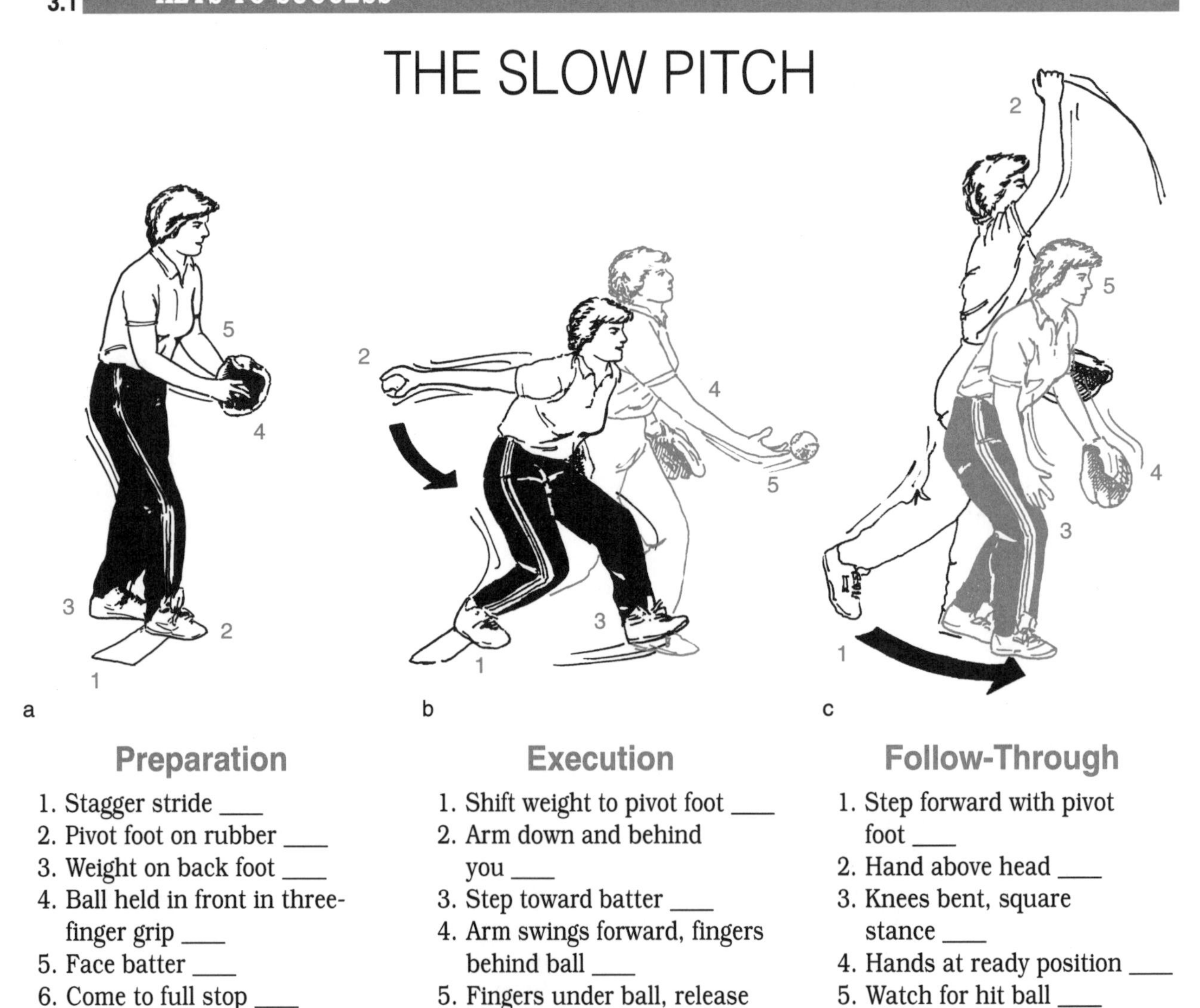

Preparation

1. Stagger stride ___
2. Pivot foot on rubber ___
3. Weight on back foot ___
4. Ball held in front in three-finger grip ___
5. Face batter ___
6. Come to full stop ___

Execution

1. Shift weight to pivot foot ___
2. Arm down and behind you ___
3. Step toward batter ___
4. Arm swings forward, fingers behind ball ___
5. Fingers under ball, release ball in front of hip ___

Follow-Through

1. Step forward with pivot foot ___
2. Hand above head ___
3. Knees bent, square stance ___
4. Hands at ready position ___
5. Watch for hit ball ___

forward spin, hold the ball with the palm up and let the ball roll off the ends of the fingers on the release. To cause a backward spin, hold the ball with the palm down, the back of the hand toward the batter, and release the ball by pulling up on the seam with the fingers and flicking the hand up. To make a ball spin clockwise or counterclockwise, hold the ball with your fingers pointing to home plate, resting along one of the four seams. For a clockwise spin, start the release with the palm down, thumb next to the body, and sharply rotate the wrist so the palm comes up and the thumb rotates up and away from the body. For a counterclockwise spin, start the release with the palm up, thumb away from the body, and rotate the wrist so the palm goes down and out, ending facing away from the body with the thumb toward the ground.

How to Execute the Modified Pitch

The technique for pitching the modified pitch is similar to both the slow pitch and the fast pitch in some aspects. Both the slow and modified pitch require an underhand delivery of the ball to the batter, but can have no windmill- or slingshot-type motion. The preparation phase is the same as for the fast pitch. Take your preliminary position (as when taking the signal from the catcher) and *heel and toe* the pitching rubber (see figure 3.2a). Stand with the pivot foot in a

FIGURE 3.2 KEYS TO SUCCESS

THE MODIFIED PITCH

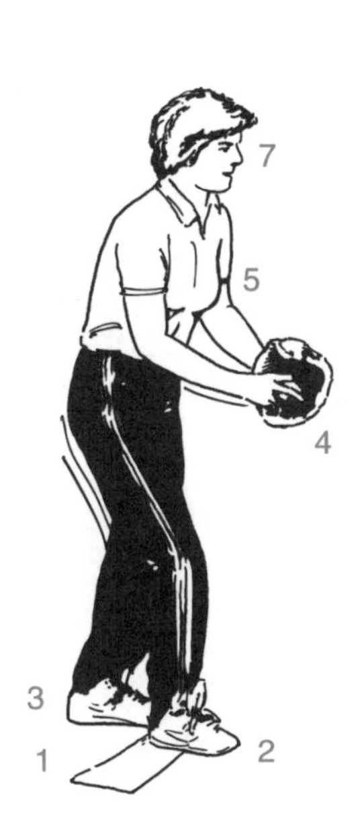

a

b c

Preparation

1. Heel and toe rubber ___
2. Pivot foot in front ___
3. Weight on back foot ___
4. Ball in both hands in front, two-finger grip ___
5. Face batter ___
6. Come to full stop ___
7. Focus on target ___

Execution

1. Shift weight to pivot foot ___
2. Arm down and to rear ___
3. Open hips and shoulders ___
4. Arm swings forward ___
5. Step toward batter ___
6. Close hips and shoulder ___
7. Release ball at hip ___

Follow-Through

1. Step forward with pivot foot ___
2. Hand above head ___
3. Knees bent, square stance ___
4. Hands at ready position ___
5. Watch for hit ball ___

slightly open stance at the front edge of the pitcher's plate so that the ball of the foot is on the ground in front of the plate and the heel is fully in contact with the plate. The toes of your non-pivot foot should be touching the back edge of the plate and pointed toward home plate. The shoulders must be in line with first and third bases, and the hands separated with the ball held in either the hand or the glove. Next, bring your hands together and come to a full one-second stop with the ball in front of your body. Because the modified pitch can be thrown with some speed, the two-finger grip (see figure 1.2, page 10) is preferred over the three-finger grip. As you begin your delivery, swing your arm backward and open your hips and shoulders so that they face third base (for a right-handed pitcher). As you bring your arm down and forward into the release zone, close your hips and shoulders by driving the hip on your pivot-foot side forward so that your hips and shoulders rotate squarely to face home plate as you release the pitch. The release of the ball is accompanied by a step toward the batter with the non-pivot foot (see figure 3.2b). The ball may not be outside your wrist at any point in the delivery, and at the point of release your elbow must be locked. These rules prevent the slingshot delivery. As with the follow-through for the slow pitch, after releasing the ball, bring your pivot foot forward and assume a balanced, square fielding stance (see figure 3.2c).

How to Execute the Fast Pitch

Unlike the hitter's game of slow-pitch, fast-pitch is a pitcher's game. The baseball adage that good pitching will beat good hitting is equally applicable to fast-pitch softball. Amateur Softball Association Hall of Fame pitchers Bertha Tickey, Joan Joyce, Donna Lopiano, Lorene Ramsey, and Nancy Welborn dominated women's fast-pitch games in the 1960s, '70s, and '80s. The 1996 U.S. women's Olympic team pitchers Lisa Fernandez, Michele Granger, Lori Harrigan, Michele Smith, and 17-year-old high school pitching sensation Crista Williams continue the dominance of pitching in women's fast-pitch. The legendary Harold (Shifty) Gears, Sam (Sambo) Elliott, and Al Linde, in addition to Johnny Spring and Herb Dudley, likewise dominated the men's fast-pitch game from the 1950s through the '80s. The speed of the softball pitch equals that of the overhand baseball pitch—elite pitchers can pitch a ball in the 90-mile-per-hour range.

It is not within the scope of this book to present extensive information on how to develop and train pitchers for the highest level of fast-pitch competition. On the other hand, the Joan Joyces, Lisa Fernandezes, Shifty Gearses, and Johnny Springs of the world began at some point in their lives to learn the fundamentals of fast-pitch pitching. If you want to begin to develop the windmill pitch, the material in this book will help you get started.

The secret to the windmill pitch is *the perfect circle.* Just as the blades of a windmill rotate in a perfect circle around its axle, the arm of the windmill pitcher traverses a similar circle. In addition, that circle must be in a direct line to the target area of home plate. Imagine a large hoop standing on its edge at the pitching rubber with the leading edge pointed toward a corner of home plate. If you gave that hoop a push, it would roll in a straight line to the target. During the windmill pitch, the same idea holds true, except the hoop is raised above the ground so that the bottom edge is at a height between your hip and your knee. The axle is your shoulder. The target point at the plate is also above the ground, somewhere between the batter's armpits and the top of the knees, over home plate. As you begin your pitch, the ball starts at the bottom of that hoop, then moves forward, up, over the top, and down the backside, and is released as your arm passes your hip, back where it began—at the bottom of the circle. This is the perfect circle.

Some other movements of your body must occur in order to have the ball, as it is held in your hand, traverse that perfect circle. Official fast-pitch rules regarding the starting position on the pitching rubber vary according to gender. When learning the windmill pitch, it is recommended that you heel and toe the pitching rubber as described under "How to Execute the Modified Pitch." Most pitchers will dig a slight hole in front of the pitching rubber where the ball of the pivot foot contacts the ground. This allows the pivot foot to push off against the front edge of the pitching rubber as the pitch is delivered, thus giving additional force to the pitch. The slightly open stance of the pivot foot enables you to fully open your hips at the top of the circle, making the perfect circle possible. Your shoulders must be in line with first and third base as you assume your position on the pitching rubber prior to starting the pitch.

When taking a signal from the catcher, the ball may be held either in the hand or glove, but the hands must be separated. Prior to starting the pitch, you must bring the hands together and come to a one-second stop, holding the ball in both hands. The most relaxed position for the required stop is with the hands together, elbows straight, and arms resting against the front of the body. The ball is held so that you can take the appropriate grip for the pitch. To prevent the batter and the base coaches from seeing the grip you have on the ball (thereby giving the pitch away), cover the ball with your glove so that the back of the glove is toward the batter.

The pitch starts with the separation of the hands after the stop. Once you separate your hands to start the pitch, you cannot rejoin them. Initiate the pitching motion by starting the ball, still covered by the glove, forward and up the front side of the circle (see figure 3.3a). At the same time, begin to open your hips and shoulders (right-handed pitcher—rotate hips and shoulders so you face third base) and shift your weight onto your pivot foot (see figure 3.3b).

FIGURE 3.3 **KEYS TO SUCCESS**

THE WINDMILL PITCH

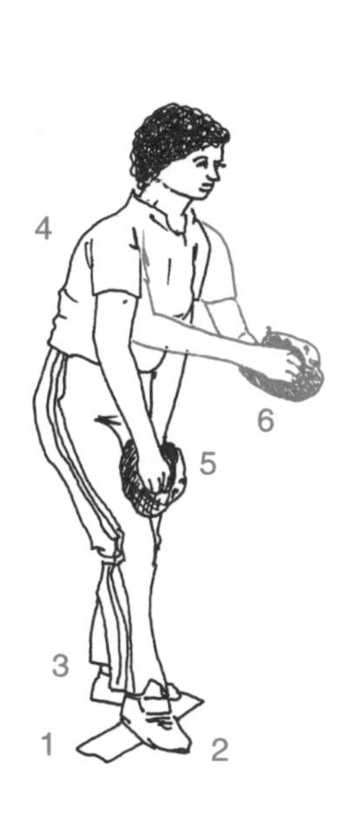

a

b

c

Preparation

1. Heel and toe the rubber ___
2. Pivot foot slightly open ___
3. Weight on back foot ___
4. Shoulders in line with first and third bases ___
5. Ball in both hands with stop in front ___
6. Start ball forward with both hands ___

Execution

1. Shift weight to pivot foot, knees bent ___
2. Open hips and shoulders ___
3. Arm fully extended, back of hand to batter ___
4. Close hips and shoulders ___
5. Elbow relaxed ___
6. Step toward batter, plant foot with flexed front leg ___
7. Drive off pivot foot ___
8. Release ball by thigh ___

Follow-Through

1. Step forward with pivot foot ___
2. Hand above head ___
3. Knees bent, square stance ___
4. Hands at ready position ___
5. Watch for hit ball ___

When your hand is at the top of the circle, your hips and shoulders are open, your weight is fully on the pivot foot, and your knees are slightly bent. Your arm should be fully extended with the ball held in the fingertips in a tight two-finger grip (see figure 1.2). The hand should be rotated so the back of the hand is toward the batter. As your hand starts the downswing on the back side of the circle, your hips and shoulders begin to close, and your head should be steady with eyes looking at the catcher's glove target. Keep your chest up and your torso in alignment with your shoulders. Do not lean forward. Your weight begins to shift forward as you begin the step toward home plate with the non-pivot foot. During the downswing, your pitching elbow should be relaxed and slightly bent. The knees are still bent and the front foot begins to plant (be sure the step is on, not over, the line of flight of the ball).

At the point of release, your hips drive to a fully closed position (belt buckle toward the batter), and at the same time the pivot foot pushes hard off the pitching rubber. Your arm is straight. Your torso and chest are erect, not leaning toward the batter. With a strong wrist snap, the ball is released. Your weight is balanced over the slightly flexed front leg.

In the follow-through, your pivot foot and leg must come forward to a balanced fielding position in which both feet are parallel facing the batter. Your hand should finish above chest level (for a fastball) and away from your body, having followed the path of the front edge of the hoop (see figure 3.3c).

The technique described in the previous paragraphs is the basic windmill delivery from which various types of pitches (such as the rise and the drop) can be thrown. The grip and the direction height of the arm on the follow-through, however, vary with the specific pitch thrown. Following is a brief description of the variations used for throwing the change-up, the drop, and the rise.

The Change-Up

A good companion pitch to the fastball for the beginning pitcher is the change-up. The two most common grips for throwing the change-up are the palm grip and knuckle grip, and the easier is probably the palm grip. Instead of holding the ball in the fingertips, force the ball into the palm of the hand and grip it with all four fingers and the thumb (see figure 3.4a). Use your regular fastball motion and delivery. The friction caused by the ball coming off your palm and fingers

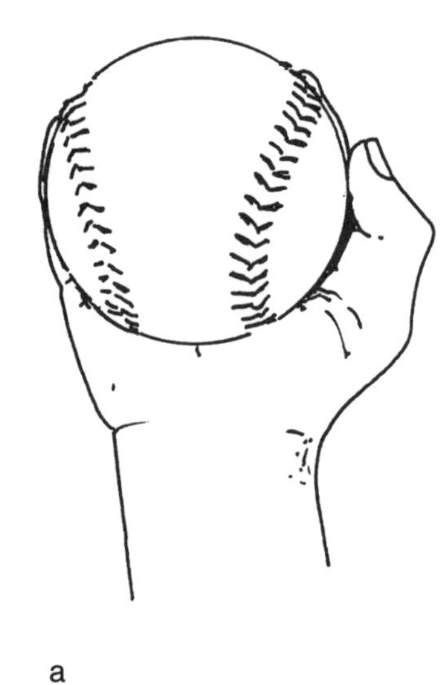

a

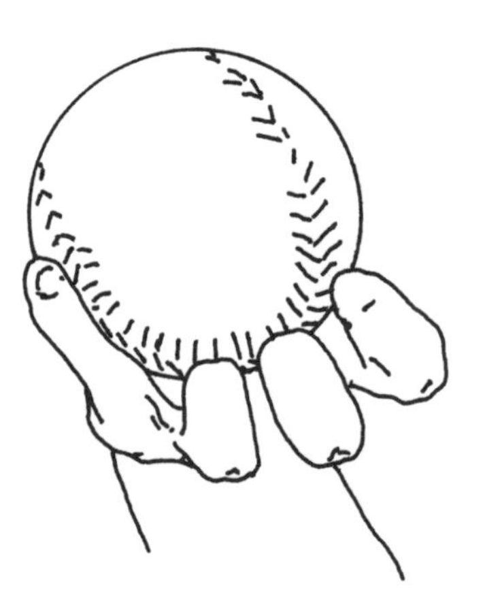

b

Figure 3.4 *(a)* Change-up palm grip; *(b)* change-up knuckle grip.

will slow the speed of the pitch and provide an effective change-up. For the knuckle grip, hold the ball with your knuckles across a seam (see figure 3.4b). (The knuckleball grip is especially difficult if you have a small hand and are throwing the 12-inch softball.) Again, use your regular fastball motion and delivery. The knuckles (rather than your fingertips) will slow the pitch and result in an effective change-up.

The change-up is effective because it disrupts the timing of the batter. That is why the motion and delivery of the change-up must be the same as for the fastball. The batter's timing is keyed to the motion. If you try to throw a change-up or an off-speed pitch by slowing your arm speed, the batter is immediately able to pick that up and adjust the timing of the swing.

The Drop

Batters can more easily adjust the timing of their swing to hit fast, straight pitching than they can to hit a ball that is moving up or down as it approaches the plate. The drop pitch, as the name implies, approaches the plate straight and flat like a fastball, then breaks sharply down or "drops" as it gets to the plate. As with the change-up, the batter is only fooled by the pitch if it looks like a fastball as you release it and it approaches the plate like a fastball. A ball that "dies a natural death," dropping to the ground in a slow arc all the way from the pitcher's hand to the plate, is not going to fool any batter!

The drop ball has a top-to-bottom forward spin. Grip the ball with two or three fingers held close together across one of four seams. The thumb should be on a seam on the side of the ball opposite the fingers (see figure 3.5). Upon release, the fingers are under the ball and the thumb is on top.

Take a shorter stride, and release the thumb first and let the ball roll off the fingertips with a slight lifting action (sometimes called the *peel method*) so that you start the ball spinning forward and your fingers come over the top of the ball as it is released (see figure 3.6). The follow-through of the arm is low, just above the waist and slightly across the body.

The Rise

The rise ball is a strikeout pitch. Experienced pitchers seldom throw the rise ball in the strike zone. The key to an effective rise is to make it look like a high fastball until it breaks sharply up just in front of the plate. At that point, the batter has already committed

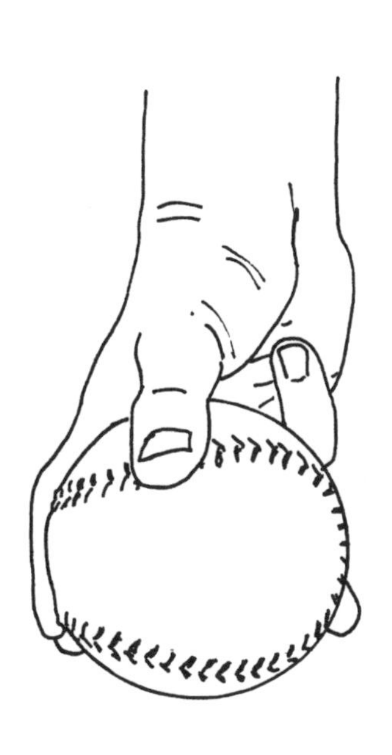

Figure 3.5 Drop-ball grip.

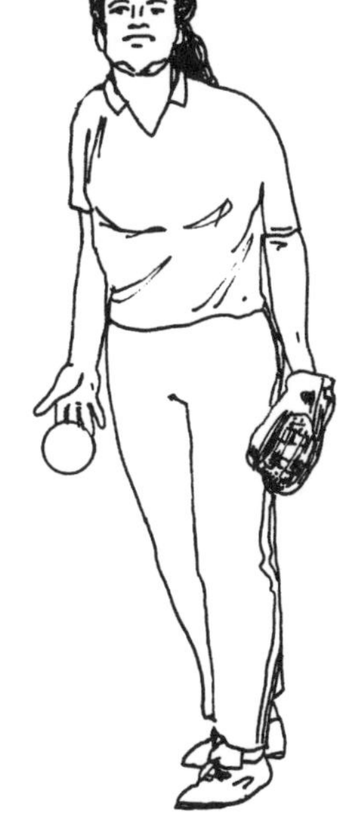

Figure 3.6 Drop-ball release.

to the swing path for the high fastball, and the pitch jumps over the bat. The rise ball must have a reverse (backward) spin. Grip the ball with the middle finger along the length of one of the four seams on the raised part of the seam. Place the index finger next to the middle finger, either flat or with the tip of the finger on the ball. The thumb is on a seam opposite the fingers (see figure 3.7).

Take a slightly longer stride, and increase the lateral lean of the trunk toward the pitching arm—this will get the throwing-side hip out of the way of the arm and allow your hand to get low and under the ball. Release the ball with the hand under the ball and away from the body. Rotate the wrist outward so the thumb goes up and to the rear and the middle finger pulls up against the seam, causing the backward rotation of the ball. The release motion is similar to turning a door knob. On the follow-through, reach out, up, and back. The follow-through is high, toward the target spot, and out in front of the body (see figure 3.8).

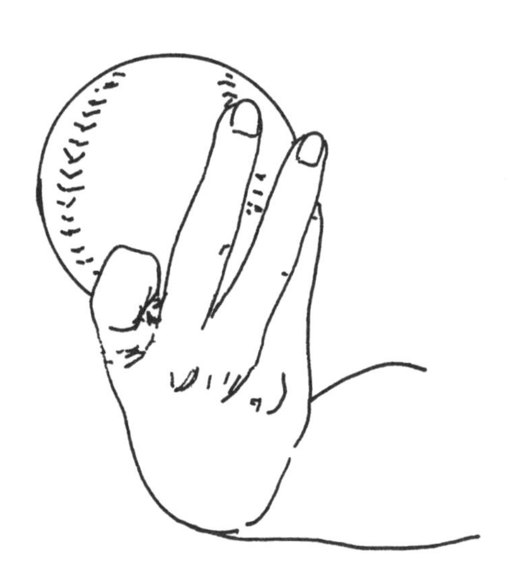

Figure 3.7 Rise-ball grip.

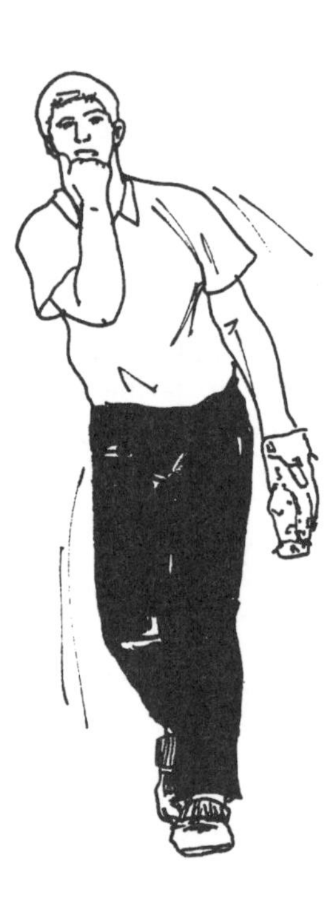

Figure 3.8 Rise-ball release.

PITCHING SUCCESS STOPPERS

Pitching errors usually occur because of improper timing of the release of the ball or incorrect travel path of the arm, hand, and ball. These errors produce an incorrect arc or distance in the slow pitch or an off-target delivery of the ball in modified and windmill pitching. Another common error is failure to get into a good fielding position after releasing the ball. This error can be hazardous to your health! For your own safety, be sure to assume a correct fielding position after you pitch the ball. The most common pitching errors for the slow pitch, modified pitch, and windmill pitch are listed here, along with suggestions on how to correct them.

Error	Correction
Slow Pitch	
1. The ball travels in too high an arc.	1. You are holding onto the ball too long. Release the ball as your hand passes your hip, and aim at a point 12 feet above the ground, two-thirds of the distance to home plate (about 33 feet).
2. The ball travels with no arc.	2. You are releasing too soon. (See Correction 1.)
3. The ball goes too long or falls short of the target.	3. The amount of force is incorrect. Try to drop the ball onto the back point of home plate.
4. You get hit with the batted ball.	4. Be sure to assume a good fielding position at the end of the pitch.
Modified Pitch	
1. Your pitched ball does not have much speed.	1. Open your hips and shoulders on the backswing, and drive them closed as you release the pitch.
2. As a right-hander, you consistently pitch the ball outside to a right-handed batter.	2. Make sure your arm does not come across your body as you release the ball and follow through.
Windmill Pitch	
1. The pitch is consistently high.	1. Release the ball earlier.
2. The pitch is off-line both inside and outside.	2. Have someone stand behind you and check "the perfect circle" in the line of direction to home plate.
3. The pitch has little speed.	3. Open your hips and shoulders at the top of the circle, and forcefully close them at the release.

SLOW-PITCH DRILLS

1. Wall Pitch

Place marks on a wall 1, 6, and 12 feet from the floor. The 6- and 12-foot lines are the pitching-height lines. The area between the floor and the 1-foot line is the target for the pitch. Place a mark on the floor 50 feet (or the official distance for your slow-pitch age group) away from the wall; this mark is your pitching rubber.

When you are pitching in a regulation game, the ball must travel within a 6- to 12-foot height limitation. In order for a strike to be called, the pitch, if not hit by the batter or caught by the catcher, would land on the ground just behind the back part of the plate. Aim your pitch to traverse an arc with a peak between the two highest lines marked on the wall (higher than 6 feet, but not above 12 feet) and to hit the wall between the 1-foot mark and the base of the wall. Hitting the base of the wall in this drill is like having the pitch come down just behind the plate.

Stand on the pitching rubber with your throwing-side foot. Pitch the ball 10 times using the techniques described in figure 3.1; remember to follow all three phases of the Keys to Success.

Success Goal = 7 on-target pitches out of 10 attempts ___

Success Check

- Stagger stride with pivot foot on the "pitching rubber" ___
- Shift weight to pivot foot as arm swings down and to rear ___
- Step toward wall (batter) as ball is released ___
- Bring pivot foot to square stance, hands at ready fielding position ___

To Increase Difficulty

- Mark the target area the width of the plate; aim the pitch for the inside corner or the outside corner.
- Place a bucket at the base of the wall; try to get the pitch to hit the wall and go into the bucket.

To Decrease Difficulty

- Shorten the distance of the pitch.
- Focus mainly on the execution phase by having a partner field the ball as it comes off the wall.

2. Up and Over

With a partner, position yourselves across from one another on opposite sides of the outfield fence. Each person stands about 25 feet from the fence. (The distance between you, 50 feet, is the regulation slow-pitch pitching distance.) Adjust the distance for your age group.

Pitch the ball back and forth over the fence, using it as a guide to work on the correct arc of the pitch. Pitch at least 20 balls, trying to get 10 consecutive pitches that clear the fence and go to your partner. Your partner should not have to move to catch the pitch. Your partner will pitch the balls back to you. If you get 10 consecutive pitches before you reach 20 attempts, keep going and see how many times in a row you can pitch successfully.

Success Goal = 10 consecutive pitches clearing the fence and going to your partner out of 20 attempts ___

Success Check

- Take one step with non-pivot foot toward partner as the pitch is released ___
- Use the three-finger grip, hand under the ball, and release ball past hip ___
- Follow through with pitching hand above head ___

To Increase Difficulty

- Place two ropes, one at 12 feet and one at 10 feet high, at the midpoint of the pitching distance. Pitch the ball the regulation distance so that the ball goes between the two ropes.
- Place spins on the ball.

To Decrease Difficulty

- Shorten the distance of the pitch.

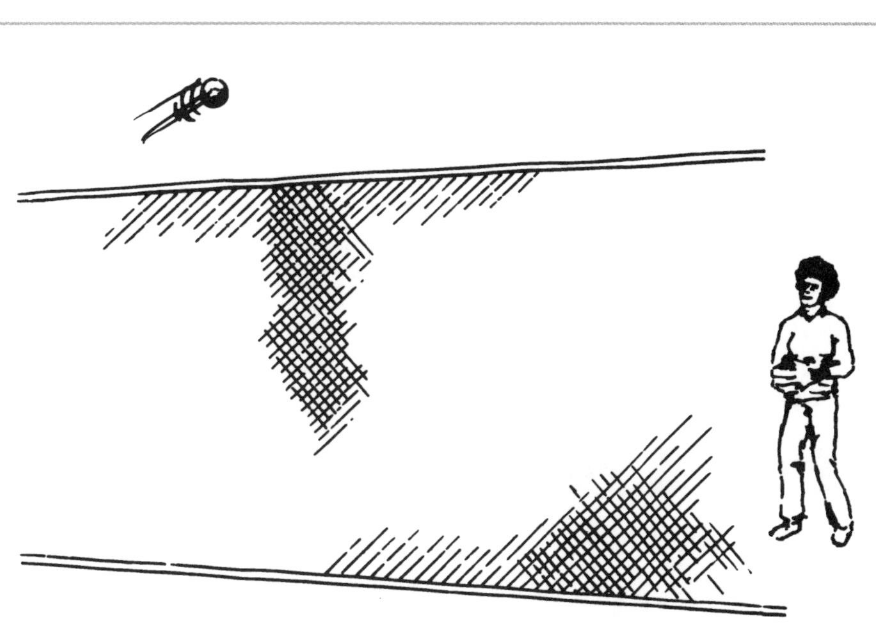

3. Ball in the Bucket

Place an empty bucket, milk crate, or similar container 50 feet away from your pitching rubber. Using correct technique, pitch the ball into the bucket. If you are working alone, use 10 or more balls so that you do not have to retrieve each pitch. If you are working with a partner, stand 50 feet apart, each with a bucket, and pitch one ball back and forth. Adjust the distance for your age group.

Pitch 10 pitches. Score 2 points if a pitch goes into the bucket (even if it pops out!) and 1 point if a ball hits the bucket on the fly. A pitch must traverse the regulation arc in order for the points to count. Partners should judge for one another. (If you are working without a partner, you can do this drill over the outfield fence to help you judge the regulation height of the pitch.)

Success Goal = 14 points on 10 pitches ___

Success Check

- Bend knees and use legs to aid in lift for the pitch ___
- Hand follows through high, directly in line with bucket ___
- Focus on target (bucket) throughout pitch ___

To Increase Difficulty

- Use two smaller buckets set the width of the plate apart, and alternate pitching to each bucket.

To Decrease Difficulty

- Shorten the distance of the pitch.
- Use a bigger bucket (or a big cardboard box or laundry basket).

MODIFIED- AND FAST-PITCH DRILLS

4. Fence Pitch

These first few exercises are lead-up practices to the full-motion drill at the end of drill 4. Do 10 repetitions of each and then repeat the set.

a. Finger Snaps: Stand 4 feet away from a fence (or wall) with your glove side toward the fence. Hold the inside of your pitching-hand wrist with your glove hand and release the ball at your waist toward the fence by use of the fingers only. Your fingers will move across your body from right hip to left hip (if you are right-handed).

b. Wrist Snaps: Move back from the fence an additional 2 feet, and move the glove up your pitching arm to a spot just above the wrist. Move your wrist back and forward two times and then "throw" the ball at the fence using a strong wrist-snap motion, again releasing about waist height.

c. Half Butterfly: Move back from the fence another 2 feet. In the same glove-side-to-fence position, raise the glove and pitching hands to the side and up to a position above your head with the thumbs pointed down. Swing your pitching arm down, then snap and release the ball just below the waist.

d. Full Circle: Stand in the same glove-side-to-fence position. Your glove hand faces out toward the fence, and your pitching hand swings up, out, and around in a full circle, releasing the ball with the wrist and finger snap at the bottom of the circle.

Stand 10 feet away from a fence. Although the regulation pitching distance for women's fast pitch is 40 feet (43 feet for women's intercollegiate), in this drill you'll stand closer to the fence so you'll be less likely to pitch the ball over the fence. Mark an area on the ground the size of the pitcher's rubber so that you can face the fence and heel and toe the rubber when pitching in this drill. Using either the modified or windmill delivery (this drill is appropriate for both), pitch the ball at the fence. The goal for this practice is to develop a relaxed, free-swinging pitching delivery, not to work on accuracy. Concentrate on the Keys to Success in figure 3.2 or 3.3, depending on the delivery style you are attempting to develop. Be sure your arm goes through the full range of motion for the pitch. Focus on opening and closing the hips and shoulders, getting the appropriate timing of the step, and using the proper wrist and finger snap with the release of the ball.

Success Goal = 10 pitches with correct form (as shown in figure 3.2 or 3.3) out of 20 attempts ___

Success Check

- Heel and toe the rubber, two-finger grip, full one-second stop with hands together ___
- Weight shift to pivot foot, arm travels in line of direction to the plate (the fence) to the rear and forward for modified; perfect circle for windmill ___
- Open hips and shoulders at top of backward swing for modified and at top of circle for windmill ___
- Close hips and shoulders at bottom of swing as the ball is released ___
- Snap the fingers and wrist as the ball is released ___
- Follow through in the direction of the fence and assume fielding position ___

To Increase Difficulty

- Pitch the ball against a wall instead of a fence.
- Catch the ball with your glove hand as it rebounds from the wall.

To Decrease Difficulty

- Start in open position (right-hander facing third base), arm at top of the backswing or top of the circle, and pitch by completing the downswing. Bring the hips and shoulders to closed position and push off with your pivot foot as you release the pitch. Finish by coming to a balanced fielding position.

5. Speed Practice

Stand 10 feet away from a fence, as in the previous drill. Add to the setup a large target such as a hula hoop or a beach towel attached to the fence with the bottom of the target about 2 feet from the ground. In this drill, the target is only meant to give you feedback on the consistency of the line of flight of your pitches. Do not aim at the target. Proceed as in the previous drill by continuing to focus on swinging your arm freely and going through the full range of motion for the delivery you are developing. Also, continue to work on opening your shoulders and hips at the top of the backswing and closing the shoulders and hips timed with the release. As your release begins to become more consistent, your pitches should begin to "cluster" around the target. When you begin to feel more comfortable with the full pitching motion, use this drill to work on developing more speed in your pitch. Increase your arm speed and the pushoff with your pivot foot. Because you are not using a real pitcher's plate, to facilitate the pushoff dig a small hole in the ground and place the ball of your pivot foot against the back edge of the hole. Again, just use the target to give you information on the consistency of your pitches as you continue to work on speed development.

Success Goal = 10 pitches with correct form (as shown in figure 3.2 or 3.3) out of 20 attempts with increased delivery speed ___

Success Check

- Arm goes through full range of motion ___
- Arm speed increases ___
- Pushoff from pivot foot results in increased pitch speed ___
- Pitches with increased speed cluster in general area of target ___

To Increase Difficulty

- Move farther away from the fence.
- Decrease the size of the target.

To Decrease Difficulty

- Move closer to the fence.
- Increase the size of the target.

6. Hit the Strike Zone

Continue with the setup of drills 4 and 5 by placing a target the size of the strike zone for an average-size batter on the fence at an appropriate height from the ground. While maintaining the delivery speed of your pitches, attempt to pitch the ball into the target area. Do not sacrifice speed for accuracy. To be an effective pitcher, you must have both. Your ability to throw accurately with speed will increase with practice. Pitching from the pitching rubber at regulation distance, using a catcher and a strike zone made out of string attached to a frame that is placed on top of home plate, provides a more realistic gamelike practice setting for you to practice pitching. However, practicing at less than the regulation distance provides you with a better opportunity to develop the relaxed, free-swinging arm motion you want to have as a pitcher. As your arm motion becomes more comfortable, gradually move back from the fence until you reach the regulation pitching distance for your level of play.

Success Goal = 10 on-target pitches out of 20 attempts using correct form and a delivery that matches speed attained in non-target practice ___

Success Check

- Form matches that shown in figure 3.2 or 3.3 ___
- Delivery speed equals that attained in non-target practice ___

To Increase Difficulty

- Pitch from regulation distance.
- Make the target area a 6-inch border all around the four sides of the strike zone.

To Decrease Difficulty

- Shorten the pitching distance.
- Increase the size of the strike-zone target.

7. Four Corners

This drill allows you to practice your pitch location. In a game, you never want to pitch the ball in the middle of the plate. Depending on the game situation and the batter's strengths and weaknesses, you want to be able to pitch the ball to specific spots in or just out of the strike zone. Pitch from the pitching rubber with your catcher positioned behind home plate. Have the catcher give you her glove target in the four corners of the strike zone. At first, you may want to work a set sequence (for example, 10 pitches to the low inside corner, next 10 pitches to the low outside corner, next 10 pitches to the high inside corner, and so on). As your accuracy increases, ask your catcher to randomly select the corner target.

Success Goal = 7 on-target pitches out of 10 attempts ___

Success Check

- Focus on catcher's glove target ___
- Keep good arm speed ___
- Push off pivot foot ___
- Keep torso upright ___

To Increase Difficulty

- Change target corner after each pitch.
- Randomly order the target corners.

To Decrease Difficulty

- Pitch 10 pitches to one corner before changing target corner.
- Shorten the pitching distance.

8. Call Balls and Strikes

After practicing form, distance, and accuracy of the slow pitch, the modified pitch, or the windmill, you are ready to practice pitching in a more gamelike setting. This drill combines pitching with the hitter's tracking the ball (watching it from pitcher's release until it crosses the plate).

Set up in groups of three—one pitcher, one catcher, and one batter. In this drill, the pitcher and the batter score points, and the catcher is the drill facilitator. The pitcher is practicing the pitching technique, while the batter is practicing watching the pitched ball and making judgments about its position as it comes into the hitting contact zone.

As the batter stands in position at home plate, the pitcher tries to pitch strikes to the catcher crouching behind the plate. The batter doesn't swing, but calls the pitches balls or strikes, according to the official strike zone (the space over home plate, between the batter's back shoulder and front knee for slow-pitch; and between the armpits and top of the knees for modified-pitch and fast-pitch). The catcher must verify each call. Any pitch about which the catcher disagrees with the hitter is judged a "no-pitch" and does not count as either a ball or a strike. Two calls resulting in no-pitch judgments during a single turn at bat, though, put the batter out, resulting in a point for the pitcher. (One turn at bat consists of the batter's taking either four balls or three strikes.)

Although the batter does not swing at the pitch, she should assume a regular batting stance holding a bat. The catcher should wear a mask and full protective gear in case a pitch accidentally hits the held bat and is tipped back at the catcher.

The pitcher receives 1 point for every strikeout (three strikes before four balls on six or fewer consecutive pitches); the batter receives 1 point for every base on balls (four balls before three strikes on six or fewer consecutive pitches). Rotate roles (pitcher to catcher, catcher to batter, batter to pitcher) after 3 points are scored by one person. If particular persons are working on becoming pitchers and catchers, it may be advisable to rotate pitchers only into the pitching position and catchers only into the catcher's position.

Success Goal = Score 6 points before your opponent does ___

Success Check

Batter:

- Maintain a square stance while holding the bat with hands back ___
- Focus on the ball from pitcher's hand until it crosses the plate ___
- Call the pitch as it crosses the plate ___

Catcher:

- Give the pitcher a target with the glove ___
- Move the target around the corners of the strike zone ___

Pitcher:

- Focus on the catcher's target ___
- Use correct form as shown in figure 3.1, 3.2, or 3.3 ___

To Increase Difficulty

- Batter calls the pitch when it is in her hitting contact zone (opposite her front foot).
- Count only pitches on the corners and reduce the size of the strike zone.

To Decrease Difficulty

- Reduce the distance of the pitch.
- Increase the size of the strike zone.

GAME-SITUATION DRILLS

Additional drills that call for pitching in simulated game situations can be found in Step 4: drills 10 through 15 give the pitcher an excellent opportunity to pitch to live batters who have a specific task to accomplish during a turn at bat.

Your development as a pitcher, whether it be in slow-pitch, modified-pitch, or fast-pitch, is dependent on the various opportunities you have to develop correct form and technique, and then the opportunities you have to apply that technique in simulated game situations. The ultimate goal of becoming an effective pitcher in real games is only attainable if you are willing to put in many hours of practice to develop those skills. Going from pitching at targets to game-simulated practice is a very important practice progression for pitchers to take before pitching in a real game situation. You should find these game-situation drills challenging and fun. In these drills, you should first try to pitch the ball so the batter can have the opportunity to be successful. For instance, if the right-handed batter's task is to hit the ball behind the runner (for example, to right field), assist the batter by throwing strikes on the outside corner of the plate. As the batter's skill increases, you can then try to pitch the ball in areas that make his task more difficult (in the previous example, you would pitch the ball inside).

PITCHING SUCCESS SUMMARY

In the game of softball, the pitcher is *the boss!* In fast-pitch softball, pitching is considered by most experts to be at least 85 percent of the game. No-hitters and one-hitters with one or two runs determining the winner of the game are common in elite-level fast-pitch softball games. If you have ever experienced a game in which the pitcher walks batter after batter, walking in run after run, you know the frustration every person, including the pitcher, has in this game situation. The old baseball adage "good pitching will beat good hitting any day" is also applicable for slow-, modified-, and fast-pitch softball games. Although the slow- and modified-pitch games are more of a hitter's game, pitchers contribute to the winning effort of the team in a way similar to that of a fast-pitch pitcher. They do so by putting a spin on the ball and by pitching to the corners of the plate, thus forcing the batter to hit a pitch out of his strike-zone strength area.

Your development as a modified- or slow-pitch pitcher will take considerable practice, but is an easily attainable goal. Ask an experienced observer using the Keys to Success checklists (see figures 3.1 or 3.2) to watch you pitch and help you make appropriate corrections in your pitching motion. On the other hand, if you wish to become an elite fast-pitch pitcher, you must be willing to spend years developing that skill. It is not within the scope of this book to take you to that elite level. However, using the skill-development drills—especially the game-situation drills in this and the next chapter—will help you get started in the right direction. If your desire is to become an elite fast-pitch pitcher, seek out and attend clinic and camp opportunities that have well-known pitching experts on their staffs.

To become a skilled pitcher, you must be willing to spend hours and hours developing your skill. At the beginning of your development, you must practice long hours and pitch in game situations sparingly. Your development as a pitcher requires more mental toughness than that needed for any other position in softball. If pitching is what you want to do, then go for it—be the boss!

STEP 4 HITTING

Hitting is the first offensive softball skill to learn. As the *batter,* you are the person from the offensive team who is up at bat. Being at bat and attempting to hit a pitched ball is the start of every offensive play in a game. Hitting is a complex skill—in a very short period of time, you must make many judgments about contacting a moving object (the ball) with another moving object (the bat). It is therefore helpful, when learning to hit, to simplify the hitting process by breaking it down into components. Begin by eliminating the movement of the ball as a factor—use a *batting tee* (a device that allows you to practice the hitting technique with a stationary ball). When you have developed some confidence and skill in contacting the ball with the bat, you are ready to hit a pitched ball or a *soft toss,* which allows you to practice hitting a ball tossed from a short distance.

Why Is Hitting Important?

The goal of offensive play in softball is to score runs. As explained in "The Game of Softball" (page 1), an official game of softball is won by the team scoring the greater number of runs in seven innings of play. A run can be scored only when a batter gets on base, progresses around the bases, and crosses home plate safely. Although there are several ways for a batter to get on base, hitting the ball is the most fun. Once there are runners on base, hitting the ball is an important technique for *advancing* the runners (causing them to move to a base closer to home plate) and, eventually, scoring runs. Probably the most fun of all is to hit the ball to a place that allows you (and any runners on base) to advance more than one base at a time (a double, a triple, or a home run).

How to Hit

Hitting involves moving the bat from a stationary position behind the back shoulder into the path of the ball, making contact with the ball out in front of the front foot, and following through by completing the swing while keeping the body in a balanced position. There are many different theories for hitting: swing level, swing down on the ball, swing up at the ball, keep two hands on the bat during the follow-through, take the top hand off the bat on the follow-through, and so on. There are also many different forms of hitting, depending on the game situation and the type of pitching you are facing. Slap- or punch-hitting against fast pitching, place-hitting to take advantage of gaps in defensive positioning, and hitting behind the runner to advance that person to the next base are examples of forms of hitting that are used in specific situations (they will be covered in Step 7). The following description of hitting technique is fundamental to all hitting used in specific game situations, and therefore should be mastered before attempting any of the adaptations. It is presented at this early point so that as you strive to develop your hitting skill using the various hitting drills, you will have an understanding of the complete technique and a mental picture of what hitting a ball entails.

Stand with your feet shoulder-width apart and your knees slightly bent. (If using the batting tee, stand so that your front foot is opposite the post of the tee). Take a grip on the bat so that the middle row (second row) of knuckles of both of your hands line up. To achieve this grip, bend over, put the barrel end of the bat on the ground, and place your hands on the grip end of the bat so that it angles across the palms of both hands. Lift the bat up, maintaining this hand position on the bat, and check the alignment of the middle (second) knuckles of both hands (see figure 4.1).

Hold the bat with your middle knuckles aligned, and hands located shoulder-high and away from and behind your body (away from the pitcher). Your front arm is parallel to the ground, straight but relaxed. Your back elbow is raised up from your side with the upper arm parallel to the ground (see figure 4.2a). Hitting a ball involves swinging the bat into the path of the ball and making contact with the ball. However, two very important movements of your body must occur prior to starting to swing the bat. As the pitch leaves the pitcher's hand (timing will vary depending on the speed of the pitcher), take a slight step (often called the *stride*) with your front foot, pointing your toes in the direction of the second baseman (see figure 4.2a). Next, begin to turn your hips toward the pitcher by pivoting on the ball of your back foot and the heel of your front foot. As the hips turn, start the bat swing by leading with the front elbow into the swing path or path of the ball. Keep the wrists cocked so that the barrel end of the bat trails the hands while you begin to extend your arms and move your hands forward. Keep your head down and watch the ball.

Figure 4.1 Proper grip.

A major determinant of effective hitting is your position at the *contact point* (see figure 4.2b). At the point of contact, when the bat meets the ball, your hips are square to the pitcher (belt buckle toward the pitcher), your arms are extended, and your head is down with your eyes focused on seeing the ball hit the bat. Your front leg is straight. Your back leg is bent and your weight is centered over your back knee. Swing the bat "through" the ball. Do not shift your weight onto your front foot during the contact unless you are just using a punch swing against extremely fast pitching. (*Note:* your weight shifts forward onto the front foot at the end of the follow-through so that you can take your first step out of the batter's box toward first base with your back foot.)

Continue your swing after your bat contacts the ball. Stopping your swing on contact is like trying to run out an infield hit and stopping on first base rather than running over the base. In order to stop *on* the base, you must slow down prior to getting to the base. This usually results in the ball beating you to the base, thereby putting you out. When hitting, stopping your swing on contact means you have had to slow down your swing prior to contacting the ball, resulting in a less forceful hit. To complete your swing, roll your wrists so that the thumb of your top hand points to the ground as you force the bat to wrap around your body (shoulders on a high pitch, waist or knees on a low pitch). Chin position is a good indication of proper head-down position throughout the swing. In the starting position, as you wait for the pitcher to begin the pitch, your chin should be contacting your front shoulder. On the follow-through or completion of the swing, your chin should be contacting your back shoulder, which has rotated forward (see figure 4.2c). Finally, hold onto the bat!

How to Hit the Ball Off the Tee

Hitting the ball off the batting tee is one of the easiest ways to work on achieving some of the Keys to Success for hitting technique—specifically the hip turn, including the footwork and the total body position

FIGURE 4.2 **KEYS TO SUCCESS**

HITTING

Initiating the Swing

1. Square stance ___
2. Middle knuckles aligned ___
3. Knees bent ___
4. Hands back, back elbow up ___
5. Focus on ball ___
6. Step with front foot, point toes toward second baseman ___
7. Initiate hip turn ___
8. Lead swing with front elbow ___

Contact Point

1. Hips square ___
2. Arms extended ___
3. Front leg straight ___
4. Back leg bent ___
5. Weight centered over back knee ___
6. Focus on ball ___
7. Roll wrists

Completing the Swing

1. Weight centered ___
2. Swing through ball ___
3. Hips square ___
4. Hands wrap around shoulder ___
5. Chin on shoulder ___

at the contact point. Because the ball is stationary as you attempt to make contact, you do not have to adjust your swing to the changing positions a tossed or pitched ball would have as it approaches. This allows you to focus on those aspects of the complex act of hitting that need the most work.

Take a square stance, with the toes of both feet equidistant from the edge of home plate—or in this case, the plate part of the batting tee. Because the contact point in hitting is opposite your front foot (see figure 4.2b), take your initial batting stance with your front foot directly opposite the post of the tee. Stand at such a distance from the tee that as you swing the bat to the contact point, the center of the barrel of the bat is over the post of the tee, as shown in figure 4.3. Adjust your position at the tee by taking a few practice swings without a ball on the tee. Then you are ready to add a ball, follow the Keys to Success in figure 4.2, and practice hitting using the batting tee hitting drills.

In addition to providing a beginning method of practicing hitting technique, the batting tee can be used effectively by more experienced players to work on problem areas in their swing. Focusing on the ball on the tee will help the batter who lets the head "fly" during the swing to keep it down and steady, thereby achieving good focus on the ball at the contact point. The player having difficulty hitting an inside pitch can set up at the batting tee so the contact point is appropriate for an inside pitch. This provides effective practice on hitting that type of pitch.

Figure 4.3 Adjust distance from the batting tee.

If you feel comfortable with the bat in your hands, and know the key points about the swing and can consistently execute them, you can bypass the batting tee practice and progress to practicing hitting using a soft toss or a pitched ball.

How to Hit the Soft Toss

You can practice your hitting stroke and work on its timing by swinging at a moving ball that is tossed to you from the side, or a *soft toss*. You must now judge the path of a ball that is tossed to you by a person standing a short distance from your side. You must also judge the timing of your swing so that the bat arrives at the contact point at the same time as the tossed ball. These judgments made on the short-distance path of a ball tossed by someone else are viewed by some as a preliminary step to judgments you must make when hitting a pitched ball. The toss is made from the side for the safety of the tosser. For that reason, you may find the soft toss more difficult to hit than a softly pitched ball from someone in the regular pitcher's position. If that is the case, practice hitting a softly pitched ball before attempting the soft-toss drills. For the experienced hitter, the soft-toss drills provide an opportunity for a lot of swings at the ball because the accuracy of the pitcher is not a factor in your opportunity to practice your hitting technique.

The soft toss really involves two skills for two people: tossing the ball and hitting the ball. Your ability to toss the ball properly is extremely important for two reasons. The batter cannot hit unless the ball is tossed correctly; the ball *must* come down ahead of the front foot of the hitter. In addition, your own safety as tosser requires proper execution; if you toss the ball too far toward the hitter's back foot, the batted ball could be hit back at you.

The tosser and hitter face each other with the hitter in a batting stance and the tosser kneeling on the ground about 8 to 10 feet directly opposite the hitter's *back* foot. When tossing, toss the ball with a gentle down-up motion of your hand and arm. This should make the ball loop toward the batter, coming down into the hitter's contact zone and about 2 feet from the front foot. Toss the ball as if you

Figure 4.4 Correct tossing position for the soft toss.

wanted it to land on an imaginary batting tee off the batter's front foot (see figure 4.4—remember, the tee is only imaginary).

When hitting a soft toss, stand with your feet shoulder-width apart in the same batting stance as when hitting off the tee. After your partner tosses the ball, take the same swing at the ball as you did at the tee. Initiate your swing with a slight step with your front foot. Time your swing so that you contact the ball about waist-high and opposite your front foot. To protect the tosser, you must hit balls tossed only into the hitting contact zone, which is in front of and opposite your front foot. Do *not* swing if the toss does not drop to a position opposite your front foot. Hitting a ball tossed toward the midline of your body, despite the fact that it might be in the strike zone, could result in the ball's hitting the tosser. After contacting the ball, complete your swing by wrapping your hands, still holding the bat, around your shoulders (see figure 4.5a-c).

How to Hit a Pitched Ball

Your challenge in hitting a pitched ball is to predict the flight of the pitched ball and time your swing to make contact with the ball in your hitting contact zone. All of the techniques discussed previously are applicable to hitting a pitched ball. The grip with the middle knuckles aligned, the proper step and hip turn, full arm extension at point of contact, and an appropriate follow-through must be executed without a lot of thought as you work on hitting a pitched ball. When hitting a pitched ball, your focus is on tracking the path of the ball and timing your swing to intercept the ball at the contact point, which is out in front of your front foot. Another judgment you must now make is to determine whether the pitched ball will be a *ball* (outside the strike zone) or a *strike* (in the strike zone). These judgments of *tracking, reading,* and *reacting* are much like those you had to make when fielding a ground ball and especially when fielding a fly ball.

FIGURE 4.5 **KEYS TO SUCCESS**

HITTING A SOFT TOSS

Initiating the Swing

Tosser:

1. Kneel opposite hitter's back foot ___
2. Ball in throwing hand ___
3. Focus on target opposite front foot ___

Hitter:

1. Square stance ___
2. Knees bent ___
3. Two-hand grip, middle row of hitter's knuckles aligned ___
4. Hands and bat back ___
5. Weight on back foot ___
6. Head down, focus on ball ___

a

Contact Point

Tosser:

1. Lift hand and arm ___
2. Release ball up and forward ___
3. Watch ball drop to target area ___
4. Watch hitter make contact ___

Hitter:

1. Step with front foot to open stance (point toes to second baseman) ___
2. Hips start pivot, heel of front foot, ball of back ___
3. Hips square at contact ___
4. Back knee bent, front leg straight ___
5. Weight over back knee ___
6. Arms and wrists extended ___
7. Head down, focus on ball ___
8. Back shoulder to chin ___

b

Completing the Swing

Tosser:

1. Relax arm ___
2. Watch the hitter's technique ___

Hitter:

1. Roll wrists ___
2. Hands wrap around shoulder ___
3. Chin on shoulder ___
4. Weight over bent back knee, front leg straight ___
5. Hips square ___

c

HITTING SUCCESS STOPPERS

Most errors associated with using the batting tee occur because of improper body positioning. Do not stand at the tee with the midline of your body opposite the post of the tee. Remember, your contact point for hitting is ahead of your body and toward the pitcher, at the distance of your front foot. Because the teed ball is stationary, you should position yourself so that your front foot lines up with the post of the tee.

Errors that occur when hitting the soft toss are usually caused by a poor toss. At this point, the hitter should have the basic swing under control. A poor toss, however, will make it impossible for even an experienced hitter to have success with soft-toss hitting. The major hitting error encountered with soft-toss hitting practice is a problem with timing and tracking the ball. Timing and tracking errors are also the two most common causes of error when hitting a pitched ball. Other hitting errors are usually caused by lack of concentration, failure to watch the ball go into the contact point, and problems in one or more of the specific hitting techniques, such as grip, swing path, or contact point.

The most common hitting errors, with suggestions on how to correct them, are listed below.

Error	Correction
Hitting Using the Batting Tee	
1. You contact the ball on the handle close to your hands, or you have to bend your elbows for the bat to meet the ball.	1. You are probably standing with the post of the tee opposite the middle of your body. Move your stance so your front foot is opposite the post.
2. You cannot reach the ball when you swing.	2. Move closer to the tee, in the position described in Correction 1.
3. You hit the tee instead of the ball.	3. Keep your back shoulder up; do not drop your back elbow as you swing.

Error	Correction
Hitting the Soft Toss	
Tosser: 1. The ball goes in a straight line.	1. Make the ball traverse an arc to get to the target spot. Make your toss motion down and up, not back and forward.
2. The ball goes toward the midline of the hitter.	2. If you are directly facing the hitter, be sure your hand and arm motion is to the side and forward toward the hitter's front foot. Or, in your kneeling position, turn toward the hitter's front foot. Now make your hand and arm go down-up and straight forward toward the target spot.
Hitter: 1. You miss the ball completely.	1. Watch the ball go from the tosser's hand to your bat.
2. You just tip the ball up in the air or down to the ground.	2. Try to contact the *middle* of the ball with your bat.
Hitting the Pitched Ball	
1. You consistently pop the ball up.	1. Shorten your stride. Eliminate any loop in your swing (dropping the barrel of the bat below the horizontal swing path prior to contact, causing a low-to-high swing path at contact).
2. You consistently hit ground balls.	2. Check for a high-to-low swing path. Lower your starting hand position to a height just slightly above your back shoulder.
3. You have no power in your swing.	3. Swing through the entire range of motion. Start your hands well back by your back shoulder, not in front of your body.

HITTING DRILLS

The following hitting drills are categorized and presented in three sections: drills using the batting tee, drills using a soft toss, and drills using a live pitch. Although the drills are in a progressive order within a category, they are not to be viewed as being presented in a natural progression whereby you would start with the first drill and progress to the last.

As indicated in the introduction to this chapter, the batting tee is especially advantageous for a novice hitter because it allows the person to focus on the fundamentals of the hip turn and the swing path without the added attention to tracking the ball. It is also a useful practice aid for the experienced hitter having difficulty with a particular phase of the hitting action. To develop your hitting technique, select drills from the various categories that meet your specific needs for practice.

If you are a less experienced hitter just beginning to develop your hitting technique, you will find it helpful to move back and forth in hitting practice between using the batting tee and using live pitching, probably at a modified distance. Hitting is an extremely complex action. Utilizing the variety of practice opportunities presented in these drills should afford you the chance to develop into an effective hitter.

BATTING TEE DRILLS

1. Batting Tee With Net or Fence

Position the batting tee 10 feet from a hanging net or fence. Take a stance beside the tee so that the line of flight of the batted ball is toward the net or fence. Using a bucket of 10 regulation balls, place a ball on the tee, assume your correct batting stance beside the tee, and hit the ball off the tee into the net or fence.

If you are working with a partner, one person (the ball feeder) should stand with the bucket of balls on the side of the tee opposite the hitter and place the ball on the tee. *Caution*: Hitter, wait until the feeder removes her hand from the ball and steps back from the tee before you swing at the ball.

Feeder, watch your partner hit the ball. Using the points from each of the three phases of the Keys to Success shown in figure 4.2, give feedback to the hitter about his technique. Switch roles after hitting the bucket of balls. Repeat the drill so that each of you hits 20 balls.

Success Goal = 16 hits with correct form out of 20 swings ___

Success Check

- Square stance with front foot opposite the tee ___
- Focus on the ball ___
- Initiate hip turn, pivot feet ___
- Swing through the ball ___

To Increase Difficulty

- Use the bottom hand only to make the swing.

To Decrease Difficulty

- Go through the full swing motion with no ball on the tee.

2. Target Practice

Mark three lines on the net: one that is 2 feet from the ground, another 4 feet from the ground, and the third 8 feet from the ground.

Using the same procedures as in drill 1, hit 10 balls below the 2-foot line, 10 between the 4- and the 8-foot lines, and 10 above the 8-foot line. To hit the low target (attempting to hit a ground ball), use a high-to-low swing path. To hit the middle target (attempting to hit a line drive), use a horizontal swing path. To hit the high target (attempting to hit a fly ball), use a low-to-high swing path.

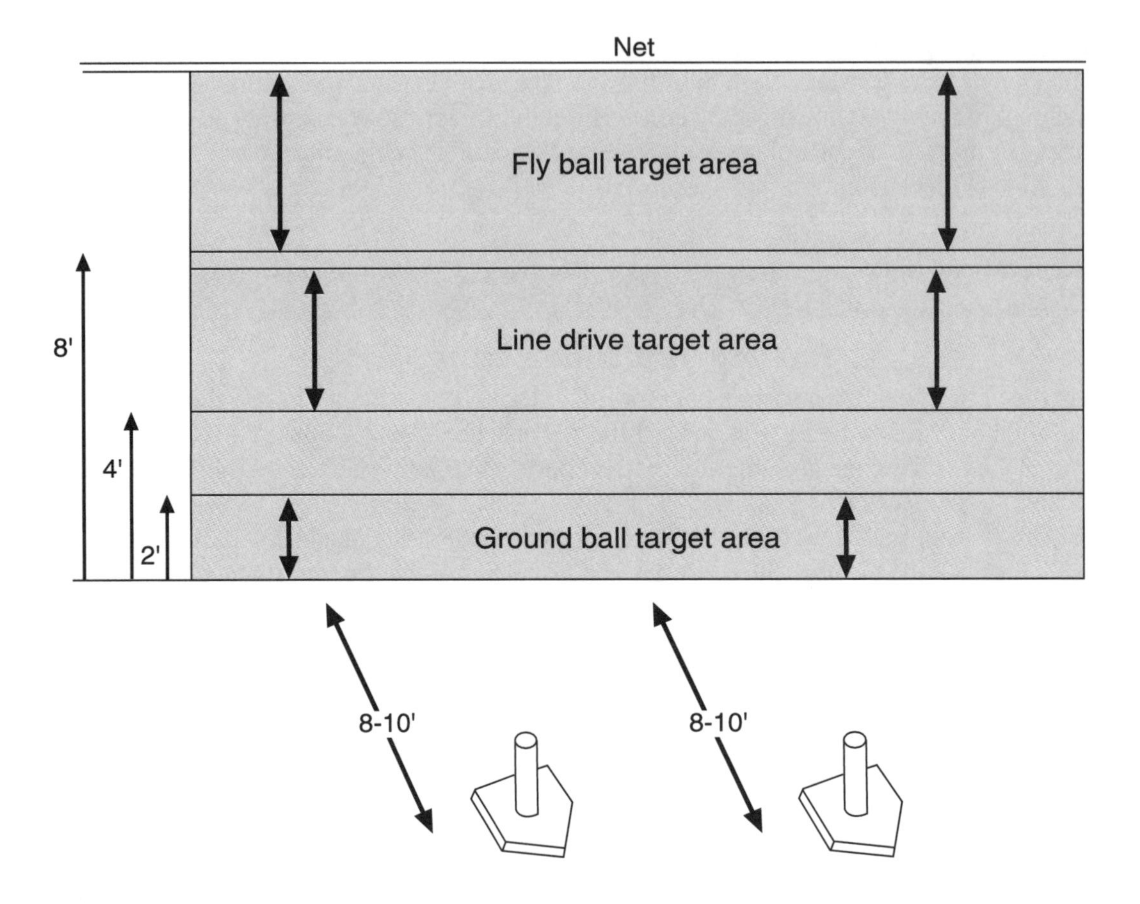

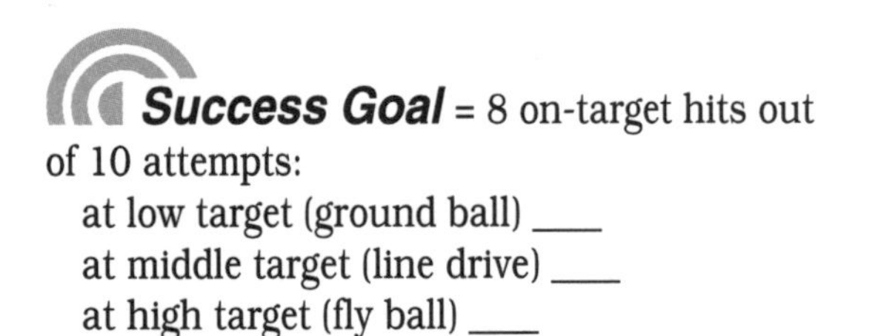

Success Goal = 8 on-target hits out of 10 attempts:

at low target (ground ball) ___
at middle target (line drive) ___
at high target (fly ball) ___

Success Check

- High-to-low swing for low target ___
- Horizontal swing for middle target ___
- Low-to-high swing for high target ___

To Increase Difficulty

- Vary the swing path on each hit.
- Have the ball-feed partner call the hit to be made.

To Decrease Difficulty

- Close your eyes and practice the three swing paths.
- Focus on only one target area.

3. One-Hand Swing

Put the tee at the center height setting. Stand with your regular grip on the bat. As you swing at the ball, let go of the bat with your top hand and make contact with the ball while holding the bat with your bottom hand only. Be sure to complete the full swing with the one hand. Try to hit the ball at line-drive height or lower. Hit 10 balls to the net. Collect the balls and repeat (or if you have a partner setting balls on the tee, switch roles). Count the number of balls that go line-drive height or lower from swings in which the bat does not hit the tee.

Success Goal = 16 line drives out of 20 swing attempts that do not hit the tee ___

Success Check

- Hit the middle of the ball; make full contact ___
- Swing through the ball; do not stop your swing upon contact ___
- Take a full turn on the ball; hips face the net at contact ___

To Increase Difficulty

- Hit to fly ball and ground ball targets in addition to hitting line drives.

To Decrease Difficulty

- Keep top hand on the bat with a loose grip to help guide the bat through the swing path.

4. Low Ball/High Ball

Adjust the height of the batting tee to work on the low pitch, then the high pitch. Hit 10 balls at each height. Then change roles if a partner is setting balls on the tee for you, or go collect the balls if you are practicing alone. Strive for clean hits (no bat contact with the tee).

If the tee you are using has an adjustment to move the ball inside and outside, add those variations in combination with high and low to double your practice (high inside, high outside, low inside, and low outside).

Success Goal = 8 cleanly hit balls out of 10 attempts at each height ___

Fixed center-post tee
at low setting ___
at high setting ___

Adjustable center-post tee
at low inside setting ___
at low outside setting ___
at high inside setting ___
at high outside setting ___

Success Check

- Keep your head down and focus throughout your entire swing, first on the ball on the tee and then on the top of the post that held the ball ___
- Use high-to-low or low-to-high swing path, depending on tee setting ___
- Start your hip turn before your arm swing ___
- Hips square and arms extended to hit the ball at the point of contact ___

To Increase Difficulty

- Adjust the tee, if possible, to place the ball on the corners of the plate: low inside, low outside, high inside, and high outside.
- If using a tee with a fixed center post, adjust your stance to place the ball in the relative inside and outside positions just described.

To Decrease Difficulty

- Take your stance so that the ball is in the middle of the strike zone.

SOFT-TOSS DRILLS

5. Soft Toss With Net or Fence

With a partner, position yourselves as hitter and tosser 10 feet from a hanging net (or blanket). Position yourselves so that the batted ball hits the net. The tosser has a bucket of 10 fleece, cloth-covered, or regulation balls. (For more experienced hitters, have 10 or 20 old tennis balls available also. Tennis balls are smaller and therefore more difficult to track and hit. Be sure the holes in the mesh of the net will block tennis balls before you try this drill with them.)

Conduct the drill using the techniques outlined in the Keys to Success (see figure 4.5) for both the hitter and the tosser. The hitter switches places with the tosser after hitting 10 balls. Repeat the drill two times, for a total of 20 hits for each partner.

Note: Using the backstop or outfield fence and regulation softballs for the soft-toss drill was an accepted practice for years. Recently, though, there has been litigation because of the ball's rebounding off the fence and hitting a participant. Consequently, using the bare fence for the drill is not recommended. However, it is possible to hang a large, thick, gymnastic-type mat on the fence that absorbs the force of the hit ball and dramatically limits the rebound.

Success Goal = 20 on-target tosses and 17 hits that go directly into the net (on good tosses) out of 20 attempts ___

Success Check

Tosser:

- Toss ball to hitter's contact zone ___

Hitter:

- Extend arms and wrists ___
- Hips square at contact ___
- Hit only balls tossed opposite your front foot ___

To Increase Difficulty

- Use a smaller ball.

To Decrease Difficulty

- Use a larger ball.

6. Bat-Eye Coordination

For this drill, you need about 15 golf-ball–size Wiffle balls as well as a wooden wand, a broom handle (cut to bat length), or a stickball bat. *Caution*: Be sure that anything you use to hit with has a taped hand grip that enables you to hold onto it. If you are making your own "bat," do not use plastic tape or any other slick or slippery material for the grip. Cloth-backed adhesive tape works well.

This drill is like drill 5, but must be performed in an unobstructed area. It is also helpful to do the drill in groups of three—the third partner uses a container to retrieve the Wiffle balls as they are hit. Rotate roles after the hitter has had a minimum of 15 swings.

The key to hitting a smaller ball is to track it carefully into the contact zone. Do not overswing (swing too hard); just try to make solid contact with the ball. This is a difficult skill, and you should practice it often if you find you are swinging and missing the ball in games.

Success Goal =
12 on-target tosses out of 15 attempts ___
10 full-contact hits (ball goes forward) out of 15 attempts ___

Success Check

Tosser:
- Toss ball waist-high opposite hitter's front foot ___

Hitter:
- Head down, watch ball go into contact zone ___
- Make solid contact ___
- Don't overswing ___

To Increase Difficulty
- Tosser varies the position of the tosses within the contact zone.
- Hitter uses bottom hand only on the swing.

To Decrease Difficulty
- Increase the arc of the toss.
- Use a larger "bat," such as a Wiffle-ball bat.

7. Hit the Ball Where It's Tossed

This drill is set up like the previous drill, except that you use 10 regular softballs and a real bat. The hitter and tosser position themselves for the ball toss. The third partner takes the empty bucket to the field to retrieve the hit balls.

The tosser must now adjust the height of the tosses in the order given in the Success Goal. The batter hits high balls with the low-to-high swing pattern, which should produce fly balls. The hitter practices hitting low balls with the high-to-low swing pattern, which should produce ground balls.

When fielding a grounder, the third partner uses proper ground ball fielding technique. Catch a fly ball with correct fly ball fielding technique. Put the fielded balls into the bucket. After a set of 10 tosses to the hitter, rotate roles. The fielder brings the bucket to the tosser position. The hitter takes the empty bucket out to the fielding position. The tosser moves to the hitting position.

Success Goal = 7 correct hits out of 10 attempts on each of the following swing patterns:
fly ball hits on high tosses (low-to-high swing) ___
ground ball hits on low tosses (high-to-low swing) ___
appropriate fly ball or ground ball hits on random high or low tosses ___

Success Check

Tosser:
- Accurate tosses at appropriate height for hitting task ___

Hitter:
- Swing path low-to-high for fly ball ___
- Swing path high-to-low for ground ball ___

Fielder:
- Get into position to field the ball with two hands ___

To Increase Difficulty
- Use only the random order Success Goal.

To Decrease Difficulty
- Focus on only one swing path.

PITCHED-BALL DRILLS

Any of the following drills that involve hitting the pitched ball can be done as combination drills, with fielders practicing the skills of fielding ground balls and fly balls, throwing, and catching. If drills are done in groups of two or three, you must make a provision for collecting the hit balls. Using a large plastic bucket with a handle for ease in carrying is recommended. You can also use a plastic milk crate, but it is more difficult for one person to carry.

If throwing is not one of the practice tasks when fielders are used, use two buckets. Start with a full one by the pitcher and an empty one in the field. Collect the fielded balls in the bucket in the field. Have the players who are rotating into and out of the hitting role ferry the buckets in and out.

8. Bleacher Ball Drop

You need a partner for this drill. The hitter places a glove on the ground (to simulate home plate) approximately 2 feet away from the end of a set of bleachers. The hitter stands at "home plate" facing the bleachers with the front foot opposite the plate. The hitter takes a couple of practice swings to make sure the bat covers home plate but will not contact the bleachers during the swing. The partner stands at the end of the bleacher, slightly in front of and above the head of the hitter. The partner in the bleachers should have a bucket of 20 balls (regulation if outside; Wiffle or fleece if inside).

The partner drops the ball so that it angles down toward the back edge of the plate, simulating the slow-pitch pitch, or drops it straight down on the front edge of the plate, simulating a modified or fast pitch. The hitter swings, hitting the ball as it comes into the contact zone. Hit 10 balls, then change roles. Collect the balls after both partners hit. Repeat the sequence. This drill can also be set up to include fielders.

Success Goal = 8 hits beyond a target distance of 100 feet out of 10 attempts ___

Success Check

Tosser:
- Drop the ball into the hitter's contact zone ___

Hitter:
- Time the swing, hit the ball in the contact zone by the front foot ___
- Keep head down, see the bat hit the ball ___

Fielders:
- See the ball as it leaves the bat ___
- Quickly move into position to field the ball with two hands ___

To Increase Difficulty

- Prior to dropping the ball, the tosser specifies the type of hit that must be executed (fly ball or ground ball).
- Use specific targets at varying distances and directions.

To Decrease Difficulty

- Do not use a target distance.

9. Call Balls and Strikes

Game play requires that hitters be able to read the pitch that is being delivered. It is critical that a hitter not waste an at-bat by standing and watching three strikes go by or swinging at pitches that are not in the strike zone. Hitters need to practice watching the ball come from the pitcher so they can tell a strike from a ball.

This drill requires a group of three—a hitter, a pitcher, and a catcher. The pitcher stands at an appropriate regulation pitching distance from home plate. The catcher is in the catcher's position behind home plate in full gear. The hitter takes her regular batting stance at the plate with a bat.

The pitcher should be focusing on proper pitching technique and attempting to throw strikes during this drill. The pitcher pitches a regulation softball. The batter takes a stride and initiates the hip turn and shoulder turn only—keeping hands and arms still and not swinging at the ball. The batter watches the ball pass over (or by) the plate and calls a ball if the pitch is outside the strike zone or a strike if the pitch goes into the strike zone. The catcher verifies the call of the pitch. Remember, the strike zone is the area over home plate between the batter's back shoulder and the front knee for slow-pitch, and between the armpits and the top of the knees for fast-pitch and modified-pitch. Rotate roles after 10 pitches.

Success Goal = 8 agreed-upon calls (hitter and catcher) out of 10 pitches ___

Success Check

Pitcher:

- Throw strikes, but try to hit the corners ___

Hitter:

- Take the stride and initiate the hip and shoulder turns only, *not swinging the bat at the ball* ___
- Watch the ball from the pitcher's hand to the catcher's glove and accurately call a ball or a strike ___

Catcher:

- Accurately verify the call of the pitch by the batter ___

To Increase Difficulty

- Hitter calls the position of the pitch (for example, high outside) in addition to calling a ball or strike.
- Hitter calls the type of hit that is dictated by the pitch (only on strikes, see Step 7); for example, if the pitch is inside, pull the ball; if outside, hit to the opposite field; if low, hit the ball on the ground; if high, go for the home run.

To Decrease Difficulty

- Use an umpire to verify the batter's ball-or-strike call.
- Catcher calls the pitch and batter verifies the call.

10. Making Contact

This drill requires a group of three, with additional fielders optional. Set up as in the previous drill. The catcher *must* wear complete catching gear. The hitter takes a full swing at each strike pitch and attempts to make contact with the ball. When hitting, focus on contacting the ball out front, opposite your front foot. Watch the ball all the way to the bat. Take a smooth, fluid swing at the ball. Just make contact—do not try to hit the ball hard. Hit the middle of the ball. Hit the ball where it is pitched.

Score each hit according to the ball's path as follows:

Landing zone	Settle zone	Contact points		Hits		Points scored
Foul	Foul	1	×	___	=	___
Infield A	Infield A or B	2	×	___	=	___
Infield B	Infield B	3	×	___	=	___
Infield A or B	Outfield	4	×	___	=	___
Outfield	Outfield	5	×	___	=	___

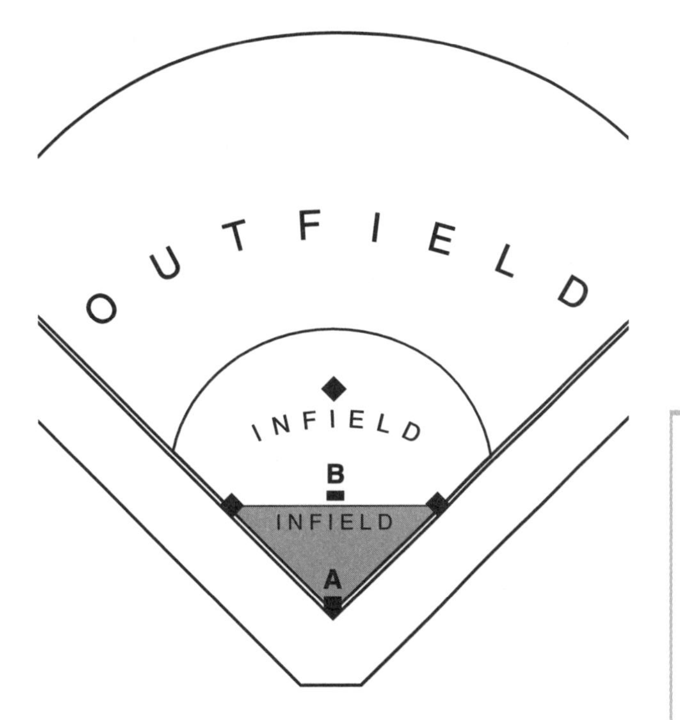

Success Goal = 25 points on 10 strike pitches ___

Success Check

- Hit strikes ___
- Meet ball out front ___
- Just make contact ___

To Increase Difficulty

- Hit outside pitch to opposite field, pull inside pitch.

To Decrease Difficulty

- Do not use the scoring chart—instead, count 1 point for every hit that goes anywhere in fair territory.
- Score any ball that lands in fair territory and ends up in the outfield.

11. Between the White Lines

This drill is set up as the two previous drills are. The hitter attempts to hit a fair ball into the outfield—but distance is not the focus. Instead, you should focus on making contact and keeping the ball in play. It is not often that the home run wins the game. In fast-pitch softball, the home run is difficult to hit and occurs less frequently than in slow-pitch. Consequently, it is more important to be able to hit the ball and keep it in play. In other words, when the ball is hit into the field of play, baserunners have the chance to advance and either score or become threats to score. As the hitter in this drill, make up game situations for yourself; for example, you need a base hit with two outs and a runner on third; or with no outs and a runner on second, you must hit the ball to right field to advance the runner to third base; or with one out and a runner on third, a long fly ball will score the run.

Success Goal = 8 fair hits ending up in the outfield out of 10 hits ___

Success Check

- Smooth, fluid swing ___
- Head down, watch the ball to the bat ___

To Increase Difficulty

- Place-hit the ball.

To Decrease Difficulty

- Don't use imaginary game situations, just try to make solid contact and put the ball in play in fair territory.

12. Hitting Line Drives

Mark the outfield with two curved lines going from foul line to foul line, one 100 feet and the other 130 feet from home plate. The area between the lines is the target landing area for line drives.

The hitter attempts to hit a line drive that would clear the infield but land in front of the outfielders. In addition to landing in the target area, a successful hit must be judged to be a line drive (it must traverse a relatively horizontal path) and not a fly ball. If available, a trained observer can make the judgment, or participants in the drill can judge.

Timing of the swing is critical for success in this drill if hitting against an arc-trajectory pitch such as in slow-pitch. The ball must be contacted above the waist as it drops through the strike zone. The swing must be horizontal, and the middle of the ball should be contacted. If practicing with a pitcher using a flat pitch, ask the pitcher to keep the pitches above the waist.

Success Goal = 6 balls landing in the target area out of 10 hits ___

Success Check

- Swing path is horizontal ___
- Contact is made in the middle of the ball ___

To Increase Difficulty

- Hit the line drives to selected spots within the target area (for example, to right field).

To Decrease Difficulty

- Increase the depth of the target area.

13. Hitting the Gap

From home plate, mark two fan-shaped alleys (a narrow strip of the field). One alley goes through the shortstop position to the left center-field fence, and the other goes through the second baseman's position to the right center-field fence.

The hitter attempts to hit the ball into these target areas and all the way to the fence. A hit into these alleys (gaps in coverage by the defensive setup) will most often result in a safe trip to first base, advancing any baserunners one or more bases.

Score each on-target hit according to the ball's path as follows:

Landing zone	Settle zone	Points		Hits		Points scored
Infield alley	Short outfield	1	×	___	=	___
Outfield alley	Outfield	3	×	___	=	___
Outfield alley	Outfield fence	5	×	___	=	___

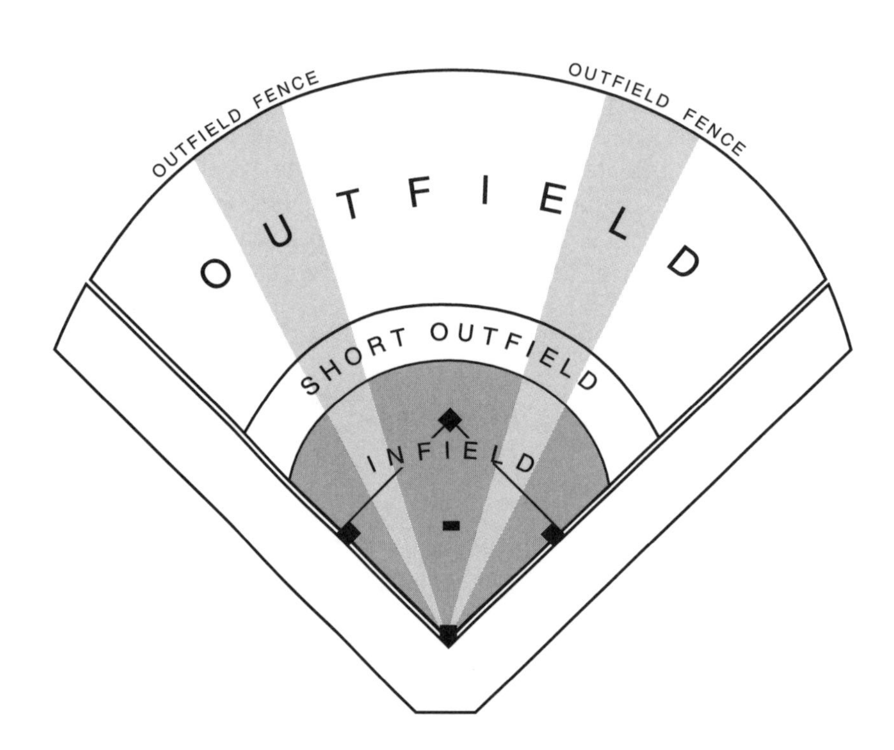

Success Goal = 20 points on 10 hits ___

Success Check

- Adjust stance and swing to hit to opposite-field alley ___
- Full hip turn and arm extension at contact ___

To Increase Difficulty

- Based on the pitch location, hit the ball to the appropriate alley.
- Hit behind the runner (see drill 14).

To Decrease Difficulty

- Increase the size of the alley.
- Don't use the point system, just attempt to hit the ball in the alleys.

14. Hitting Behind the Runner

Use the alley marking to right center field from the previous drill as one target area. For the second target area, start with the right-field foul line as one of its boundary lines; from the foul line at the outfield fence, go into fair territory 30 feet and mark the target's inside boundary line from the fence to home plate.

The hitter attempts to hit the ball to these right-side targets. In a game situation, a runner on first or second base could advance to third or beyond when you "hit behind the runner" into these alleys.

To hit to the right side, the right-handed hitter should close the batting stance slightly (so the left foot is closer to home plate than the right foot) and delay the swing, making contact when the ball is toward the back of the plate. The pitcher can help facilitate this drill by pitching the ball to the outside part of the plate (for a right-handed batter).

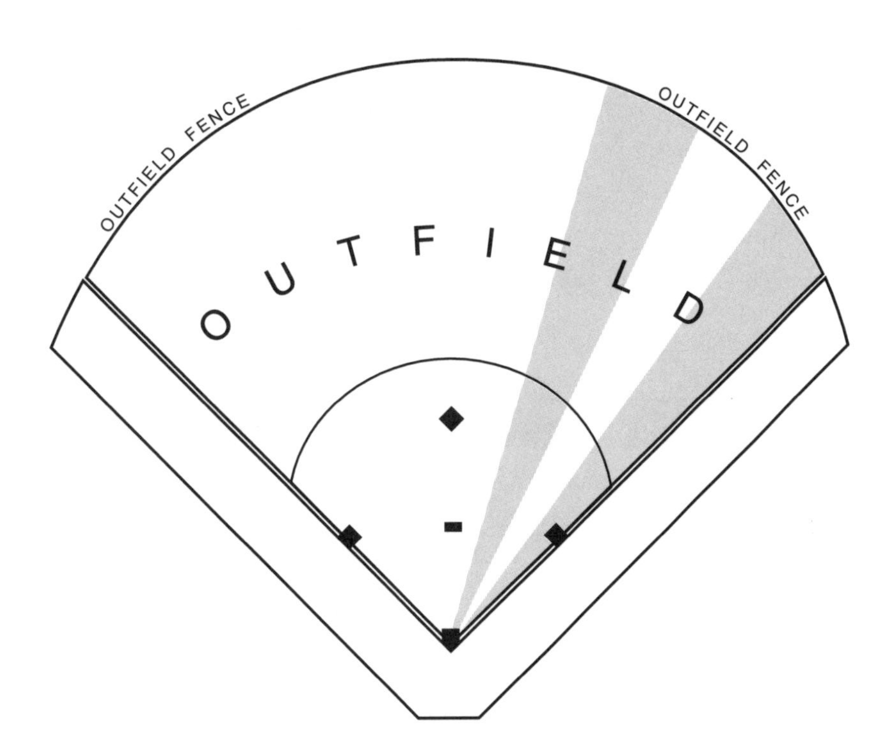

Success Goal = 8 balls landing in the outfield portion of either target area out of 10 hits ___

Success Check

- Adjust stance and timing of swing to hit to right-field targets ___
- Swing through the ball, hit line drives or ground balls ___

To Increase Difficulty

- Select one of the two targets to hit to.

To Decrease Difficulty

- Use a batting tee.

15. Situation Play

Again, a pitcher, catcher, and hitter are needed. However, this is a "let's pretend" drill. A pitcher and a hitter alternate setting hypothetical game situations for the hitter. For example, one player says, "There's a runner on third base and no one out in the bottom of the seventh inning with the score tied." The batter attempts to execute a hit (or even an out) that would produce positive offensive results for the hypothetical situation.

The pitcher attempts to get the batter out. Using the regulation three strikes (an out) and four balls (a base on balls), the batter has one turn at bat to accomplish a given task. Judgments on hits must be made as to whether they would be base hits or outs of various kinds, and whether catchable fly balls would be deep enough to advance a runner, and so on.

The batter scores 1 point for each turn at bat that produces a positive offensive result for the specified situation. A base on balls is always a point for the batter. The pitcher scores 1 point when the batter fails to produce a positive result (that is, makes an out that doesn't advance a runner). Players change roles after six situations have been completed (each player has set three situations).

12 situations ___

Pitcher:

- Throw accurately enough for a "game" to occur ___

Hitter:

- Make appropriate offensive choice to address the situation and execute the required skill at least half the time ___

HITTING SUCCESS SUMMARY

Stepping up to the plate with runners in scoring position and getting a base hit or laying down the perfect bunt is the epitome of *fun* in offensive *fun*damentals. Another aspect of the fun in hitting is the opportunity you have as the hitter to match wits with the pitcher. In a game situation, the pitcher is trying to prevent you from successfully accomplishing your task. The pitcher will try to pitch to your weakness and stay away from your strength. In order to match wits with the pitcher, you need to know your strengths and weaknesses as a hitter. And, especially in fast-pitch, you need to know the strengths and weaknesses of the pitcher. Learn the tendencies pitchers have in pitching to batters, particularly to you, in certain game situations. With two strikes on you, is the pitcher's *out* pitch a rise ball, a drop, a high-inside fastball, or a change-up? Does the pitcher repeat the same pattern of pitch placement for each batter? Does the defense play you to pull the ball? The mental aspect of hitting, so important if you are going to be a strong and successful hitter, is also a fun part of the game for the offensive player.

The individual nature of the sport of softball is just as apparent in the offensive phase of the game as it is in the defensive phase. When you are in the batter's box facing the pitcher, attempting to accomplish the offensive task at hand, no one else can help you. You and you alone must make the judgments and execute the skill technique to produce the desired result. Ask your coach, a teammate, or an experienced observer to evaluate your hitting technique using the Keys to Success checklists: figure 4.2 for hitting, figure 4.5 when hitting soft tosses, and both checklists combined when hitting a live-pitched ball.

Remember the importance of the correct contact position: hips square to the pitcher, arms and wrists extended, contact the ball in front of the front foot, and keep the head down and see the ball hit the bat. Use the appropriate swing path for the pitched ball and for the task to be accomplished. Be a relaxed hitter. Be aggressive, want to hit, outguess the pitcher. Hitting is fun!

STEP 5 BASERUNNING

Now that you have learned several offensive and defensive skills, let's go on to another important offensive skill—baserunning. As a good baserunner, you have many opportunities to contribute to the success of your team. Major league ball players like Lou Brock and Maury Wills were valued for their baserunning skills more than their hitting skills. The success of the 1996 U.S.A. Olympic softball team in its quest for the gold medal in Atlanta was in large part due to the baserunning abilities of players like Dot Richardson and Laura Berg. Laura has great speed, while Dot's success is due to her smart baserunning decisions. Once you hit the ball, you must run to first base. *Batter-baserunner* is the official rulebook term identifying the batter who, one way or another, has finished a turn at bat and is moving from home plate to first base. By definition, the term *batter* refers only to the person at bat and does not describe the person running to first base. Technically, then, as the batter, say you hit a ground ball to the shortstop. As you run to first base, you become the batter-baserunner until you either reach first base safely or are put out there. You become a *baserunner* when you have reached first base without having been put out.

Why Is Baserunning Important?

Baserunning is the only way you can advance around the bases and score a run. Your degree of baserunning skill often makes the difference between your being safe or out on a play. Thus, correct baserunning technique is essential to your team's offensive success. Baserunning technique is the same whether you are playing in a fast-, modified-, or slow-pitch game. However, the rules for baserunning are different for fast- and slow-pitch games.

Running is a fundamental locomotor skill you probably learned as a young child. However, *baserunning* is a skill specific to softball and baseball that involves more than simple physical running skills: you must exercise good judgment in executing those skills. The physical skill is the development of maximum speed in short distances as you run around a 60-foot square. Traveling the shortest distance possible, despite the fact that making a 90-degree turn at each base is impossible, is the tactical baserunning skill. In both fast- and slow-pitch games, you may overrun first base and home plate, but must stop on second and third base when advancing directly to those bases. When baserunning in fast-pitch softball, you may leave the base the moment the pitcher releases the pitch. This allows you to be off the base when the ball is hit, thus shortening your distance from the next base at the moment of the hit. In slow-pitch softball, though, you may not leave a base until the ball is hit or crosses home plate; thus, you must run the full distance to the next base after the ball is hit.

You must also know when and how to run. Will you try to advance, or will you return to the base you just rounded? Will you slide or stand up coming into a base? These and many other questions relate to your ability to use good judgment when baserunning. Once you get on base, sound baserunning techniques and good judgment make it possible for you to score runs—and win games!

How to Overrun First Base

When you have hit a ground ball playable by an infielder, you must get out of the batter's box as quickly as possible and run at top speed *over* first base. Remember that first base and home plate are the two bases you may overrun. (The *batter's box* is the marked area at home plate in which the batter must stand when making contact with the ball. You are out if you step on home plate as you contact the ball with the bat; not because you stepped on home plate, but because you were out of the batter's box when you hit the ball.)

After hitting the ball, take your first step out of the batter's box with your back foot (see figure 5.1a). You begin with your back foot because your swing follow-through puts weight on your front foot. Your run to first base *must* take you into foul territory (outside the base line) and into the alley that starts halfway between home and first. If you run from home plate to first base in fair territory and are hit by a thrown ball, you are out.

As a left-handed batter, your first step with your back foot should be very close to being in foul territory because most of the left-handed batter's box is in foul territory on the first-base side. You would step into fair territory only if batting in the very front of the box, in which case you need to get to the foul side of the baseline as soon as possible. If you are a right-handed batter, you must make a conscious effort to start your movement to first base toward the foul line, and not run directly at the base from

FIGURE 5.1 **KEYS TO SUCCESS**

OVERRUNNING FIRST BASE

Preparation

1. First step with back foot ___
2. Get to foul territory ___
3. Accelerate quickly ___
4. Get to top speed before reaching base ___
5. Look to coach, *then* focus on base ___

a

Execution

1. Run on foul ground ___
2. Continue running at top speed ___
3. Don't break stride ___
4. Focus on base ___
5. Contact front corner of base ___

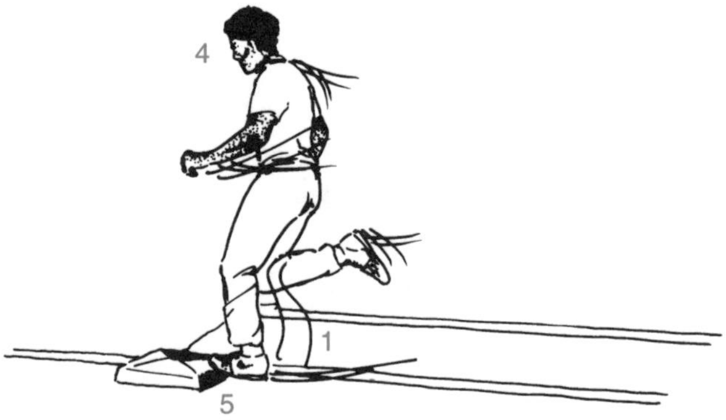

b

Follow-Through

1. Bend knees ___
2. Short steps ___
3. Lean back and stop ___
4. Turn to left ___
5. Go directly back to base ___

c

the point at which you complete your swing follow-through.

Once you are on the foul side of the first-base foul line, run directly over the first-base bag, touching it with your foot on the front corner that is on the foul line (see figure 5.1b). Overrun the base at full speed, traveling in a straight line (follow the foul line). Then start to slow down by bending your knees, taking short steps, and leaning back until you can easily come to a stop. Turn to your left, toward fair territory (see figure 5.1c). If you have been called safe, return *directly* to the base. If, as you turn toward the field of play, you see that the ball has been misplayed, make a judgment about whether you should continue toward second base. Once you *make an attempt* to go to second base, you are no longer allowed to return to first base freely and may be tagged out.

Figure 5.2 Rounding the base.

How to Round a Base

You round a base when you think you might be able to advance beyond it or you know you are advancing beyond it because of an extra-base hit. The technique used for rounding a base is designed to let you take the most direct route around the bases. When you are about 15 feet from the base, curve your path to it by swinging out to the right about three strides, then heading back in toward the base. The pattern you run looks like the outside edge of a spoon—thus the term *spooning* is sometimes used for rounding a base. As you cross the base, lean toward the infield and make contact with the *inside* corner of the base with your left foot (see figure 5.2).

If advancing to the next base, continue in a direct line toward that base. If you decide you cannot safely advance to the next base, take only a few steps past the base you just rounded, bend your knees, shift your weight back, and come to a stop. Retreat to the base by walking backward to it, keeping your eyes focused on the person with the ball.

When rounding a base in a game, you cannot return freely to it; instead, you are liable to be tagged out. If the ball is thrown to the person covering the base you have rounded, get back to the base to avoid being tagged; otherwise, you will be out.

BASERUNNING SUCCESS STOPPERS

Errors in overrunning first base usually occur in one or more of four stages: leaving the batter's box, getting into foul territory, the speed of overrunning the base, and the turn to return to the base. Leaving the box with the back foot taking the first step makes acceleration easier. Moving into foul territory as soon as possible eliminates the possibility of your being called out for being hit by a thrown ball while in fair territory. Running at top speed over first base, slowing down, and turning to the left to return to the base make it possible for you to see the field of play and determine whether you have the opportunity to advance another base because of a defensive misplay.

The primary cause of error when rounding a base is failing to swing out to the right in a small arc as you approach the base. Even though the shortest distance between two points is a straight line, it is impossible to run at full speed from home to second making a right-angle turn at first base. If you do not run in a small arc before the base, you will have to make a large, wide arc after crossing the base. That takes more time. The most common baserunning errors when overrunning first base and using the rounding-the-base technique are listed below, along with suggestions on how to correct them.

Error	Correction
Overrunning First Base	
1. You start to run out of the batter's box using your front foot.	1. At the end of your swing's follow-through, be sure your full weight is on your front foot, so your rear foot is free to move.
2. You run all the way to first in fair territory.	2. *Don't!* Get over into foul territory as soon as possible.
3. You leap for the bag or take short and long strides just before reaching first base.	3. Maintain stride, and contact the front outside (foul line) corner of the base with either foot.
Rounding a Base	
1. You end up out in the right-field grass when making the turn at first base.	1. You started your rounding turn too late, probably *at* the base. Start your turn 15 feet before the base.
2. You slow down at the base so you can make the turn.	2. Be sure to swing out to the right 15 feet before the base and head to the base at full speed.

How to Advance When on Base

As indicated previously, baserunning rules differ for slow- and fast-pitch softball. Leading off on the pitch and stealing are allowed in fast-pitch (see Step 7), but not in slow-pitch. However, advancing *into scoring position* (second or third base) is very important in any type of softball game. Once you have gotten on base and are stopped, you want to increase your chances of attaining the next base on a hit by your teammate, or by stealing in fast-pitch. The faster you can get to the next base, the more likely it is that you will beat a throw and arrive safely. When standing on first, second, or third base with a teammate up at bat, you take a position with one foot (usually your dominant or takeoff foot) in contact with the edge of the bag closest to the next base (see figure 5.3). We'll discuss other leadoff stances in Step 7.

Your other foot is either in a forward stride position ahead of the base, or just behind your takeoff foot and next to the base. Select the most comfortable foot position, and, most important, the position that provides you with the quickest and strongest movement off the base. If not stealing, turn your head to watch the batter so that you can see the ball as it goes over home plate or is hit. If stealing, watch the pitcher so that you can time your pushoff from the

Figure 5.3 Initial baserunning posture for rapid acceleration.

base with the ball leaving the pitcher's hand. Another technique is to focus on the pitcher's striding foot and time your pushoff with that foot contacting the ground.

At the moment the ball is hit in slow-pitch, or the ball is released in fast-pitch and you are stealing, leave the base by pushing off with the foot that is in contact with the base, taking your first step with your rear foot. Run directly toward the next base. Either stop at that base or round it, depending on the circumstances.

Another situation affects the manner in which you leave a base. There is a rule in softball that applies when a baserunner is on base with less than two outs and a fly ball is hit. You, the baserunner, must be in contact with the base when the fly ball is caught, or you can be put out by a throw to the base. You may leave the base on the fly ball, but you must return to the base if the fly ball is caught. If you go too far from the base on a fly ball, the fielder who catches the fly will throw it to the base you left on the hit. Then, if the ball is in the hands of the fielder covering the base, and he tags you or even merely steps on the base before you get back to the base, you are out.

When leaving the base on a ball that is hit into the air, you must decide how far from the base you can venture. If you are on first base and a fly ball is hit to right field, you should go no more than two or three steps off the base (8 to 10 feet). This is because the right fielder or the short fielder has only a short throw to put you out at the base if the ball is caught. On the other hand, if a fly ball is hit to left field when you are on first base, you can go nearly half the distance to second base. Then, if the ball is dropped, you will be that much closer to second base; if the ball is caught, you should be able to beat the throw back to first base.

When you are on second or third base, the same principles apply. If a fly ball is hit to an outfield position close to the base you are on, you must not venture too far toward the next base. On the other hand, if the fly ball is hit to an outfield position far away from the base you are on, you can leave the base and venture farther toward the next base.

You must decide how far you can progress toward the next base on a fly ball and still be able to get back to your original base before the throw if the ball is caught. If the fly ball is not caught or if any ground ball is hit, your job is to run at maximum speed to the next base and either stop or round it and go to the next base. This is the judgment and decision-making of baserunning—one of the most challenging and fun parts of softball offense.

Tagging Up and Advancing on a Caught Fly Ball

Another important baserunning tactic is tagging up and advancing to the next base after a fly ball is caught. This opportunity usually occurs when the ball is hit deep into the outfield. For example, as the baserunner on second base, you would immediately return to second base on a deep fly ball that can be caught by the right fielder. Once the right fielder touches the ball, you may break contact with second base and advance to third base. Make sure you don't leave second base *before* the fielder touches the ball. The play on you is a tag play, so you must beat the throw to the base and avoid being tagged out. The same tagging-up strategy applies when you are a runner on third base and a fly ball is hit to any deep outfield position. In such case, you would not only be advancing a base, you would be scoring a run.

How to Slide

Previously, you learned that you may overrun first base and home plate, but must stop on second and third base when advancing to those bases. Sliding into a base where you must stop is the fastest way to get to that base because you do not have to slow your run in order to stop at the base. Sliding into a base is also an effective way to avoid a tag when the play is not a force-out (when the baseman has to tag you with the ball rather than just catching the ball and touching the base). You are not allowed to remain on your feet and crash into a defensive player who has the ball or is about to catch the ball to make a play on you at that base, such as at home plate; therefore, you must slide whenever that situation arises. Sliding involves lowering your body to the ground while in full running stride so that you go into a base feet-first. Head-first sliding into a fielder or base is not recommended, as serious injury can occur to the head, neck, arms, and hands. When you are approximately 10 feet from the base and still running at full speed, throw your shoulders back and lift your legs, turning slightly to the side on which you want to slide. Keep your hands up and contact the ground with your body fully extended as explained in the various situations that follow.

Techniques for sliding vary, but some general principles apply to sliding in most situations. On a close tag play, slide away from the tag and present a very small target for the tag. On a throw from the center fielder to second base, slide to the infield side of the base on your left side and hook the corner of the base closest to the pitcher with your right foot (see figure 5.4a). If the throw is coming from the infield (for example, from the catcher), slide to the outfield side of the base on your right side and hook the base with your left foot (see figure 5.4b).

The straight-in (or down-and-up) slide is used when you can see that the throw will not arrive in time to put you out; however, you still need to maintain full speed into the base to assure reaching it safely. Correct execution of this sliding technique also brings you to a standing position so that if the throw is off-target and goes past the base, you are ready to advance to the next base. In order to end up facing in the direction of the next base, you should slide on your left side. As you lower you body into the slide, contact the ground with the outside of your upper leg or left buttock and the outside part of your lower leg just below the knee. The front of your knee should not contact the ground. Bend your left leg so that the front of your entire lower leg or shin comes up against the base. Keep your right leg straight and lift it slightly so that your foot clears the base (see figure 5.5a). Your forward momentum will be slowed as your left leg contacts the base. Your forward momentum will then be transferred to vertical lift, causing your body to come up over the base and allowing you to stand with your right foot on the far side of the base (see figure 5.5b). You are now in a position to advance to the next base if the situation presents itself.

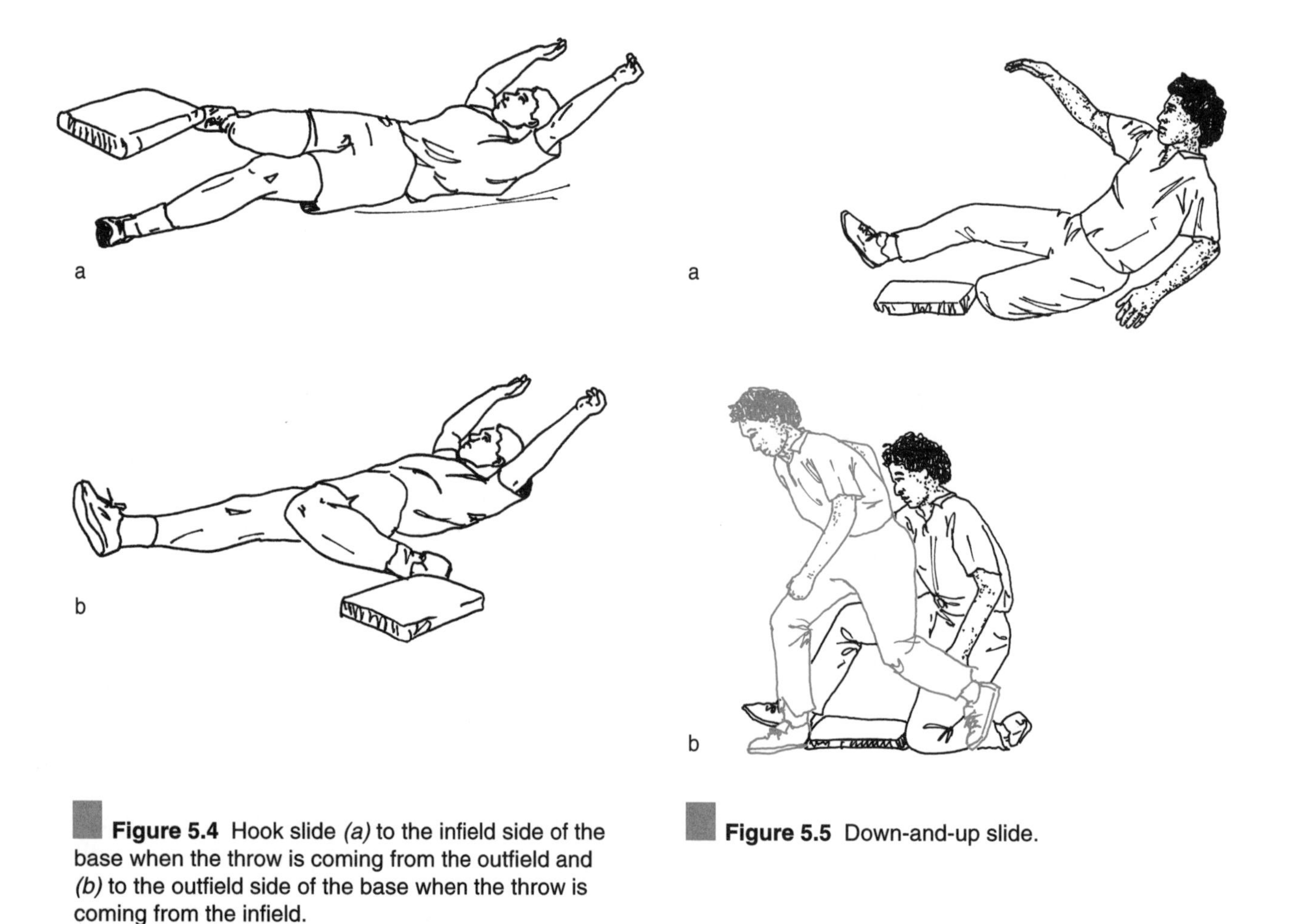

Figure 5.4 Hook slide *(a)* to the infield side of the base when the throw is coming from the outfield and *(b)* to the outfield side of the base when the throw is coming from the infield.

Figure 5.5 Down-and-up slide.

SLIDING SUCCESS STOPPERS

Sliding mistakes usually occur during the takeoff or the landing. In the takeoff there should be a smooth transition from an upright forward-lean running position to a backward-lean, body-extended, flat-out position. A common mistake is jumping into the takeoff rather than lowering into it. When you jump into the takeoff you elevate your body, which makes for a greater distance to fall to the ground. Therefore, you not only have a much harder landing, but also you are slower getting to the base. Another common mistake is starting your slide too close to the base; a late takeoff will cause you to slide into the base forcefully, risking injury.

Sliding on the wrong side of the body, especially for the down-and-up slide, is a typical landing problem. When sliding into a base with the option of going on to the next base, the landing should be on the left side so that when you pop up you are facing the direction of the next base. If you slide into second base on your right side, you will come up facing right field rather than third base!

Error	Correction
1. You jump into the slide.	1. *Don't!* Lower your body and fully extend.
2. You land on your hands.	2. Throw your hands and arms up as you start to slide.

BASERUNNING DRILLS

Prior to trying any of the baserunning drills that call for a sliding option in the next section of this step, practice sliding using the following suggestions.

Sand Walk-Through

1. In a large sand area, such as a long jump pit (or the beach!), sit down in the sand in the position shown in figure 5.5a. Be sure you are turned slightly onto your left side so you are resting on your left buttock and the outside of your bent left leg. Lean back and put both hands up in the air over and behind your head. Try to *feel* where your legs, hips, seat, and arms are when you are in this sliding position.
2. Next, while walking through the sand, gradually bend your knees, lower your hips, throw your right leg forward (don't jump), bend your left leg, and fall back onto the sand in the same position you were in in step 1. Be sure your hands are up over your head as you land—don't reach down to catch yourself with your hands. Try this a few more times, each time increasing your walking speed. Remember, *do not jump* into the landing sliding position and do not catch yourself with your hands.
3. When you feel comfortable assuming the landing position in the sand, move to one of the following techniques for practicing sliding.

Sliding Practice on Wet Grass

This is a great option for a nice hot summer day! Using plenty of water, wet down a thick grassy area that is free from any hazards such as glass and rocks. Wear an old pair of sweatpants or other long pants that you don't mind getting wet and grass-stained, and take off your shoes so that you can run in socks. *Do not wear cleats*! Place a loose base (with no spikes attached), a carpet square, or a similar flat object in the middle of the wet grass area to represent a base. Take a starting position 30 to 35 feet away from the base and run toward it. When you are 10 to

12 feet away from the base and while still running at top speed, lean back, lower your body, bend your left leg, throw your right leg out and forward (keeping your right foot off the ground), and land in the same position you assumed in the sand. Make sure you throw both hands up over your head and tuck your chin to your chest so you don't hit the back of your head on the ground. You should end up sliding into the base. If you didn't make it to the base, you probably weren't running fast enough when you started your slide. If you took the base with you in your slide, you may have started your slide too late or too close to the base. Be sure to start your slide at least 10 feet from the base and let your slide take you to the base.

If no water is available, put a large piece of plastic or cardboard on the grass and slide on that. Another option is to wait for a warm, rainy day!

Snow Sliding

If you live in an area that gets snow, a great way to practice sliding is on grass that is covered with just a few inches of snow. If the snow is too deep, it is too hard to run. Set up your practice area and use the same technique as you did for sliding on wet grass.

1. Leave the Batter's Box

With a bat, assume your regular batting stance in the batter's box. Swing at 10 imaginary pitches, using the technique described in figure 4.2 for hitting. Emphasize the end of the follow-through. On each swing, make sure your weight is on your front foot, your front knee is bent, and your body is leaning toward first base. Drive out of the batter's box, taking the first step with your back foot, and release your top hand and hold the bat with your bottom hand as you start toward first base. Drop (do not throw) your bat on the ground in foul territory as you take your second or third running step. Take several full strides toward first base (until you get into foul territory and have taken two more strides down the line for a right-handed batter, four for a left-hander).

Success Goal = 5 consecutive sequences using correct technique in the swing, in leading out of the box with the rear foot, and in getting into foul territory within 10 feet of home plate ___

Success Check

- Take the first step out of the batter's box with the back foot ___
- Get into foul territory within 10 feet of home plate ___

To Increase Difficulty

- Increase the distance of the run to first base.

To Decrease Difficulty

- Make the swing, drive out of the box, and take the first three steps in slow motion.

2. Over the Base

Initiate this drill exactly as you did the previous drill. Swing at imaginary pitches and drive out of the batter's box with the rear foot. Instead of stopping after several strides, though, continue to run to first base. Do not slow down before you get to the base. After crossing first base, turn left and return to the base. *Do not turn out to the right after crossing first base or return directly to home plate—go back to first base!* Execute the skill according to the techniques outlined in figure 5.1.

If other runners are practicing with you, quickly leave first base after you have completed your correct return to the base. Get well out of the baseline so that you will be out of the way of the next runner.

Success Goal = 10 consecutive error-free sequences ___

Success Check

- Run in foul territory within the alley markings ___
- Continue running at top speed until *over* the base ___
- Come to a controlled stop ___
- Turn to the left and return directly to the base ___

To Increase Difficulty

- Use a regulation base.
- After crossing the base and turning to the left, make a move toward second base, hesitate, and then continue eight steps at full speed toward an imaginary second base.
- After crossing the base and turning to the left, make a move toward second base, change your mind, and run back to first base (the outfield baseline corner) and stop on the base.
- Using a batting tee, hit a ground ball and run to first base.

To Decrease Difficulty

- Use an indoor base so the height of the base does not make you afraid of tripping over it.
- Decrease the distance so you can maintain full speed.
- Go from home to first base without using a bat in the swing.

3. Tee Ball and Run

In a game, you will have to hit a real ball and run to first base. We will simulate this situation by having you hit the ball off the batting tee and run to first base.

Set up a batting tee at home plate. Hit a ground ball off the batting tee and run to first base. If you are working alone, have a bucket of 10 balls so that you can hit all 10 (running to first base with each hit) and then collect them all.

If you are working with a partner, hit the ground ball to your partner. Run to first base using correct technique. Your partner fields the ball and puts it into the bucket. When you have hit five balls and run to first base five times, change roles with your partner. Repeat the drill until you have each hit and run out 15 grounders. You may increase or decrease the difficulty of this drill by using the same ideas as outlined in drill 2.

Success Goal = 10 ground balls hit and correctly run out in 15 attempts ___

Success Check

- Run in foul territory within the alley markings ___
- Continue running at top speed until *over* the base ___
- Come to a controlled stop ___
- Turn to the left and return directly to the base ___

4. Overrun Base With First Baseman

You need to practice overrunning first base when the first baseman is there attempting to catch the thrown ball. This is when it is critical that you contact the front foul-line side of the base as you overrun it. You must be sure that you do not go across the center of the bag, because you may collide with the person making the catch.

This drill has two parts, and requires three participants. You are the batter-baserunner, one partner is the fielder, and the other partner is the first baseman. The ball is hit from the tee. Place a bucket of 10 balls beside the tee. The fielder has an empty bucket in which to place the fielded ground balls.

a. No-throw: You hit the ball to the fielder (who is standing at the shortstop position) and run to first base. The first baseman stands with one foot on the second-base side of the bag, leaning toward the shortstop. The first baseman reaches as if a throw were coming. The fielder fields the ball, but holds it. The fielder then watches to see whether you crossed the foul-line corner of the base. After you have completed five hits and runs to first base, rotate roles. Repeat the drill. Continue the drill until each of you has made five hits and runs to first base.

b. Throw: This time the fielder (still in the shortstop position) throws the ball to the player at first base after fielding the ball. The bucket is moved to the infield side of the first baseman (be sure that it is out of the way of both the first baseman and the batter-baserunner). Hit a ground ball to the fielder. The hit should make the fielder move no more than two steps to field it. After you hit the ball from the tee, run to first base. The shortstop fields the ball and throws it overhand to the first baseman. Try to beat the throw to first base. The first baseman drops the ball into the bucket. If the throw is off-target, the first baseman should just let it go; do not move toward it. The batter-baserunner must wear a batting helmet.

After five hits and runs to first base, rotate positions. Repeat this portion of the drill until you have each had 15 turns to hit the ball and run to first base. Count the number of times you get to first base safely (you beat the throw there or the first baseman does not catch the ball).

Success Goal =

a. 4 runs to first base with foot contct on foul-line corner of base out of 5 attempts ___
b. 7 times safe at first base out of 15 attempts ___

Success Check

- Run in foul territory within the alley markings ___
- Maintain full, consistent stride when contacting the base ___
- Contact the front corner of the base that is on the foul line ___
- Turn to the left and return directly to the base ___

To Increase Difficulty

- Try to hit a ground ball that requires the infielder to move two or three steps to the right or left to field.
- Make a game of the drill variation in which the ball is thrown to the first baseman (see drill 5). Play this game with four players (shortstop, first baseman, two batter-baserunners). One team is composed of two batter-baserunners. The other team consists of the shortstop and the first baseman. Keep score: 1 point for each run to first base in which the batter-baserunner is safe. Each player on the baserunner team gets five times at bat, then the two batter-baserunners rotate to the fielding and first-base positions. Keep track of the number of points you score as a team.

To Decrease Difficulty

- Use an indoor base.
- Decrease the distance to first base.
- Use the drill variation with no throw.
- Swing without the ball and batting tee.

5. Safe or Out

Let's play a game using the drill we just did. Do everything you did in the previous drill, but now keep score.

The batter must hit the ball off the tee as a ground ball in the range of the shortstop, making the shortstop move no more than two or three steps to the side or forward to field the ball (otherwise, the two defensive players score 1 point each). If the hitter makes it to first base safely on a good grounder, he gets a point. If the shortstop and first baseman combine to get the batter-baserunner out (the first baseman having the ball in the glove while contacting first base before the runner contacts the base), each of them gets a point.

Do the hit-and-run sequence five times, then rotate positions. Continue the game until each player has hit the ball 15 times. Keep track of your points.

Success Goal = Score more points than your partners ___

Success Check

Hitter:

- Hit goes within the range of the shortstop ___
- Reach first base safely ___

Shortstop:

- Field the ball cleanly ___
- Make a successful throw to the first baseman ___

First baseman:

- Catch the ball while contacting first base ___

To Increase Difficulty

- Fungo hit the ball (see Step 8).
- Extend the range expected of the shortstop.

To Decrease Difficulty

- Roll the ball directly at the shortstop.

6. Swing Out

To round a base, start running directly at a base. When 15 feet from the base, swing out to the right of the baseline and run in a semicircular path to the base. Cross the inside corner of the base, heading in the direction of the next base. Continue running for several strides past the base, then stop.

If practicing on a regulation softball field, start 30 feet from first base and round the base at full speed. Slow down 10 to 15 feet past the base. Walk or jog to a position 30 feet from second base and repeat the drill. Continue in this fashion around all the bases, including home. Pay attention to the size of the semicircular path you need to take to be able to cross the base heading in the general direction of the next base. Make sure you use the technique shown in figure 5.2.

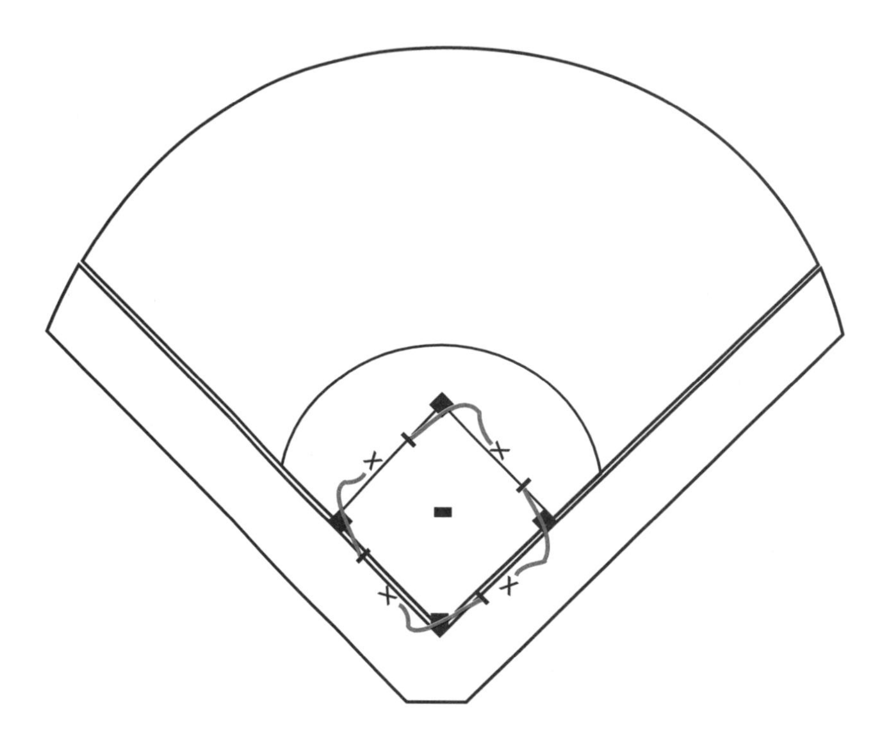

If practicing with just a single base set on the ground or floor, turn around when you have run 20 feet past the base and repeat the drill going to the same base. Swing out to the right of the base each time and cross the base from right to left. After four repetitions, you will be back to your original starting position.

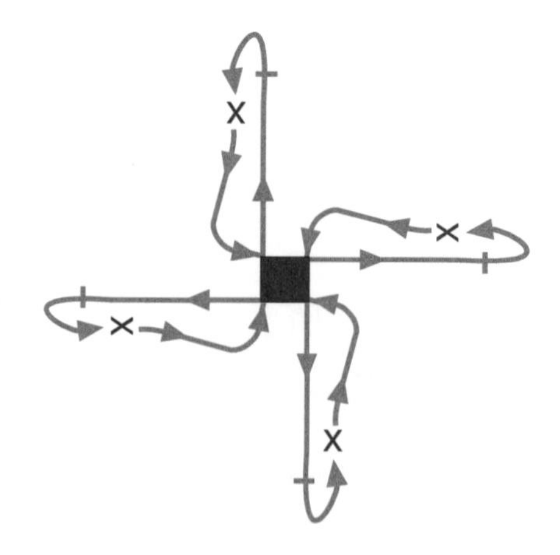

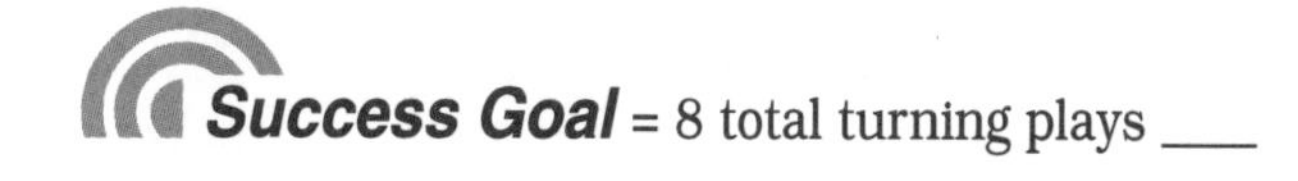

Success Goal = 8 total turning plays ___

Success Check

- Swing out to the right when within 15 feet of the base ___
- Lean to the left and head toward the base ___
- Contact the inside front corner of the base with left foot ___

To Increase Difficulty

- Decrease the allowable arc size.
- Increase the speed of the approach and the rounding of the base.
- Reduce the length of the jog between bases so that ultimately you are running the length of the entire baseline.

To Decrease Difficulty

- Decrease the speed of the approach to the base.
- Decrease the distance from the base that you run in the approach.
- Begin with a relatively large arc and gradually reduce the size of the arc while maintaining medium speed.
- Jog through the entire rounding-the-base pattern.

7. Single, Double, Triple, Home Run

You need a partner who will time you with a stopwatch for this drill. Start at home plate. Using a bat, swing at an imaginary pitch and, using the technique described in figure 5.2, run out a single rounding first base. Retreat to first base with the correct technique. Return to home plate.

Next, swing and run out a double, rounding first base and stopping at second base as you would in a game. Slide into the base, or run full speed to within 10 feet of the base, bending your knees, shifting your weight back, and taking smaller steps to come to a stop on the base without overrunning it. Return to home plate. Continue the drill with a triple, rounding first and second base and stopping at third. Return to home plate.

Finish the drill sequence by running out an inside-the-park home run. When you hit the ball over the fence for a home run, you may simply jog around the bases, waving to the crowd. On an inside-the-park home run, though, the ball remains in play, and you must arrive at home plate before the defense gets the ball there to tag you out. Therefore, you must use good baserunning technique to beat the throw to the plate. Round all three bases, running at full speed all the way from home to home. Remember, you can overrun home plate, so don't slow down to stop on the plate. Run full speed *over* home plate.

Success Goal = 12 points based on the allocations on the following page ___

Distance run	Time range (seconds)	Points
Home to first	More than 4.5	1
	4.0–4.5	2
	3.5–3.9	3
	Less than 3.5	4
Home to second	More than 11.0	1
	10.0–11.0	2
	9.0–9.9	3
	Less than 9.0	4
Home to third	More than 15.0	1
	14.0–15.0	2
	13.0–13.9	3
	Less than 13.0	4
Home to home	More than 20.0	1
	19.0–20.0	2
	18.0–18.9	3
	Less than 18.0	4

Success Check

- Take first step with the back foot ___
- Run at top speed *over* the base when overrunning first base ___
- Spoon out prior to crossing the base when advancing to next base ___

To Increase Difficulty

- Hit a soft tossed ball for each part of the drill.

To Decrease Difficulty

- Reduce the distance between bases.

8. React to Base Coach

In a game situation, the batter-baserunner is assisted by the first-base coach in deciding whether to overrun or round first base. A baserunner going to second base looks to the third-base coach for direction. At first base, the coach usually tells the batter-baserunner to round the base and look for the ball when the ball goes through the infield. The batter-baserunner must look at the coach within 15 feet of reaching the base in order to receive the base coach's instructions in time to round the base if necessary.

This drill is designed to help you develop your ability to react to the coach and the call she is making. You need a partner for this drill: you be the batter-baserunner, and your partner is the coach. You swing at an imaginary pitch and run to first base. The base coach tells you either to overrun or to round the base, randomly calling "round and look for the ball" or "overrun." You react to the base coach by following the call. Run to first base five times. Count the number of times you react correctly to the call of the coach. Switch roles.

Success Goal = 4 correct actions at first base out of 5 attempts ___

Success Check
- Accelerate quickly ___
- Look at the base coach, then focus on the base ___
- Execute the called play at the base ___

There is little one can do to increase or decrease the difficulty of this drill. Simply proceed to the next drill. If you have difficulty with this drill, continue to practice it.

9. Double to the Outfield

For this drill, you need three people. You are the batter-baserunner; one person is an outfielder situated behind the shortstop position; and the other person is a second baseman, situated to the outfield side of second base. You need a bucket of five balls and a tee at home plate, and an empty bucket near second base.

Hit five line drives off the tee into the outfield beyond shortstop. Run, round first base, and decide whether to run to second base. The outfielder fields the ball and throws it to the player at second base, who drops the ball into the empty bucket after the play is completed. As batter-baserunner, try to make the correct decision: either go back to first, or get to second base before the ball is caught by the second baseman (no tag is necessary in this drill—however, you may work on your sliding skills when going into second base). Count the number of times you make the correct decision by remaining at first base or advancing safely to second.

After five hits, rotate roles. The hitter goes to the outfield, taking the empty bucket to second base on the way out. The outfielder goes to second base. The second-base player goes to home, taking the bucket of five balls to hit. The goal of this drill is primarily making appropriate decisions; therefore, there is no need to increase or decrease the difficulty of the drill.

Success Goal = 3 correct decisions out of 5 hit balls ___

Success Check
- Reach the base before the ball does when deciding to go to second base ___
- Remain at first base when the ball would arrive at second base before you ___

10. Overrun or Round Game

Now we make the practice very similar to a game situation. For this drill, six players are needed. Two players are hitters, one is the base coach, a fourth player is the shortstop, the fifth player is the left fielder (behind shortstop), and the sixth player is the second baseman. Set a bucket with five balls at home plate, and an empty bucket near second base.

The batters alternate hitting the ball off the batting tee, attempting to get the ball by the shortstop and into deep left field. Upon hitting the ball, the batter runs to first base and reacts to the call of the base coach. If the ball goes by the shortstop, the base coach calls, "Round the base and look for the ball!" If the ball is fielded by the shortstop, the base coach calls "Overrun the base!" The batter-baserunner does as the coach signals. If the call is to round the base, it is then up to the baserunner to decide whether to return to first base or to try to advance to second base. When advancing to second, the baserunner has the option of practicing his sliding skills.

The fielders attempt to field the ball as it comes to them. If the outfielder fields the ball, she throws it to the second baseman, who drops it in the bucket; the shortstop returns fielded balls to home. After five hits by each batter, rotate positions: one batter to shortstop (the second batter remains at bat and hits another round), shortstop to outfield, outfield to second base, second base to base coach, and base coach to batter. Continue the drill until each player has hit the ball 10 times (the first hitter to rotate out to shortstop needs to rotate into the hitting position in order to complete 10 hits).

The goal of this game is to get as many doubles as you can. Count the number of times you make it safely to second base. See whether you can get more doubles than any of the other players in your group. As in the previous drill, the goal of this drill is primarily making appropriate decisions; therefore, there is no need to increase or decrease the difficulty of the drill.

Success Goal = 6 hits are safe doubles out of 10 attempts ___

Success Check

Hitter:

- Respond appropriately to the coach's call ___
- After contacting the base, look for the ball and focus on the play ___
- Make appropriate decision whether to advance to second or return to first ___

Outfielder:

- Field the ball cleanly and make an accurate throw to the second baseman ___

Shortstop:

- Field the ball cleanly and hold the runner at first base ___

Base coach:

- Make the appropriate call for the batter-baserunner ___

BASERUNNING SUCCESS SUMMARY

Scoring runs is the ultimate goal of a softball team when its players are on offense (at bat). Your ability to run the bases efficiently and effectively contributes to your team's ability to score runs. Getting into scoring position in softball means getting to second base or, even more important, getting to third base. In slow-pitch softball, as in baseball, a single will usually score a runner from second base. However, in fast-pitch softball, because the outfield distances are shorter than in baseball and the outfielders do not play as deep as in slow-pitch softball, you are not as likely to score from second base on a single. In fast-pitch softball, a baserunner who is a threat to steal a base gives the pitcher an extra something to be thinking about besides trying to get the batter out. Baserunning is fun! Sliding into a base and avoiding the tag of the fielder is one of the most exciting aspects of the game for the players and the spectators.

Ask your coach, teacher, teammate, or classmate to watch you perform the various baserunning skills in a practice or game setting. The observer should pay particular attention to the items in the checklist in figure 5.1 and the technique points identified in the descriptions of rounding a base, tagging up on a fly ball, and sliding.

STEP 6 POSITION PLAY

Different defensive players have different responsibilities, depending on the positions they play and the situations that come up in a game. When you play a position, you must read a developing situation and carry out the duties of your particular position, including covering and backing up bases, knowing which position should make the play to catch a fly ball, and how to execute force and tag plays.

Why Is Knowledge of Position Play Important?

It is important to know the duties of all the positions so that you can interact most usefully with your teammates no matter where the ball is hit or thrown. All team members should work together smoothly, rather than be confused about responsibilities.

Good position play requires an understanding of some basic concepts that are applied to the particular game and play situations as they arise. The two major categories of defensive duties are *covering* and *backing up*. A checklist later in this step includes all covering and backing-up responsibilities for each position. Only the basic concepts and some examples are described in the sections that follow. When you are *covering* a base, you are usually going to be making a *tag play* or a *force play* on a runner coming to your base. The techniques used for these plays are explained later in this step. In addition, some drills for practicing the force and the tag plays are included in this step. There are no specific drills included in this step for practicing the skills of covering and backing up. However, you will be able to apply these concepts while participating in drills in later steps.

Coverage Responsibilities

Each of the positions (9 in fast-pitch and 10 in slow-pitch with the short fielder) has a specific name, number, and coverage area. Figure 6.1 shows the regular-depth starting positions and the area coverage for each position. Note the difference between slow- and fast-pitch starting positions for the first and third basemen. Because the fast-pitch game allows the batter to bunt the ball, the first and third basemen usually assume a starting position in fair territory in front of their respective bases, closer to home plate. In the same diagram, the sections outlined by dashed lines identify the *primary area coverage* for each starting position (notice the change in the coverage area indicated by dotted lines for the first and third basemen because of their different starting positions in fast-pitch softball). The shaded areas that overlap the dashed or dotted lines identify the *interaction areas*, in which coverage responsibility is shared by adjoining positions. The diagram shows flexible approximations of these coverage areas, which may vary depending on the relative range and other skills of teammates. The term *covering* also describes the responsibility of an infielder at a base (see figure 6.2). For instance, on a ground ball hit to the shortstop, the first baseman covers first base to take the shortstop's throw and to put out the batter-baserunner. The assigned coverage in area 6 (figure 6.1), by the way, enabled the shortstop to field the ground ball without interference from another defensive player.

Priority System for Fly Balls

Any ball coming into a primary coverage area is mainly the responsibility of the defender playing the corresponding position (figure 6.1). A team's initial defense is based on the concept that each player has *jurisdiction* in his primary coverage area. Take, for example, a high pop fly hit to area 6: the third baseman, the shortstop, the second baseman, and the pitcher would all have time to move into position to

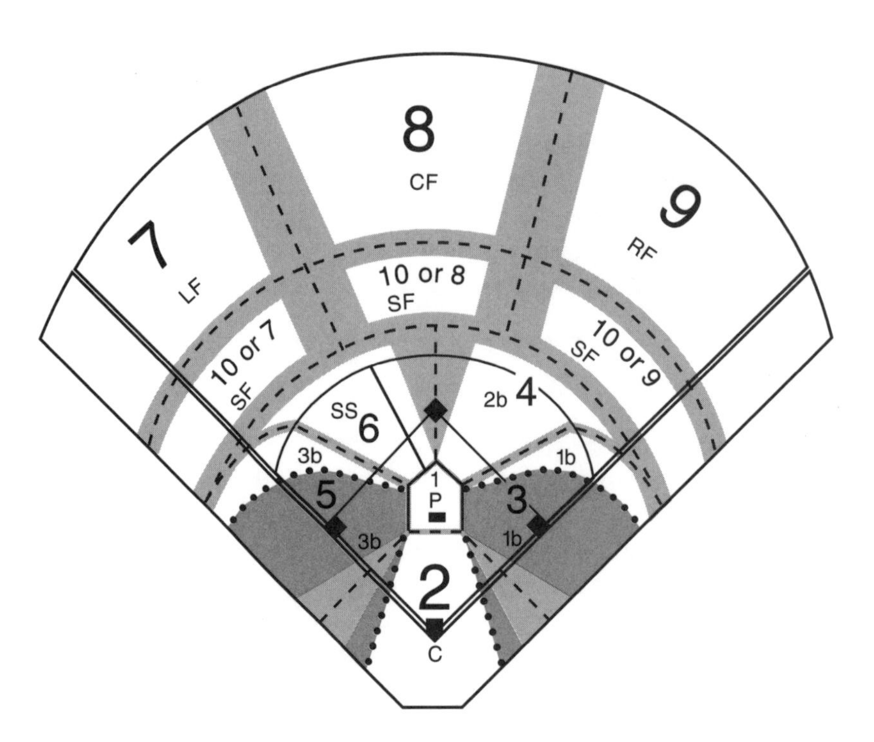

Figure 6.1 Regular-depth starting positions and area coverage. First- and third-base areas for fast-pitch are indicated by color shading.

field the ball. If they all did at once, however, there would be chaos. If everyone understands that area 6 is the responsibility of the shortstop, though, this assigned jurisdiction allows the play to be made with minimal confusion.

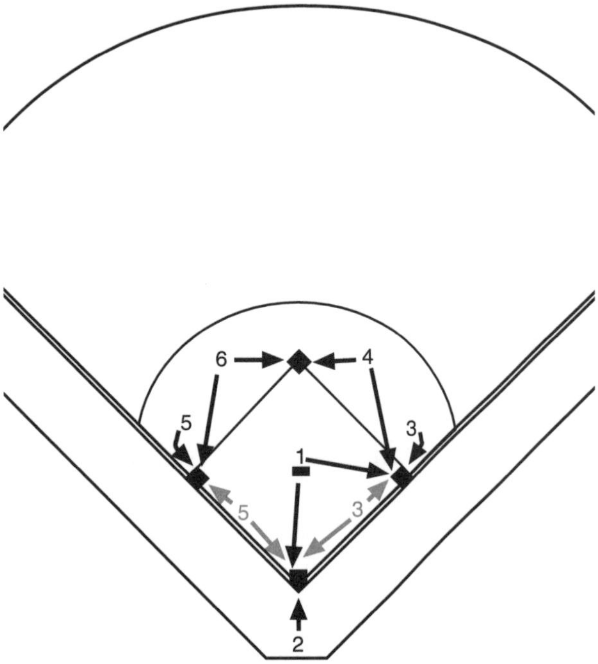

Figure 6.2 Base coverage responsibilities. The first- and third-baseman positions closest to home plate indicate fast-pitch starting positions.

Verbal signs are extremely helpful for team defense. You should always *call for the ball* on a fly ball, and even sometimes on ground balls playable by more than one fielder. Your call of "I have it!" or "Mine!" must be loud and clear enough for all players in the immediate area to hear. In fact, it is helpful to call for the ball even when it is clearly in your area of responsibility. To indicate that they understood your call, other players should then call "Take it!" or call out your name.

Determining who should play a fly ball between two areas of responsibility is more of a problem, but it becomes less difficult when a priority system is established. In general, outfielders have priority over infielders. Because they are moving in on the ball, outfielders have an easier time fielding and throwing than infielders, who are running back to the ball. When the ball is between two or more outfield positions, the fielder who would be in the best throwing position after the catch has priority. When a follow-up throw is needed, the outfielder with the strongest throwing arm has priority.

In the infield, the third baseman should cut off any ground ball he can reach while going to the left. Because it is easier to run laterally than backward, the shortstop should field any pop-up behind the third baseman. Similarly, the second baseman should field any pop-up behind the first baseman.

Following is the priority system for calling for most fly balls:

Fly Ball Jurisdiction Chart

Position number	Symbol	Player position	Has fielding priority over
1	P	Pitcher	No one
2	C	Catcher	Pitcher
3	1b	First baseman	Catcher, pitcher
4	2b	Second baseman	First baseman, pitcher
5	3b	Third baseman	First baseman, catcher, pitcher
6	SS	Shortstop	Third baseman, second baseman, first baseman, pitcher
7	LF	Left fielder	All infielders, short fielder*
8	CF	Center fielder	All infielders, all other outfielders
9	RF	Right fielder	All infielders, short fielder
10	SF	Short fielder	All infielders

* Slow-pitch only

Back-Up Responsibilities

Backing up describes support or aid given to a covering player by another defensive player. The backing-up player does not make the initial play on a runner or on a hit ball. For example, the short fielder or the left fielder backs up the shortstop fielding a ground ball. The catcher backs up the first baseman; the catcher's stopping a misplayed ball that has gone beyond the first baseman could prevent the runner from advancing to another base.

Backing up a play requires that you:

- *know* all the possible backing-up responsibilities for the specific position you are playing,
- immediately *recognize* situations for which you have backing-up responsibilities when they arise, and
- *move* into the correct back-up position.

Thus, backing up is two-thirds cognitive and one-third physical! Descriptions of back-up responsibilities for each position in this step, and game opportunity experience in later steps, will help you learn this aspect of position play. Good anticipation will help you recognize situations as they unfold.

Figure 6.3 shows the back-up positions each fielder would likely take. A back-up position is actually

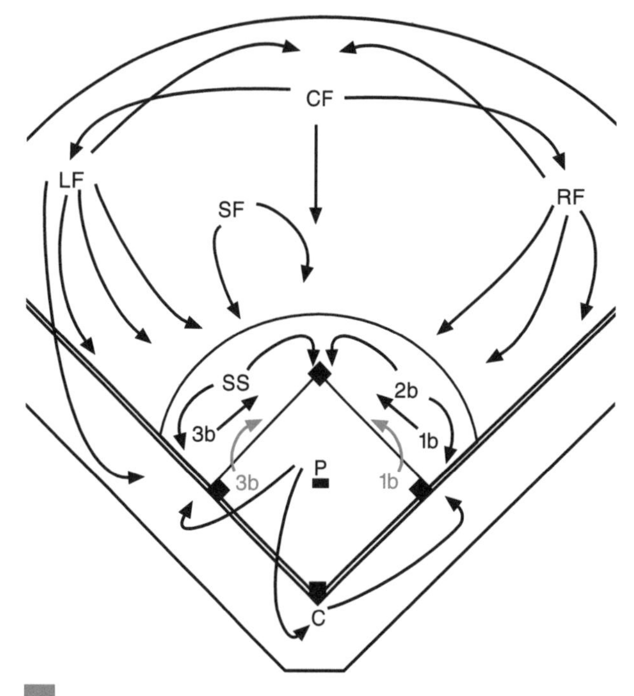

Figure 6.3 Back-up responsibilities. The first- and third-baseman positions closest to home plate indicate fast-pitch starting and back-up positions.

determined by the path of the ball. The back-up person must get in direct line with the source of the ball (the throwing fielder or the hitter) and its receiver (the fielder covering a base or the fielder making a play on the hit ball; see figure 6.4). The back-up player must assume a position approximately 15 to 20 feet *behind* the primary receiver. Remember, your role as the back-up is to catch a misplayed ball to prevent additional advance by any baserunner; you are not trying to make the initial covering play. If you back up a play by standing too close to the covering fielder, a misplayed ball will go past you because you will not have time to react and catch the ball.

Once you catch the ball as the back-up, listen for verbal assistance from your teammates as to what to do with the ball; also, look to see what the runners, especially the lead runner, are doing. Sometimes a runner seeing an overthrow or other error will automatically dash for the next base. That is when your backing up a play really pays off, because your team then gets a second chance on the same play to get the runner out.

Special Situations

Special situations may alter the starting positions and the size of the coverage areas. For example, in playing a strong right-handed pull hitter (whose swing pulls or hits the ball to the left field), all the infielders and outfielders would be shifted around toward the left-field foul line, as shown in figure 6.5 (compare to figure 6.1). The areas covered by the left fielder and third baseman become smaller. The center fielder's area remains about the same but moves to the left; this increases the right fielder's area coverage. The second baseman's closer position to second base increases the area coverage for the first baseman.

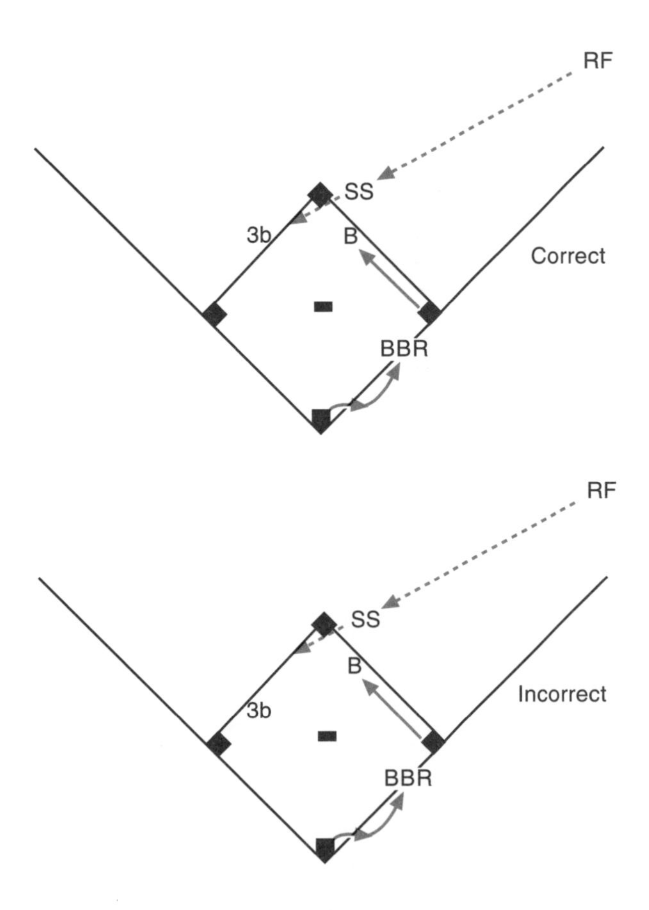

Figure 6.4 Backing up on the overthrow line.

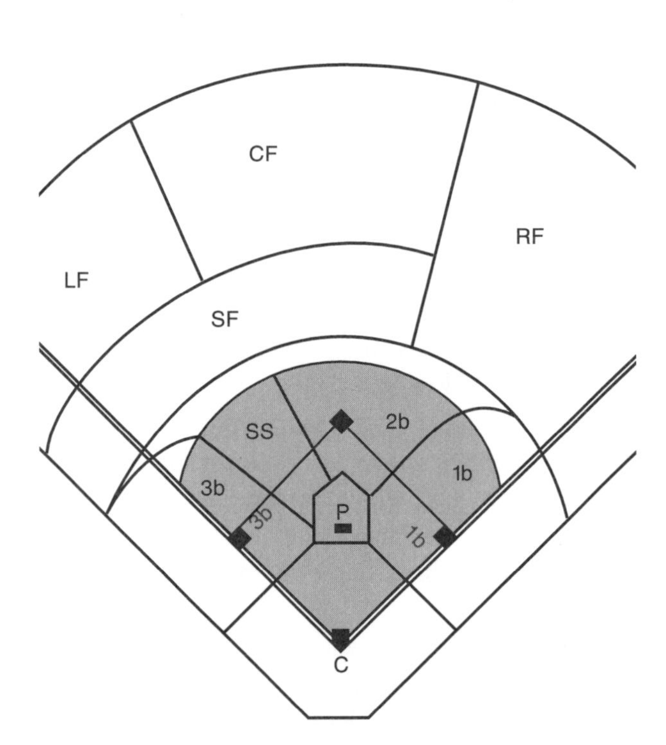

Figure 6.5 Overshift positioning for a right-handed pull hitter. The first- and third-baseman positions closest to home plate indicate fast-pitch positions.

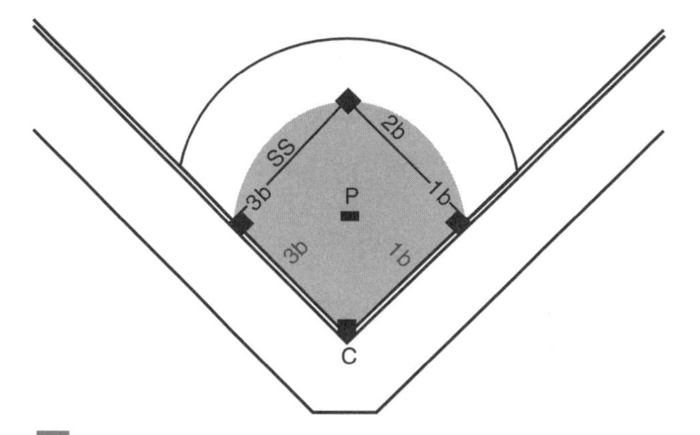

Figure 6.6 Infield "in" positioning. The first- and third-baseman positions closest to home plate indicate fast-pitch starting positions.

Another special situation comes with the bases loaded (baserunners on first, second, and third base) and less than two outs. The infielders move in a little closer to home plate (compare figure 6.6 to figure 6.1) before the ball is pitched. This is called the *infield in* position. If a ground ball is then hit to an infielder, the force play at home plate (for less experienced players) or the home-to-first double play (for those more experienced) has a greater likelihood of success. The shortened distance the ball has to travel to the fielder and the resulting shortened distance of the throw to home plate make a successful play more possible than if the fielders had stayed back in their regular-depth positions.

KEYS TO SUCCESS

POSITION PLAY

Every player has individual responsibilities on every play. Defensive position play depends on the offensive situation and the duties of the player's position. To be a successful defensive softball player, you must think about your responsibilities before each pitch.

You can certainly become a better offensive player by knowing the defensive position play concepts. If you thoroughly understand defensive positioning and likely responses, you can make offensive moves that attack the inherent weaknesses of any defensive setup.

Use the checklist below to help yourself remember what you do when playing each position. Then ask a trained observer to use the checklist to evaluate your position play during game-situation drills, modified games, or official games.

Position and number	Covering responsibilities	Back-up responsibilities
Pitcher (1)	____ Area 1	____ Home plate on outfield throws
	____ First base on hit to 1b	____ Second base on outfield throws
		____ Third base on outfield throws
Catcher (2)	____ Area 2	____ First base on infield throws
	____ Home plate	
First baseman (3)	____ Area 3	____ Second base on LF throws
	____ First base	
	____ Cutoff-throws to home from CF, RF, SF, and LF (fast-pitch only)	
Second baseman (4)	____ Area 4	____ Balls hit to 1b
	____ First base when 1b out of position	____ Second base on throws to SS from P, C
	____ Second base on double plays (DP) and force plays from 3b and SS	
	____ Second base on LF, CF, and SF throws	

(continued)

Position and number	Covering responsibilities	Back-up responsibilities
Third baseman (5)	____ Area 5 ____ Third base ____ Cutoff throw to home from LF (slow-pitch only)	____ Second base on RF throws
Shortstop (6)	____ Area 6 ____ Second base on DP and force plays from P, C, 1b, 2b ____ Second base on RF, SF throws	____ Second base on throws to 2b from P, C ____ Balls hit to 3b ____ Balls hit to P
Left fielder (7)	____ Area 7 ____ Third base on bunt to 3b with runner on first base (fast-pitch only)	____ Balls hit to CF, SF ____ Balls hit to 3b, SS (if SF not available) ____ Second base on 1b, 2b, RF, SF throws ____ Third base on C, 1b, 2b, RF, SF throws
Center fielder (8)	____ Area 8	____ Balls hit to LF, RF, SF ____ Balls hit to SS, 2b (if SF not available) ____ Second base on P,C, 1b throws
Right fielder (9)	____ Area 9	____ Balls hit to CF, SF ____ Balls hit to 1b, 2b (if SF not available) ____ First base on C throws ____ Second base on 3b, SS, LF, SF throws
Short fielder (10) (slow-pitch only)	____ Area 10	____ Balls hit to 1b, 2b, 3b, SS when SF is in nearby part of Area 10 ____ Second base when in over-throw line

Force Plays and Tag Plays

An offensive player can be put out by the defense in a number of different ways. Many of these plays fall into two categories: force plays and tag plays. A *force play* occurs whenever a baserunner must go to the next base because the batter has become a baserunner. The batter must *always* go to first base after hitting the ball. Only one baserunner may be on a base at one time; therefore, with a runner on first base, when the batter hits a grounder, the runner already on first base is forced to go to second base, and there is a force play on the batter at first base and on the baserunner going to second base.

The runner is put out in a force-play situation when the defense gets the ball to the base ahead of the runner. The ball itself need not actually come into contact with the base for a force-out, but the defensive player must have control of the ball and make contact with the base with some part of the body before the baserunner arrives (see figure 6.7).

The simple force play is *the* fundamental defensive concept in softball. In beginning-level game play, the most basic defensive strategy is to get one out at a time. When there are less than two outs and runners on base in a force-play situation, the fundamental defensive strategy is to "get the lead runner" (the runner closest to home plate). With two outs, on the other hand, the play for the third out to end the inning is normally made at first base because that is always a force-out situation.

The *tag play* is another fundamental defensive concept. A tag-play situation occurs any time a runner is not in contact with a base and is not allowed to move to any base freely. For example, a runner overrunning second base is not free to return to the base; conversely, a runner *is* free to return to the base after a foul ground ball. To put a baserunner out with a tag play, the defensive player must tag, or touch, the offensive player with the ball or with the glove holding the ball when the runner is off the base (see figure 6.8).

Why Is Understanding the Force Play and Tag Play Important?

Infielders are the defensive players who normally execute force plays and tag plays because the plays occur on the infield (at or between the bases). These plays are the basic skills for getting baserunners out (preventing them from advancing and scoring runs). It is essential that you know the tag-play and force-play concepts and be able to execute the skills to be a successful defensive player and help your team stop the offensive play of your opponents. This is

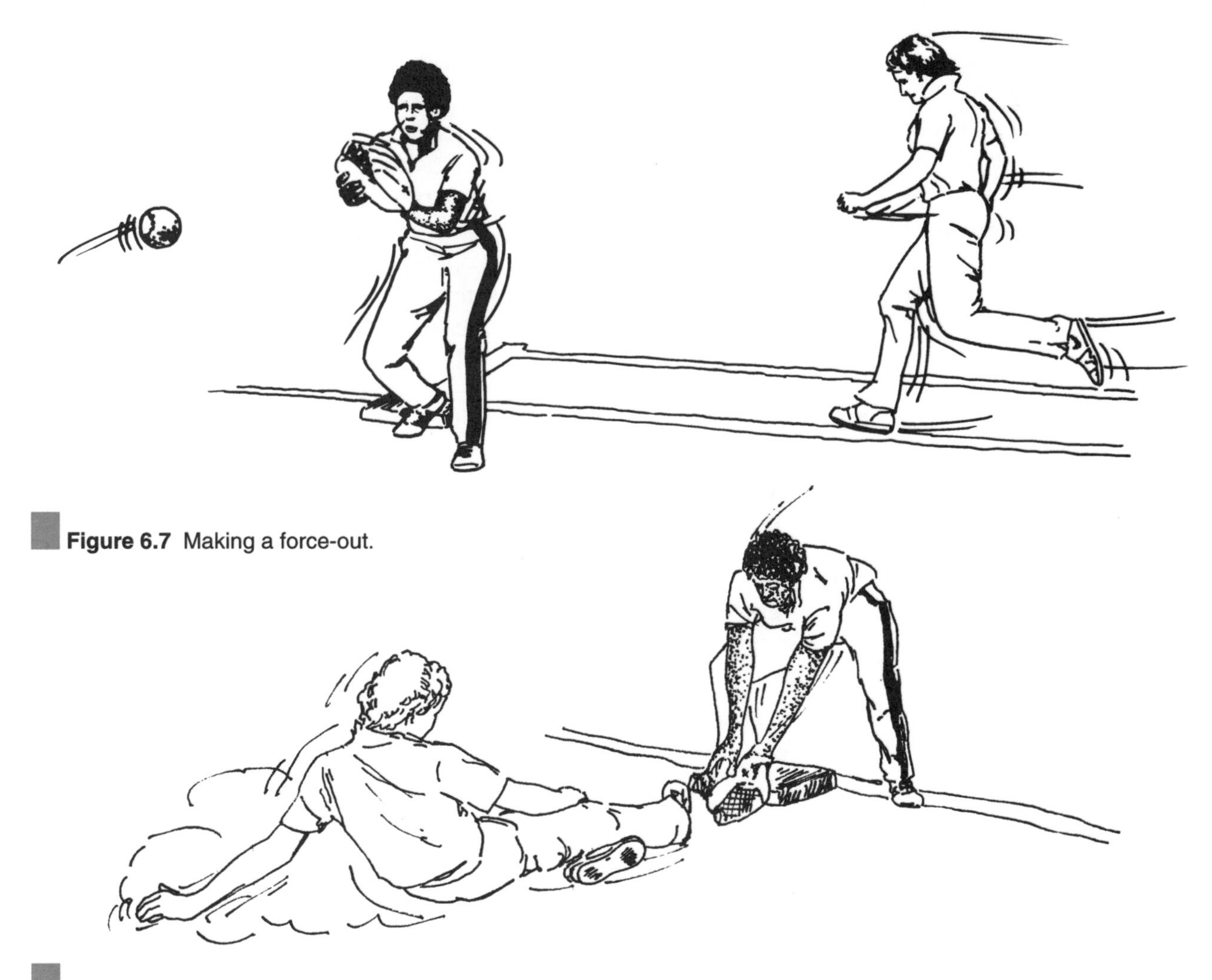

Figure 6.7 Making a force-out.

Figure 6.8 Executing a tag play.

especially important if you would like to concentrate on playing an infield position.

How to Execute the Force Play

The force play can be executed at all three bases and home plate. The basic techniques, and the fundamental principles upon which the choice of techniques is based, are the same regardless of the base. Make the throw for a force play about chest-high. As the defensive player covering the base, you should move to the side of the base nearest the source of the throw. This will shorten the throw's length, and thus the time it takes for the throw to arrive in your glove. The quicker the throw arrives, the more likely it is that you will get the out.

For example, on a force play at third base with a throw coming from the catcher, the player covering the base moves to the home plate side of third base to receive the throw, as shown in figure 6.9. On the other hand, if the throw were coming to third base from the left fielder, the covering player would stand on the outfield side of third base to receive the throw (see figure 6.10).

Once the throw is on the way and you, the covering player, know exactly where the throw will arrive, place one foot on the base and stretch out your glove hand and the other foot to meet the throw. If the throw is slightly off-target to the side, step to meet the ball with the foot on the ball side, and contact the base with your other foot. For example, if the throw is off-target to your left, step to the left with your left foot and contact the base with your right foot. If the play is going to be close, stretch as far as you can and catch the ball in your glove hand only. If the play is not going to be close, stretch a comfortable distance and catch the ball with both hands. Remember, you want to shorten the distance and time of the throw so the throw will get to you (and the base) before the runner does.

How to Execute the Tag Play at a Base

First of all, remember that the tag play is required when a baserunner is not forced to go to a base. In slow-pitch softball, the tag play is used when a baserunner overruns second or third base, or is advancing on a hit ball and is not forced to do so. Following are three examples of situations that dictate that a tag play be executed when the baserunner goes into a base when not forced to:

1. With no runner on first base, a runner on second base tries to go to third base on a ground ball hit to the second baseman.
2. A runner attempts to score from second base on a base hit.

Figure 6.9 Third-base coverage on a force play with a throw from the catcher.

Figure 6.10 Third-base coverage on a force play with a throw from the left fielder.

3. A runner tagging up on a fly ball tries to advance a base.

In fast-pitch softball, the tag play is also used when a baserunner attempts to steal a base.

The throw for the tag play should arrive just below the knees of the covering player. The runner will probably be sliding into the base, so the throw should be low, and close to the runner. This minimizes the time it takes for the covering player to move the glove and ball into position to tag the baserunner.

There is more than one acceptable technique for covering the base for the tag play. The method recommended places you in a position at the base where you can tag the runner, but where your chances of getting knocked down are limited. As your skill increases, and if you then choose to become more aggressive in your play, you may wish to actually block the base from the runner with your body as you make the tag play. For now, though, let's give the runner an open path to the base.

Your exact position at the base will depend on the path the runner is taking to the base—for instance, coming into third base from second base as opposed to coming back to third from the direction of home plate. The other factor that affects your exact position is the source and direction of the throw. Is the ball coming to you from the outfield, or from the infield side? In general, straddle the base or stand just to the side of the base facing the direction of the incoming runner. *Do not*, under any circumstance, place your leg between the base and the incoming runner! Leave the path to the base open to the runner.

Position yourself so that you can catch the ball and bring the gloved ball down to the edge of the base where the runner will arrive. As the runner slides in, let the runner tag himself out by sliding into the ball held in your glove. Then sweep your glove out of the way of the runner. Even if the runner does not slide, the runner's foot must get to the base—*tag the foot*. Don't reach out to tag the runner on the chest only to find out that the feet slid into the base before you tagged the chest (see figure 6.11).

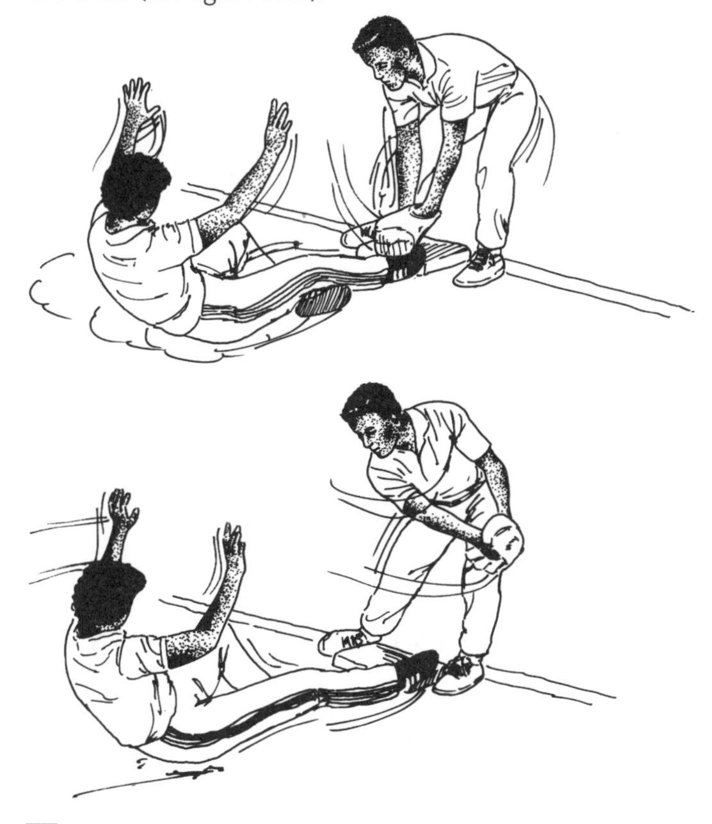

Figure 6.11 At a base, tag the foot and hold onto the ball!

How to Execute the Tag Play Between Bases

When you have the opportunity to tag out a player who is running past you between bases, you have a fairly easy play. The baserunner will be standing up, so you will have little trouble reaching her to make the tag. Hold the ball securely in both hands (the ball in your glove) to reduce the chance of dropping it. Tag the baserunner with the back of the fingers of your glove. Immediately pull both hands away so the contact with the runner does not knock the ball out of your glove. Hold onto the ball! (See figure 6.12.)

Figure 6.12 A tag play between bases.

FORCE-PLAY AND TAG-PLAY DRILLS

1. Mimetic Practice

Proper footwork is required as you move from an infielder's starting position to the covering positions of force plays and tag plays. Place a loose base (home plate, if called for) on the ground or floor. Foul lines are helpful in orienting your fielding position in relation to the base. If there are no lines available, place a cone about 15 feet from the base and use that cone to represent the direction to home plate; draw an imaginary foul line from the cone to your base. Remember that the base lies in fair territory, so the line (real or imaginary) goes on the left side of first base or the right side of third base (when facing home plate from your infield position).

When in the first baseman's role, position yourself slightly behind for slow-pitch or slightly in front for fast-pitch and about 8 feet to the right of the base. When in the third baseman's role, position yourself slightly behind for slow-pitch or slightly in front for fast-pitch and about 8 feet to the left of the base. When in the shortstop or second baseman's role, position yourself in regular fielding position. When in the catcher's role, position yourself about 2 feet behind the plate.

Without a ball, you will practice the footwork for force plays and tag plays at each base. The following chart lists the covering positions, the general direction, and the possible thrower with whom you will practice for force and tag plays.

Force-Play and Tag-Play Practice Situations

Covering player	*General direction and possible thrower*
1b (figure 6.13)	RF, SF, 2b, SS, 3b, P, C
2b (figure 6.14)	LF, SF, 3b, SS
SS (figure 6.15)	RF, 2b, CF, SF, 1b, C, P
3b (figure 6.16)	LF, SF, CF, SS, RF, 2b, 1b, P, C
C (figure 6.17)	RF, 2b, 1b, CF, SF, P, LF, SS, 3b

Take your regular fielding position before each repetition in the drill, then *move* into coverage position at the base to receive an imaginary throw. First you move into position to make a force play. Mimic the stretch and the ball reception. Then practice the footwork needed on throws that are slightly off-target to the left and to the right. Remember, on throws to your left, step with your left foot toward the throw and contact the base with your right foot; on throws to your right, step right and contact left.

Finally, do a series of repetitions in which you move to the base to make tag plays on imaginary throws from all positions listed on the chart. Mimic the actual tagging movements in each of the situations. Do two repetitions of the footwork practice for a force play; two repetitions for off-target throws right and left; and two repetitions for tag plays at each of the positions and for each of the throw directions listed in the Success Goal.

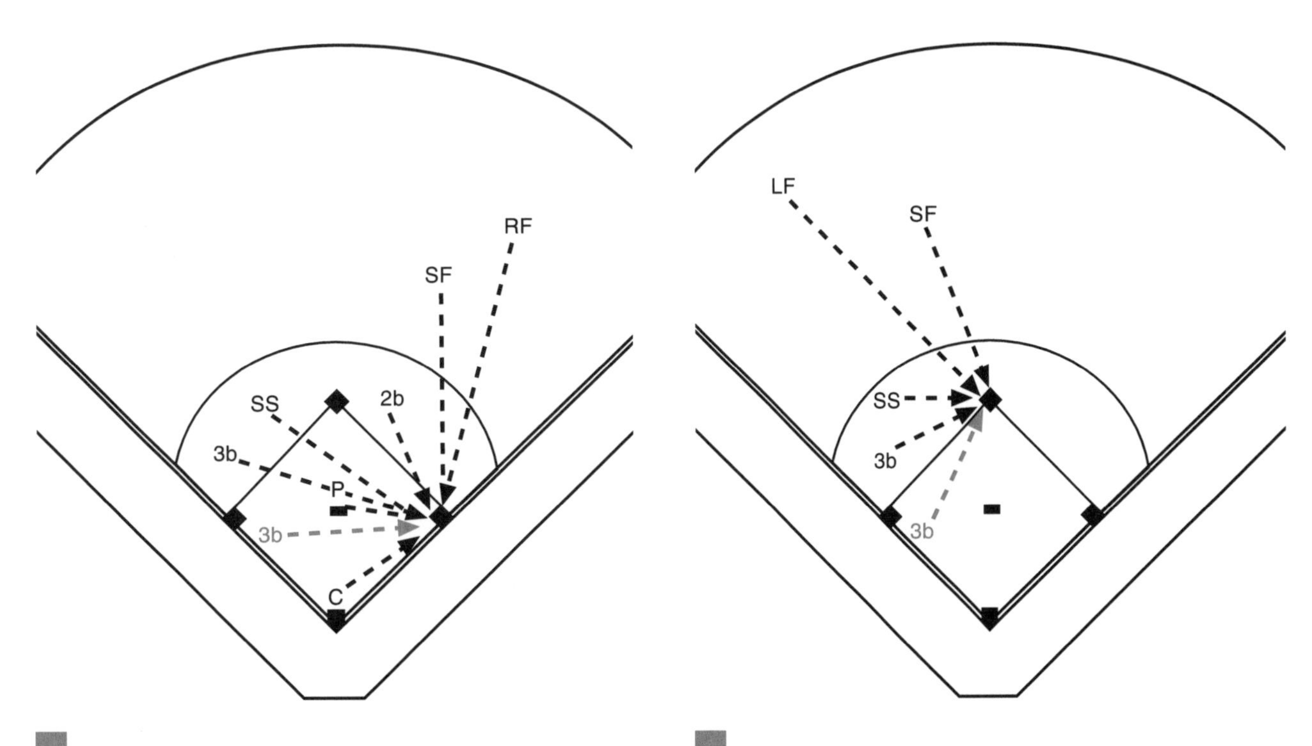

Figure 6.13 Throws to first baseman covering first base.

Figure 6.14 Throws to second baseman covering second base.

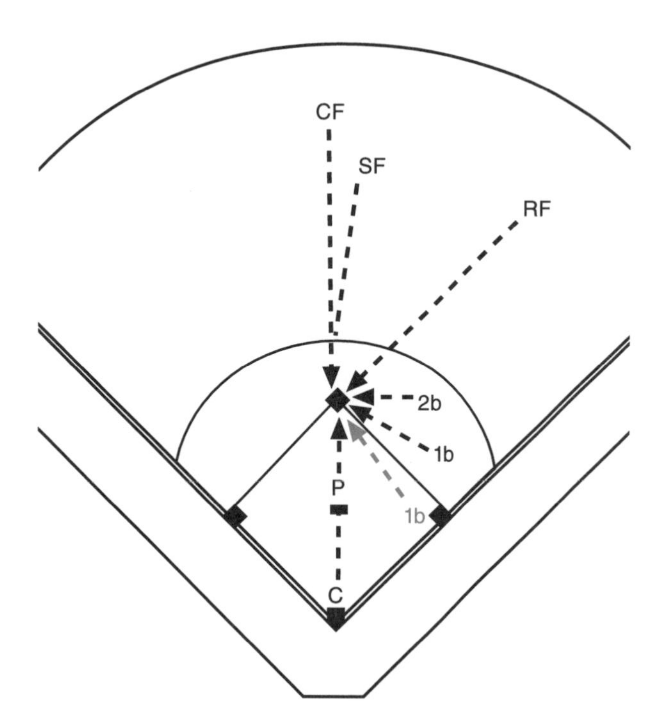

Figure 6.15 Throws to shortstop covering second base.

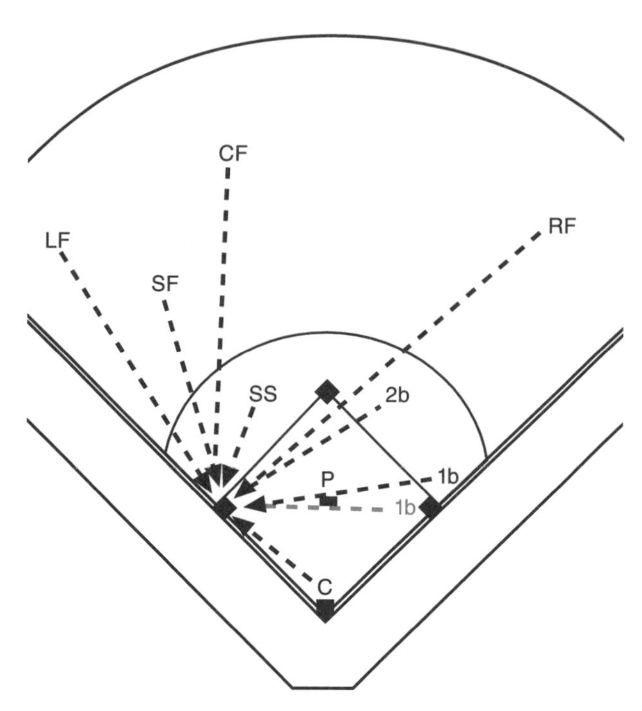

Figure 6.16 Throws to third baseman covering third base.

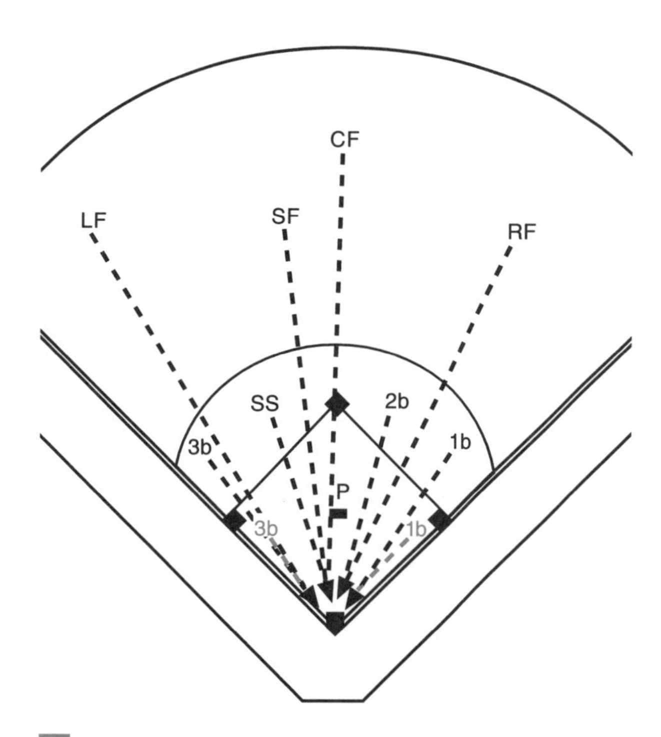

Figure 6.17 Throws to catcher covering home plate.

Success Goal = 8 total successful repetitions (2 force plays, 2 off-target throws right, 2 off-target throws left, and 2 tag plays) at each player position:

1b covering first base ___
2b covering second base ___
SS covering second base ___
3b covering third base ___
C covering home plate ___

Success Check

- Start in regular fielding position ___
- Move to ball side of base ___
- Step with ball-side foot, contact base with other foot ___

To Increase Difficulty

- Have a feeder softly toss a ball to the covering player.

To Decrease Difficulty

- Decrease the number of successful repetitions needed.

2. Force Play and Tag Play Without Runners

Two pairs of partners set up on a regulation softball field as follows: one pair of partners includes a fungo hitter (see Step 8) and a catcher at home plate; the other pair has a fielder to whom the ball will be hit and a fielder covering a base and making force and tag plays.

As the covering fielder, make two force plays and two tag plays at each of the positions listed in the "Force-Play and Tag-Play Practice Situations" chart in drill 1. Switch roles within pairs after the four repetitions (two force plays and two tag plays) have been completed. Exchange roles between pairs (fungo hitter and catcher go to two fielding positions, and vice versa) after completing all the situations listed for a particular baseman.

For more experienced players doing this drill with baserunners as suggested in "To Increase Difficulty," some added factors come into play. As the covering fielder, you must be sure that you get to the ball side of the base and set your glove as a target that can be hit by the throwing fielder without the ball crossing the path of the runner. Add to that the fact that the baserunner is bearing down on you, and you have to be a very cool player to react calmly and correctly under such conditions. For this drill variation, baserunners must always wear helmets.

Success Goal = 4 repetitions (2 force plays and 2 tag plays) at each player position:

1b covering first base ___
2b covering second base ___
SS covering second base ___
3b covering third base ___
C covering home plate ___

Success Check

- Start in regular fielding position facing the hitter ___
- Move to ball side of base to receive throw ___
- For on-target throws, catch ball with two hands ___
- For off-target throws, step with ball-side foot and contact base with other foot ___
- For very off-target throws, catch ball with glove hand only ___

To Increase Difficulty

- Add baserunners.

To Decrease Difficulty

- Have the batter throw the ball, rather than fungo hit, to the fielding player.

POSITION PLAY SUCCESS SUMMARY

Successful team defense is dependent upon your ability to read and react to specific game situations, to know your responsibilities for your position, and to know the responsibilities for all other positions as each situation develops. You need to know whether and where you have coverage or backing-up responsibility on every play. You need to know whether the ensuing play is a tag play or a force play in your coverage situation. Have your coach or teammate observe you in gamelike drills or game situations and pay particular attention to your response to various game situations. Do you usually choose the appropriate course of action for the position you are playing? Are you able to successfully execute the skills needed in a particular situation? Regardless of your level of playing experience, you can benefit from the mental and physical practice of responding to game situations.

STEP 7 OFFENSIVE SITUATIONAL PLAY

The offensive objective for a softball team is to score runs. Your team has to score more runs than the opposing team in seven innings to win a game. In order to score runs, batters have to get on base, advance around the bases, and ultimately cross home plate safely. The batter becomes a baserunner by reaching first base safely by a hit, a base on balls (walk), an error by the defense, being hit by a pitched ball (in fast-pitch), or on a fielder's choice—a play in which the defense makes a play on a baserunner other than the batter-baserunner to get an out.

The number of outs, the location of the runners on base, the inning, the score of the game, the ball-strike count, the strengths and weaknesses of the batter, and the strengths and weaknesses of the pitcher all are factors that characterize the offensive situation. These factors influence the decision of the coach or player regarding the potential choices presented by the situation, especially in fast-pitch softball. For example, in the top of the seventh inning of a fast-pitch game with the home team ahead 1-0, the pitcher walks the first batter, who is the ninth batter in the order. The next batter, the lead-off batter, lays down a bunt to the first-base side, which the right-handed first baseman fields and throws to second base for the force-out on the lead runner. The throw is slightly off-target, drawing the shortstop off the bag and leaving runners on first and second base with nobody out.

To this point in the game, the home team pitcher has allowed only a scratch infield hit and three fly balls to the outfield (one by the number-three hitter [a left-hander], two by the cleanup hitter), and has struck out 10 batters. The next batter, the number-two hitter in the batting order, is a good contact hitter and also a good bunter. Based on the performance to date of the opposing pitcher, the location of the baserunners, the fact that there are no outs in the potential last time at bat, and the strengths of the next three batters, the coach makes the decision to try to advance the runners with a bunt. She instructs the batter to square around early to see where the defense moves to cover the bunting situation and either call time and step out of the box—or, if there is no opportunity to call time, don't bunt the first pitch. Does the third baseman stay back to cover third, in which case the pitcher will play the bunt on the third-base side? Or does the third baseman come in and the shortstop move over to cover third base, leaving no cover at second? Knowledge of how the defense intends to play the bunt situation will help the batter decide the best placement for the bunted ball.

The fact that the first baseman is right-handed means she must pivot after fielding the bunt on the first-base side, thereby slightly delaying the throw to third. The right-handed pitcher would have the same problem if she were covering the bunt on the third-base side. If these two players were left-handed, the throws would be released more quickly and would add a different factor for consideration. Advancing the runners to third and second via a sacrifice bunt puts the tying runner on third base, in scoring position with only one out, for a potential sacrifice fly.

A *sacrifice fly* is a play in which, with fewer than two outs, the batter scores a runner with a fly ball or line drive. The batter is not charged with a time at bat when hitting a sacrifice fly. Because the third batter is left-handed and a good pull hitter, a fly ball to right field would not only score the runner from third, but also allow the runner on second to advance to third. Obviously, a base hit by the third or fourth batter would score at least the tying run. In fast-pitch, the sacrifice bunt is a good and often-used option to advance runners into scoring position. However, in slow-pitch bunting is not allowed, so hitting to right field behind the runners to advance them to second and third base might be the play of choice. In a coached game, the coach usually makes the decision on the play of choice. In a game where players are given the decision-making responsibility, the players involved need to go through the same thought process as described for the coach to arrive at the *best* tactic to use given the situation.

The complexity of the cognitive aspect of the game of softball for players and coaches is what makes the game so appealing to many people—they like the challenge of outthinking the opponent. Managers in major-league baseball formerly used more offensive strategy than is often observed in the current game, in which the home run dominates. Maybe the ball *is* livelier. Certainly, more hitters are bigger and stronger, and more of them are able to put the ball out of the park with one swing of the bat! The hit-and-run, hitting behind the runner, and stealing are offensive strategies used by many major-league managers today, but the sacrifice bunt is used sparingly if at all.

Why Is Advancing the Runners Important in Fast-Pitch Softball?

Fast-pitch is still a pitcher's game. Although the pitching distance has been moved back to 43 feet for collegiate women and is 46 feet for men's ASA, the increased distance has not seemed to have had the desired effect of making fast-pitch more of a hitter's game at the elite level. Because of the normal depth positioning of the fast-pitch outfielders (which is typically closer to the infield than for slow-pitch outfielders), a single going directly to an outfielder will seldom score a runner from second base. A ball hit in the gap between outfielders or over the head of outfielders will normally allow a runner to score from second base. Therefore, it is advantageous in fast-pitch softball to get runners to third base with less than two outs so that the runner can score on a single or a sacrifice fly ball. Because pitching still dominates the fast-pitch game, the sacrifice bunt and the suicide squeeze bunt (both described later in this step) are major offensive weapons used to advance runners and even to score runs. In addition, as in baseball, hitting behind the runner, the sacrifice fly, and the fast-pitch weapons of the drag bunt (bunt to get on base), push bunt, slash bunt, slap hit, hit-and-run, and stealing (all described later in this step) are offensive strategies commonly used in softball to advance the runners into scoring position and to score runs.

How to Execute the Sacrifice Bunt

In fast-pitch softball, moving runners into scoring position with less than two outs increases the likelihood of their being able to score on a base hit, on a sacrifice fly, or on an error by the defense. The sacrifice bunt is a relatively high-percentage play to advance runners into scoring position. It is typically used when there are no outs (or at least less than two outs), with a runner on first base, runners on first and second base, or, in certain instances, with a runner on second base. As the name implies, in executing the sacrifice bunt, the batter "sacrifices" his opportunity to get on base with a base hit and instead bunts the ball so that the defense, in order to get an out, must force him out at first base.

The most important part of executing the sacrifice bunt is to move from your normal batting stance (figure 7.1a) into the bunting position in the batter's box *prior* to the pitcher's beginning her windup. Do not delay your pivot. The fact that you are going to lay down a bunt need not be kept a secret from the opposing team—everyone in the ballpark knows when a situation calls for a potential sacrifice bunt. The defense will be in the preliminary bunt-defense position to defend against the possibility of the bunt before you make any move in the batter's box. If your opponent is an aggressive defensive team, as you square around they will then move into their tight bunt-defense coverage in order to be in position to make an attempt on the advancing runner at second or third base. Your responsibility is to *put the ball on the ground!* In order to have the greatest possibility of success in this endeavor, you must be in a stationary position with a good view of the oncoming ball as you make contact. Pivoting into your bunting position prior to the pitch will ensure you that good view of the ball. Successfully laying down a bunt on a pitch traveling at excessive speed while you are in the process of moving into your bunting position is virtually impossible.

Both feet must be in the confines of the batter's box when you make contact with the ball on any hit, or you will be called out. In order to keep both feet in the box while assuming your bunting position, execute your pivot by taking two steps. The first step is with your front foot stepping around, slightly back, and toward the outside edge of the box; the second step is with your back foot stepping around and into a square stance facing the pitcher. If you square around toward the pitcher moving only the back foot, you will tend to step out of the box into the area between the batter's box and home plate. You may even find yourself stepping on home plate with that rear foot, and that is certainly out of the batter's box!

Face the pitcher with knees bent and your bat held parallel to the ground at the top of your strike zone, at a relaxed arm's length away from your body (see figure 7.1b). Grip the bat loosely with the bottom hand in its regular starting position at the knob end of the bat. As you pivot your feet and raise the bat to the top of the strike zone, slide the top hand down the throat of the bat to a position just outside the grip area. As you slide your hand down the bat, release the bottom three fingers from the bat, maintaining grip contact with the index finger and the thumb. Rotate your hand so that it is perpendicular to the ground and the back of your hand faces the plate. Make an open fist with your hand in the position just described and grip the bat loosely with the edge of the index finger under the bat and the thumb at the back and slightly on top of the throat. Do not

FIGURE 7.1 KEYS TO SUCCESS

SACRIFICE BUNT

Preparation

1. Square stance as if hitting ___
2. Hands and bat back ___
3. Focus on the pitcher ___

Execution

1. As pitcher gets sign, two-step pivot to square stance facing pitcher ___
2. Bat parallel to ground at top of strike zone away from body ___
3. Bottom-hand hitting grip ___
4. Top-hand outside grip area, perpendicular to ground ___
5. Bat rests on index finger, thumb on top ___
6. Give with the bat as you contact the ball ___

Follow-Through

1. Step to first base with foot farthest from the base ___
2. Get into foul territory ___
3. Run over first base ___

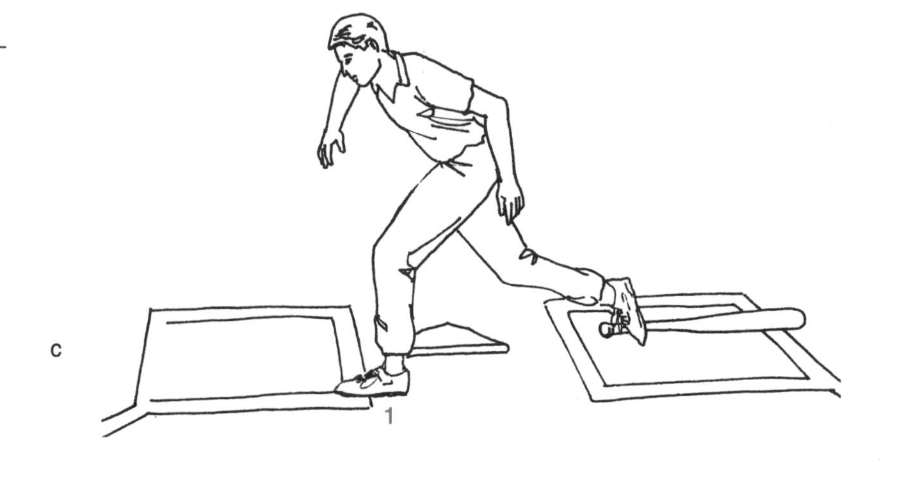

maintain your regular top-hand grip on the bat with all fingers wrapped around the bat as you prepare to bunt the ball. An inside pitch could hit the fingers of your top hand, which is very painful.

Keep your eyes focused on the ball as it leaves the pitcher's hand. The purpose of a sacrifice bunt is to advance the runners; therefore you must bunt only a strike. If you work the pitcher for a walk, you have been successful—because by advancing to first base yourself, you advance the other runners! In addition, now there is another runner on base who may potentially score.

Know your strike zone, and don't bunt at a pitch that is outside that zone. When you do bunt the ball, remember that it *must* be put on the ground—no pop-ups allowed! In order to keep the ball down, remember to hold your bat at the top of the strike zone—then any pitch that is over the bat is a ball that you can let go. Any pitch in the strike zone will be below your bat; therefore, to contact the ball you have to bring the bat down on top of the ball, which makes it easier to direct the ball down to the ground.

You want to bunt the ball down either the first or third base line, not directly at the pitcher. As you make contact with the ball, let your arms give slightly with the bat, which will help the ball drop down and roll 10 to 12 feet from the plate, not out to the fielders. Your bunt has to be placed so that a play on you at first base is the *best* choice the defense has.

After you bunt the ball, start to run to first base by taking your first step out of the batter's box with the foot that is furthest from home plate (see figure 7.1c). Be careful not to run into the bunted ball in fair territory—you'll be called out. Get into foul territory as quickly as possible and try to beat the throw to first. A sacrifice bunt doesn't mean you bunt the ball, give yourself up, and go back to the dugout! If you advance the runner and reach first base safely, your team has increased its opportunity to score runs.

Refer back to Step 6 for the different defensive alignments teams might take to defend the situation with runners on base in various positions. Prior to stepping into the batter's box, see where the first and third basemen are playing. As you pivot to face the pitcher, although focusing on the ball in the pitcher's hand, try to pick up any movement by the first and third basemen in your peripheral vision. Are they both charging the plate? If one is staying back, which one? These reads on the defense will help you decide where to try to place the bunt.

How to Execute the Squeeze Bunt

A fast-pitch team really needs to take advantage of an offensive situation in which a runner is on third base with less than two outs—advancing that runner means your team scores a run. With a good contact hitter or longball hitter at bat, the base hit or sacrifice fly to score the run are viable strategy options.

Another option used in both baseball and fast-pitch softball is a *squeeze bunt* play. The batter bunts the ball, putting it on the ground down the first or third base line in a position that makes it difficult for the defense to throw out the runner coming into home. The element of surprise for the squeeze bunt is advantageous, unlike the sacrifice bunt. The defense at first and third will tend to charge the plate when the batter shows that she is going to bunt. Because the play will be made at home, the farther away from home plate those two fielders are when the bunt is put down, the better. The pitcher is the other fielder usually involved in making a play on the bunt. That player's distance from home plate is governed by the pitching distance and can only be altered after the pitch is delivered. Because of these defensive tactics, on a squeeze bunt the batter delays moving into the bunting position in the batter's box.

To facilitate this delayed movement, the pivot is often altered from the step-around to a square stance technique to a pivot in place. The feet remain in their original position in the batter's box, but both feet pivot to point toward the pitcher, allowing the batter to square the hips and shoulders to face the pitcher (see figure 7.2). Just as with the sacrifice bunt, the batter's responsibility is to put the ball on the ground. The likelihood of a successful squeeze bunt is increased when you get a good look at the pitch coming in—just as it was with the sacrifice bunt. However, in executing the squeeze bunt, you will not have as much time to see the ball. In addition, your role can be complicated by what the runner has been instructed to do. If the runner is going home on the pitch (a *suicide squeeze*), you must protect the runner by at least contacting the ball and fouling it off, no matter where the pitch is. If the play is a *safety squeeze*, the runner will take a big lead on the pitch and continue to home only if your bunt is put down successfully, so you do not need to try to bunt a difficult pitch or one that is way out of the strike zone.

Realize, however, that if you do not bunt the first pitch when the squeeze play is called, the element of surprise is gone and you will probably be asked to hit away on the next pitch.

How to Execute the Drag Bunt

The hitter executing the drag bunt also uses the element of surprise to enhance the success of the tactic. However, this bunt is used as a means of getting on base rather than to advance a runner. The term *drag bunt* comes from the fact that the technique, when used by a left-handed batter, causes the ball to be dragged with the batter-baserunner down the first-base line (see figure 7.3). Batting from the left side is an advantage, because the batter is much closer to first base when the ball is contacted and therefore has a shorter distance to run than a right-handed batter. If that left-handed batter is also very fast on foot, and has a good eye for the ball, the drag bunt is an excellent alternative to swinging away for a base hit.

A right-handed batter can also execute a drag bunt to get on base. Although technically the right-handed batter does not *drag* the bunt down the first-base line, the bunt to get on is often called a drag bunt even for a right-handed batter. Regardless of the side of the plate you hit from, if you have good running speed and can make good contact with the ball, and

Figure 7.2 The pivot in place for the squeeze bunt.

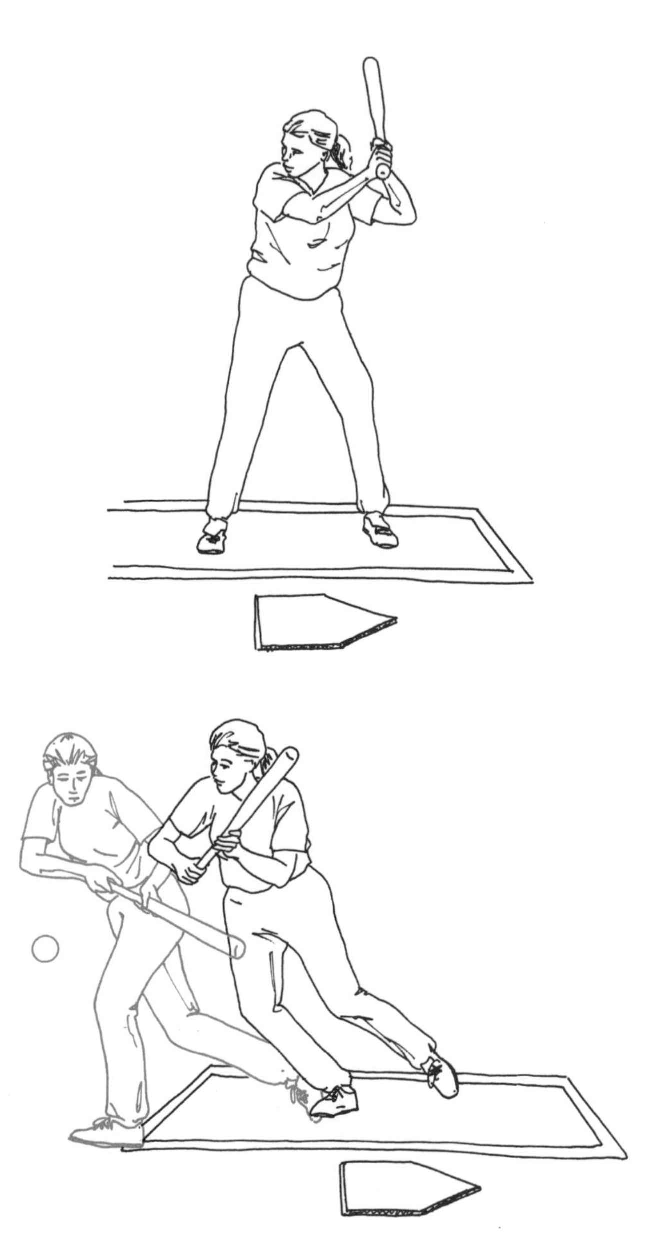

Figure 7.3 Executing the drag bunt.

the defensive players at the corners are playing back, the drag bunt is an offensive tactic you should be able to use successfully. Technique for the drag bunt varies a great deal from player to player. Many will use the same technique as previously described for the squeeze bunt. Some left-handed batters will drop the bottom hand off the bat and extend the bat to meet the ball with the top hand as they pivot and start for first base. If you use this technique, make sure you have not run out of the batter's box when contact with the ball is made. Some exceptional drag bunters will actually pivot both feet, with the weight on the front foot only and the back foot (which is taking the initial step toward first base) in the air outside of the box as the ball is contacted. This is a legal play because the foot outside the box must be in contact with the ground in order for you to be called out.

Variations on the Bunt Theme

An aggressive bunt defense will sometimes take away the sacrifice bunt option. In a bunting situation, if the first and third basemen set up their initial defensive position more than halfway to home plate, they will be approximately 25 feet from you before you square around. As you square around, they will charge the plate and stop 10 to 15 feet from you. If you bunt the ball in this situation, there is a strong possibility the defense will make the play on the runner you are trying to advance instead of on you, and the *sacrifice* will not have worked. To counteract this type of defensive play, you must be able to execute one of the following offensive alternatives. All of these techniques require you to read and react to the defense. The difficult part is that you have only a split-second to see what the defense is doing and to select and execute your choice for an alternative to the bunt.

How to Execute the Push Bunt

There are basically two different techniques to attempt when executing the *push bunt*, and the choice is sometimes dictated by the position of the runners and the resulting covering plays by the defense. With a runner on first base only, one option is to pop the ball in the air over the onrushing third baseman's head. The shortstop should be going to cover second base, so the area over the head of the third baseman should be open. This option does not work as well over the first baseman's head because the second baseman is going into that area to cover first base on the play. The other option is to try to push the ball on the ground between the third baseman and the pitcher so that the ball goes into the space vacated by the shortstop covering second base, or between the first baseman and the pitcher into the hole left by the second baseman covering first base. These two options can have a fairly high success rate if the ball is placed out of the reach of the first or third basemen who are in close to home plate. Once past these players, the pitcher is the only possible fielder. That player should be staying back in a defensive safety position for just this type of offensive play. However, if that player also comes in for the bunt, the push has an excellent chance of getting through. In addition, even if the pitcher stays back, the sacrifice itself may work. In the case of either type of push bunt, the batter successfully executing this play may well end up with a base hit. The two target areas for the push bunt on the ground could also be a target for a push bunt in the air. This is a less desirable option, because if the push bunt is not performed successfully, there is a good chance the ball could be caught in the air and a double play made by catching the advancing runner off first base.

The push bunt is executed from one of the sacrifice bunt stances; however, instead of giving with the bat as it contacts the ball to drop the ball down, push the bat into the ball to direct it into one of the target areas for the push bunt (see figure 7.4).

Figure 7.4 Executing the push bunt.

How to Execute the Slash Bunt

The *slash bunt* is used in situations similar to the push bunt, except the batter swings at the ball. It is another technique to use when the defense takes away the sacrifice bunt by virtue of their aggressive play. The resulting hit, especially if executed to the first-base side, could send the advancing runner all the way to third base.

Again, the technique players use to accomplish this play varies. In the squared-around sacrifice-bunting position in the batter's box, leave your feet where they are and merely slide your hands back together, rotate your torso back to the hitting position with hands and bat back, and take a three-quarter swing at the ball. The target for the placement of your slash bunt will be based on the same factors described for the push bunt. Keeping your feet in the squared position facilitates keeping your head still and makes it possible to better maintain your focus on the incoming pitch. If you attempt to move your feet back into your hitting stance, it is very difficult to keep the pitch in focus and initiate your swing in the time it takes for the pitch to come to the plate.

If, on the other hand, your initial bunting position is in the forward-stride position with feet pointing toward the pitcher, pivoting back to the full hitting position does not require as much movement of the entire body (see figure 7.5). Therefore, maintaining your focus on the ball is easier, and starting your swing in time is feasible. Another benefit of this skill is that by feigning a slash, you may stop the charge of the first and third basemen toward the plate and actually make it possible for you to go through with the sacrifice bunt.

How to Execute the Slap Hit

The *slap hit* is used more as a means of getting on base hitting the ball rather than as a form of bunting. It is used when you have been having difficulty making contact with the ball using a full swing against a very fast pitcher.

Assume an open stance in the batter's box with the bat held slightly in front of your back shoulder. As the ball comes in, take a three-quarter swing, just attempting to make contact and put the ball in play (see figure 7.6). The open stance puts your head in a position more nearly facing the pitcher so that your ability to see the ball is improved. The bat held a little forward of the position for a full swing will allow you to take a shorter stroke at the ball, thus increasing your chances of making contact. Even if you do not get a base hit, any time you can make contact in hitting and put the ball into play, you should do so. The defense has at least one or two opportunities to make an error: one while fielding the ball and another while throwing the ball to first base to put you out. If the first baseman misplays the throw, you have three chances for arriving safely at first base! A fast left-handed runner also has a good opportunity to get a base hit by directing the slap hit to the third-base side of the infield.

Figure 7.5 Executing the slash bunt from the forward-stride pivot stance.

Figure 7.6 Executing the slap hit.

How to Execute the Hit-and-Run

This tactic would be more correctly described as a *run-and-hit,* because the runner initiates the play by running on the release of the pitch, and the hitter then swings at the pitch, attempting to hit the ball. However, the term *hit-and-run* is the term commonly used in both softball and baseball. This play is used in fast-pitch softball but not slow-pitch, because no stealing is allowed in slow-pitch softball. In some ways, the hit-and-run is much like the suicide squeeze play. The runner goes on the pitch, and the batter must protect the runner by swinging even at a bad pitch and hopefully contacting the ball.

In the case of the hit-and-run, however, the intent of the play is to advance the runner more than one base. The assumption is that the runner would advance one base on the steal and would get to the next base on the hit. It is used quite often with a runner on first base in both baseball and fast-pitch softball to advance the runner to third base. The potential success of the play is enhanced if the batter can hit behind the runner, or direct the hit to right field, because the right fielder has the longest throw to third base of the three outfielders. The term *hit behind the runner* is used because the runner would be past the area between the first and second basemen, which is where the hit to right field would go through—thus the hit would go behind the runner. In fast-pitch, the hit-and-run play is also used with a runner on second base to increase the likelihood of scoring that runner on a single.

How to Execute the Steal

Teams that have the capacity to advance runners by stealing a base have a tremendous advantage, because they do not have to waste an out on a sacrifice bunt or any other play that has the potential for producing an out. Though stealing also has the potential for making an out, good baserunners like Ricky Henderson in baseball and Dot Richardson of the U.S. Olympic softball team have a high base-stealing percentage—meaning they are safe in the majority of their steal attempts. The successful base stealer not only has the physical ability to run fast, but also has studied pitchers and their deliveries, as well as the timing of getting the jump start allowed by the rules.

In fast-pitch, the runner cannot leave the base until the ball leaves the pitcher's hand. For the runner on first base, the right-handed pitcher's hand is hidden from view by the pitcher's body. However, a study of pitching deliveries would reveal that for most pitchers, the step with the left foot (for a right-handed pitcher), which is readily visible from first base, is timed with the release of the ball. Most base stealers will time their jump off the base with the pitcher's striding foot hitting the ground.

In fast-pitch softball, you should take a lead off the base on every pitch, even if you're not intending to steal. If you've taken a lead on the pitch in a nonstealing situation and the batter hits the ball, you are several steps closer to the next base. The following techniques for leaving the base can be used for either taking a lead or stealing. The choice is usually a matter of personal preference, or, in the case of stealing, the one that gives you the quickest start.

The method of leaving the base or the runner's foot placement on the base varies—however, one of the following three techniques is used by most runners. In the *rocker* start, the runner stands behind the base with the preferred driving foot (foot that pushes off) on the front edge of the base (see figure 7.7). As the pitcher is in the windup phase of the delivery, the runner begins to shift her weight from back to front over the driving foot (the foot that leaves the base last). The first step toward the next base is taken with the back foot, and that step is timed with the release of the ball by the pitcher. This technique is sometimes called a *rolling start*, and has the advantage of putting the runner in motion prior to the release of the ball. The timing in this method is extremely important so that you do not leave the base prior to the actual release of the ball by the pitcher. Remember, if you do leave prior to the release of the ball, you are out. It is sometimes a good idea for the coach to let the umpires know which players use the *rocker* method so that the forward movement of the runner while still in contact with the base is not viewed as leaving the base too soon.

Another technique is for the runner to assume a "track start" position in front of the base, facing the base to which the runner is advancing (see figure 7.8). The back foot is on the base, and that is the foot that takes the initial step. Experiment with each foot as the foot on the base to see which one feels most comfortable and gives you the best jump off the base.

A third technique is the *crossover*. When using this method, the runner (at first base) faces home plate with the left foot on the edge of the base closest to second base. As the runner pushes off the base with the left foot, she pivots the right foot toward second base and crosses the left foot over the right, taking the first step toward second base with the left foot (see figure 7.9)

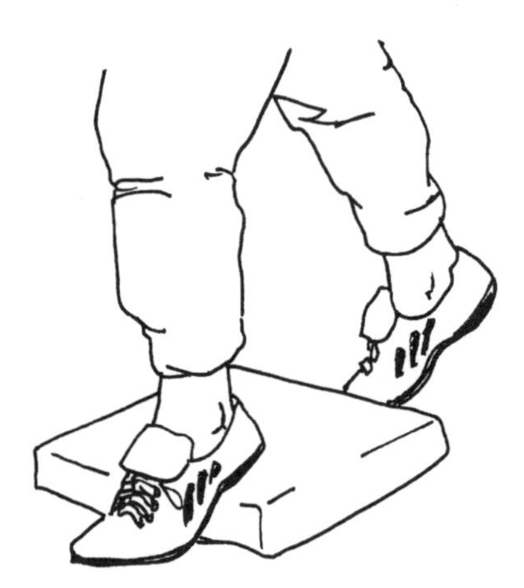

Figure 7.7 Rocker-start position.

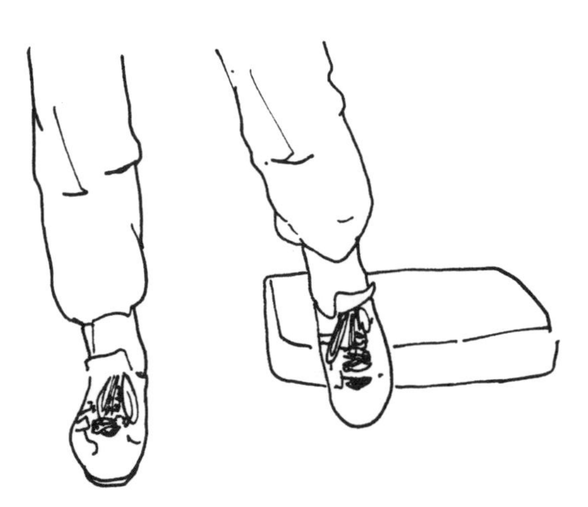

Figure 7.8 Track-start position.

Figure 7.9 Crossover-start position.

SACRIFICE BUNT DRILLS

1. Mimetic Sacrifice Bunts

You and a partner are set up as hitter and pitcher in your respective positions in the batter's box and at the pitching rubber. You, as the hitter, have a bat; your partner, the pitcher, does *not* have a ball. Assume your regular hitting position. The pitcher starts behind the pitching rubber. As she steps onto the pitching rubber to "take the sign from the catcher," use the technique described in figure 7.1 to assume the bunting position. Have your partner critique your technique of moving from the hitting to the bunting position. After 10 repetitions, rotate roles.

Success Goal = 8 correctly executed pivots out of 10 attempts ___

Success Check

- Two-step pivot ___
- Square stance facing pitcher ___
- Bat at top of strike zone parallel to the ground ___
- Bat in top hand outside grip area, resting on index finger, thumb on top ___

2. Soft-Toss Bunt

With a partner, position yourselves as hitter and tosser. The tosser has a bucket of 10 regulation balls. Conduct the drill using the techniques for the bunter outlined in the Keys to Success (see figure 7.1). The tosser may want to review Keys to Success: Hitting a Soft Toss from Step 4 (see figure 4.5 for tosser). Prior to tossing the ball for the bunter, the tosser needs to give a signal to the hitter so that he can square around to be in the correct position to bunt the ball as it is tossed. Switch places after 10 attempts.

Success Goal = 10 on-target tosses, and 8 bunts that go directly to the ground out of 10 attempts ___

Success Check

- Square stance, bat at top of strike zone ___
- Bat held well away from the body, parallel to the ground ___
- Direct the ball down to the ground ___

To Increase Difficulty

- Set up two cones 4 feet apart as targets on both the first- and third-base lines.

To Decrease Difficulty

- Use a larger ball.

3. Bunt the Pitched Ball

Set up in groups of three—a pitcher, a catcher, and a batter. The catcher must wear full catching gear. The batter takes the position in the batter's box. The catcher is behind the plate. The pitcher has a bucket of 10 balls and takes a position 15 to 20 feet from the batter in line with the pitching rubber. Prior to pitching the ball, the pitcher must signal the batter so he can pivot into the bunting position prior to the delivery of the pitch. The pitcher attempts to deliver a flat, moderate-speed pitch into the strike zone for the batter. The batter squares around into the sacrifice-bunting position and attempts to bunt the ball down the first- or third-base line. After all 10 balls are pitched, collect the balls, return them to the bucket, and rotate positions—hitter to catcher, catcher to pitcher, and pitcher to hitter.

Success Goal = 10 pitches in the strike zone and 8 bunts on the ground in fair territory out of 10 attempts ___

Success Check

- Two-step pivot with both feet remaining in the batter's box ___
- Square stance facing pitcher ___
- Bat held in loose grip away from the body ___
- Give with the bat on contact ___
- Ball comes to rest in fair territory within 10 feet of batter ___

To Increase Difficulty

- Pitcher throws from regulation distance at full speed. (Catcher must wear full gear.)
- Set up targets as in previous drill.

To Decrease Difficulty

- Pitcher moves closer to batter.
- Use a larger ball.

With the pitcher throwing at full speed from the regulation distance, this drill can be used to practice the push bunt, the slash bunt, and the slap hit. Add cones to mark the gaps at the shortstop and second-baseman positions. The batter uses the marked areas as targets for placement of the hit.

STEALING DRILL

Set up this drill with a hitter and defensive players at each infield position except first and third base. The catcher must be in full catching gear. Runners wearing batting helmets take turns stealing from first base, and runners waiting their turn should line up in foul territory behind first base. During the pitch, the runner initiates the steal as the ball leaves the pitcher's hand. The shortstop and the second baseman alternate covering second base for the tag play on the runner and backing up the throw from the catcher.

With a more experienced catcher, the batter should swing at the pitch *without making contact* in order to make the catcher's throw to second more difficult. The batter should assume a more passive role (not swinging at the pitch) when the catcher is a less experienced player. This drill also provides an opportunity for the runner to practice sliding if that is desired. The preferred slide would be a hook slide to the outfield side of second base, hooking the base with the left foot. This drill would usually be set up for the major purpose of practicing stealing. Therefore, the players at the defensive positions would be people who normally play those positions, and everyone would not rotate into those positions.

Success Goal = Runner successfully steals second base on 3 out of 5 attempts ___

Success Check

- Leaving the base is timed with the pitcher's release of the ball ___
- Takeoff corresponds to the technique selected ___
- If attempted, the slide used is a hook slide to the outfield side of the base ___

To Increase Difficulty

- Use a different takeoff technique on each stealing attempt.

To Decrease Difficulty

- Do not slide.

OTHER OFFENSIVE DRILLS

The drills in several other steps in this book, particularly Steps 4 and 8, can be modified to give you the opportunity to work on the various bunts, hitting behind the runner, sacrifice flies, stealing, and slap hits. Between the White Lines and Hitting Line Drives in Step 4 are especially appropriate for practicing the slap hit because the major focus of the drills is to put the ball in play. The Hitting the Gap drill can be used for the batter to practice the slap hit, the slap bunt and the push bunt. All of these techniques require the batter to place-hit the ball, which is the primary focus of this drill. Hitting Behind the Runner is a drill specifically designed to provide practice for the hitter using that technique. Adding fielders and baserunners to any of these drills makes it possible for those players, in addition to the batter, to practice their respective skills. Finally, the modified games in Step 9 provide opportunities for controlled and full-game practice for the specific offensive situations described in this step.

OFFENSIVE SITUATIONAL PLAY SUCCESS SUMMARY

Softball games are scored in runs. Runs can be scored only by batters becoming baserunners and then advancing around the three bases to eventually cross home plate safely. Your success as an offensive player has as much to do with your cognitive ability as it does with your physical ability. You must not only know your strike zone and the areas within that zone that are your hitting strengths, but you must also discipline yourself to swing at pitches in your strength zone—unless, of course, the pitcher has two strikes on you! However, with a two-strike count, you need to adjust your thinking and your technique to maximize your chances of getting on base. Choke up on the bat to gain more bat control. Open up your stance and shorten your swing to increase the possibility of making contact and putting the ball into play. Lay off the pitch well outside the strike zone, but don't be picky with a pitch close enough for the umpire to call a strike!

Take pride in being able to successfully execute the fundamental skill of laying down a sacrifice bunt that will move a teammate into scoring position. In slow-pitch, develop the ability to place-hit the ball with line drives into gaps in the outfield instead of hitting towering fly balls that are automatic outs. Learn to hit with power to the opposite field to take advantage of defensive overshifts defending you as a pull hitter. If you are a right-handed batter, hitting to the opposite field means you will be able to hit behind the runner to advance that runner to third when the situation presents itself.

If you are not blessed with blazing speed and therefore are not a real threat to steal a base, be a smart baserunner. Take the extra base on outfield throws to home, and be ready to advance on passed balls and overthrows. If caught in a rundown with a baserunner ahead of you, try to stay alive in the rundown so the other runner might have a chance to advance or score.

Run out every hit ball—defensive players drop balls and make throwing errors! Enjoy the challenge of executing a particular technique or tactic to successfully meet the offensive situation. Just as when on defense you want the ball to be hit to you so you can make the play, on offense you should want to be the batter up in the last inning with two outs and the winning run on third base. When called upon to sacrifice bunt, enjoy the thrill of being able to adjust your technique to slap the ball past the onrushing first baseman or push the ball over the head of the third baseman who is close enough to you to shake hands.

Softball is one of the most individual-focused team sports. You and you alone stand up there in the batter's box trying to advance a teammate into scoring position. And unlike basketball, it is a member of the opposing team who "passes" you the ball so you can carry out your part of the play. It is seldom a sympathetic pass. The pitcher is not going to intentionally give you an easy pitch to hit, so you have to successfully lay down the bunt to advance your teammate to second base. On the other hand, the teamwork involved in the hit-and-run is an example of players working together on a team to accomplish a goal dictated by an offensive situation.

Ask your coach or a fellow teammate to use the Position Play Keys to Success checklist (pages 89-90) or the Rating Your Progress sheets (pages 170-171) to help you evaluate your ability to react to offensive situational play. Continue practicing to improve the skills that are not as refined as you want them to be.

STEP 8 DEFENSIVE SITUATIONAL PLAY

Your development as a softball player depends on your ability to select and execute the appropriate skill combinations in the variety of offensive and defensive situations that occur during a game. Seldom in a team sport like softball is one skill carried out in isolation. Unlike the diver or the gymnast who does *a* dive or *a* vault, the softball player must be able to field a ground ball or fly ball and make a follow-up throw, or follow a hit with baserunning. In addition, often the technique used in one skill influences the performance of the follow-up skill.

Your focus in this step is on executing the fundamental defensive skills of fielding and throwing in typical defensive game situations, including double plays, sacrifice bunts, situations involving relay or cutoff plays, and rundowns. You know how to execute four of the basic defensive skills used in the game of softball: catching, throwing the ball overhand, fielding ground balls, and fielding fly balls. You also know the offensive skill of hitting a pitched ball and the practice skills of hitting off a tee and hitting the soft toss. In order to help you practice the combinations of defensive skills used during a game in a more gamelike setting, we'll learn a new skill: *fungo hitting.*

Why Is Fungo Hitting Important?

Fungo hitting is hitting the ball out of your own hand either onto the ground (ground balls) or into the air (fly balls). It is a skill mainly used to facilitate practice of fielding grounders and fly balls; it is not used in a game. However, it does help you with hand-eye and bat-eye coordination necessary for hitting.

Once you have learned the basics of fielding ground balls and fly balls, it is important to practice fielding balls that have come off a bat for a more gamelike experience. If the coach were the only one who could hit the ball toward a fielder, the practice opportunities would be severely limited. On the other hand, if everyone can fungo hit a ball, then half of the team will be able to practice fielding ground balls or fly balls at the same time. You will need to be able to fungo hit both ground balls and fly balls in order to fully participate in the drills in the remainder of this book.

How to Fungo Hit Ground Balls

Begin by holding a ball in the hand you place on the bottom end of the bat). Hold the bat high, back by your rear shoulder, your top hand gripping the bat as usual (it might help to use a light bat). Toss the ball out in front of your front foot so that it will drop to the position in space that it had on the tee. Once you toss the ball, quickly place your bottom hand on the bat to make your regular two-handed swing, and hit the ball. Because you want to hit grounders, let the ball drop just below waist height (as on the tee) before contacting and swinging through the ball. Be sure to start the bat high so that your swing path is high-to-low, making the ball go down onto the ground (see figure 8.1). Stand so that your tossing shoulder is pointed toward the fielder. Step toward the fielder with your front foot as you begin your swing. Watch the ball until you make contact.

If you want to get some practice fungo hitting grounders before you hit to a partner who is working on fielding, you can hit against a wall or fence. Stand far enough away from the wall so that you have plenty of time to field the rebounding ball with your tossing hand (your other hand continues to hold onto the bat).

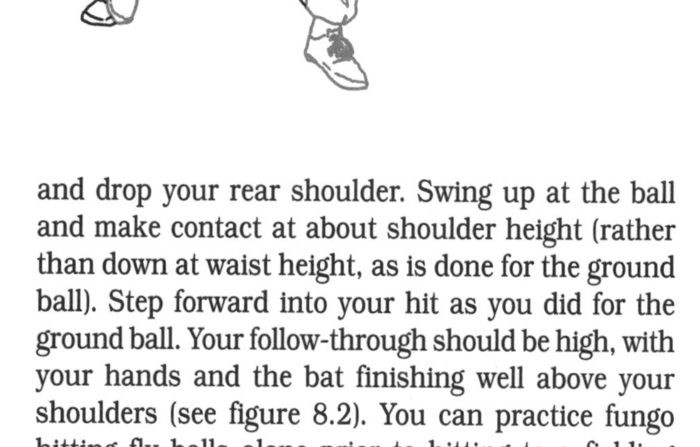

Figure 8.1 Fungo hitting ground balls.

How to Fungo Hit Fly Balls

Fungo hitting a fly ball is exactly the same as fungo hitting a ground ball, except the swing path is low-to-high rather than high-to-low. You need to toss the ball a little higher than when tossing for the ground ball, and the bat must begin the swing below your rear shoulder. Shift your weight onto your back foot and drop your rear shoulder. Swing up at the ball and make contact at about shoulder height (rather than down at waist height, as is done for the ground ball). Step forward into your hit as you did for the ground ball. Your follow-through should be high, with your hands and the bat finishing well above your shoulders (see figure 8.2). You can practice fungo hitting fly balls alone prior to hitting to a fielding

Figure 8.2 Fungo hitting fly balls.

partner, as you did for ground balls. However, rather than using a wall for practice, select a high obstacle to hit over, such as the backstop, goalposts, or even a small tree. Use a bucket of balls, hit them all over the obstacle, collect them, and hit them back. Before very long, you will be ready to use your newly learned skill of fungo hitting to provide a partner or teammate with realistic practice in fielding fly balls and ground balls.

FUNGO HITTING SUCCESS STOPPERS

Most errors in fungo hitting ground balls are caused by tossing the ball too high and by swinging too soon, thereby hitting the ball before it has a chance to drop below your waist. Most errors in fungo hitting fly balls are also caused by a poor toss, poor timing of the swing, and an incorrect swing path (it needs to be low-to-high). The most common errors that occur when fungo hitting ground or fly balls are listed below, along with suggestions on how to correct them.

Error	Correction
1. You hit a fly ball instead of a ground ball.	1. Toss the ball lower. Start your swing later. Contact the ball after it drops below your waist.
2. You hit a ground ball instead of a fly ball.	2. Toss the ball higher. Drop your rear shoulder and swing up at the ball.
3. The hit ball goes off-target.	3. Toss the ball directly opposite your front foot. Contact the ball off your front foot. At contact, feet point in the line of direction of the target. Step toward the target.
4. You miss the ball completely.	4. Watch the ball until the bat makes contact.

Why Are Skill Combinations Important?

In a game situation, there are two ways a ball can be hit off a pitch: into the air (either a line drive or a fly ball) or on the ground. The defense must field the ball however it is hit. Fielding the ground ball, line drive, or fly ball and making an overhand or sidearm throw or underhand toss to another player is a combination of actions that occurs frequently in a regulation game and is termed *defensive play.* Fly ball hits to the outfield often either advance runners into scoring position or enable them to score (*sacrifice flies*). Catching the fly ball and throwing it quickly and accurately to the proper player or base makes it much more difficult for the offensive team to move its runners ahead.

Typical game situations that require a combination of defensive skills include the following:

- Fielding ground balls, line drives, or pop-ups hit to you at one of the five infield positions (pitcher included). These hit balls can come to you at varying speeds and can be hit directly at you, to your glove side, and to your throwing side. Then you must make throws of varying distances and in a variety of directions in order to make a play at any of the bases and home plate.
- Fielding ground balls, line drives, and fly balls, and making overhand throws from the various outfield positions to a relay or cutoff person, an infield base, or home plate.

You now need to perfect your ability to use the combination skills of fielding ground balls, line drives, and fly balls and throwing in simulated game situations in order to become a complete and effective defensive player.

The first nine drills in this step, starting on page 130, will allow you to work on skills in combinations that typically occur in a game situation: fielding ground balls and fly balls, throwing the distances that infielders and outfielders have to throw, and moving in different directions to get in front of the ground balls and under the fly balls in order to make the plays. Before moving on to more advanced situations, use these drills and work with a teammate to make a force play or tag play that requires each of you to make a specific contribution to the successful completion of the play. In addition, you will have the opportunity to practice with a teammate who is either trying to make the same catch as you or is backing you up as you make the catch (drill 7). These basic concepts, strategies, and combinations of skills are used in all levels of softball. Next, we will work on more advanced defensive plays to deal with the offensive situational play described in the previous step. These plays are used by more experienced players in regulation games. If you are a more experienced player, use drills 10 through 20 (on pages 140-149) to improve your timing and technique. Step 9 describes modified games that will provide you with the opportunity to practice these defensive plays in controlled and real game situations.

If you are a player wanting to gain more experience and play at a higher level, you must increase your knowledge and physical ability to execute these plays successfully. Whether you play slow-pitch or fast-pitch, the ability to make the double play is a must if you intend to play in the infield. As discussed in the previous step, fast-pitch players must be able to lay down a variety of bunts. As a fast-pitch defensive player, you must be able to play aggressive bunt defense. In addition, a new skill, *throwing sidearm*, is introduced here because it is used by some infielders when executing the double play—one of the first defensive situational plays covered.

Why Is the Sidearm Throw Important?

The sidearm throw should be used sparingly by less experienced players because it is difficult for them to throw as accurately and with the same force as the overhand throw. At an elite level of softball, the sidearm throw is used by shortstops and sometimes third basemen when a quick-release throw is needed to make a play on a batter-baserunner at first base. However, there are instances when a less forceful throw is needed. Most players can use the sidearm throw for short-distance throws, such as the second baseman's throw to first base after fielding a ground ball, and the close feeds at any base for a single force play or first out of a double play.

The trajectory of the sidearm throw is horizontal or slightly low-to-high. Most throws should arrive to the fielder about chest-high. A short-distance overhand throw tends to go high-to-low, thus arriving at the fielder's feet and making for a very difficult catch. The short-distance sidearm throw stays horizontal or rises slightly to the fielder, arriving at the desired chest height. Although the sidearm throw is less accurate than the overhand, the shorter distance in which the throw is used reduces the likelihood of error. The sidearm throw also gets to the intended base more quickly because the thrower releases the ball from a crouched position rather than coming to the erect overhand throwing posture.

How to Execute the Sidearm Throw

As you field a ground ball, bring the ball to the throwing position; keep your back flat, knees bent, and torso parallel to the ground. If you are a right-handed second baseman throwing to first, or a right-handed shortstop throwing to second, your glove side is already pointed toward your target, so you don't need to pivot. Simply bring the ball across the front of your body, keeping your throwing arm parallel to the ground (see figure 8.3a-c). All other aspects of the throw are exactly the same as for the overhand throw.

When using the sidearm throw to your throwing-arm side—for example, the second baseman throwing to second, or shortstop throwing to third—pivot your feet after fielding the ball so your glove side is toward the throwing target, and then proceed as described for throwing to the glove side. Use the sidearm throwing drills on pages 140-142 to perfect this technique prior to going on to the double play.

FIGURE 8.3 **KEYS TO SUCCESS**

THROWING SIDEARM

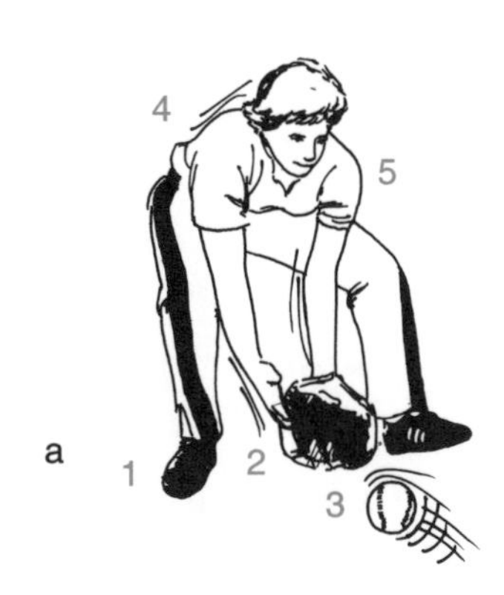

Preparation

Glove-Side Target

Throwing-Side Target

1. Feet more than shoulder-width apart ___
2. Hands low, fingers pointed down ___
3. Glove open to ball ___
4. Back flat ___
5. Focus on ball ___

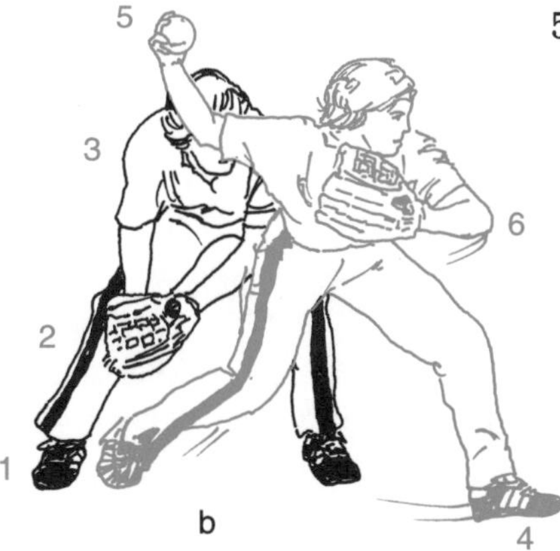

Execution

Glove-Side Target

1. Shift weight to throwing side ___
2. Start glove and hand to throwing shoulder, two-finger grip ___

Throwing-Side Target

1. Weight on throwing-side foot ___
2. Start pivot to throwing-side target ___

3. Stay low, flex at waist ___
4. Step toward target ___
5. Ball to throwing position ___
6. Glove elbow toward target ___
7. Weight to glove side ___
8. Hips square to target ___
9. Throwing arm parallel to ground ___
10. Snap wrist on release of ball ___

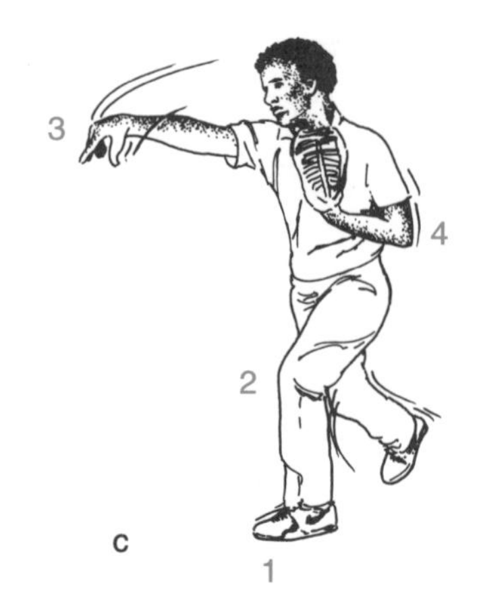

Follow-Through

Glove-Side Target ***Throwing-Side Target***

1. Weight on glove-side foot ___
2. Knees bent ___
3. Throwing arm moves horizontally toward target ___
4. Glove elbow back ___

SIDEARM THROWING SUCCESS STOPPERS

Sidearm throwing errors are usually caused by an improper point of release, and failure to keep the throwing arm parallel to the ground through the throwing movement. The most common sidearm throwing errors are listed below, along with suggestions on how to correct them.

Error	Correction
1. The ball goes to the right or left of the target.	1. Snap your wrist directly at the target, not before or after.
2. The trajectory of the ball is high or low.	2. Do not "stand up" to throw—stay low. Bend and keep your torso parallel to the ground.
3. You "push" the ball rather than throw it.	3. Lead with the elbow as you bring the ball across your body.
4. When you throw to a target on your throwing side, the ball is off-target.	4. Stay low, but pivot your torso so your glove side is toward the target.

Why Is the Double Play Important?

As less experienced players, your defensive strategy was to get one out at a time. In situations where there are fewer than two outs and runners in a force situation, the play should be on the lead runner. Now you are going to focus on the *double play*, an advanced play that calls upon the defense to get two outs from continuous action.

The most common double-play opportunity occurs with one or more runners on base in a force situation with fewer than two outs. The batter hits a ground ball to an infielder, who throws to a base to put the lead runner out, immediately followed by that covering player's throw to first base to put the batter-baserunner out. Infield double plays are made second to first when there is a lone runner on first base; third to first with runners on first and second; and home to first when the bases are loaded.

A double play occurs anytime two players are put out during continuous action. For example:

- A fly out or line-drive out is followed by the baserunner being put out after failing to tag up
- A fly out, then the baserunner is thrown out attempting to advance
- In fast-pitch, the batter strikes out, and a baserunner is thrown out trying to steal a base

However, in this step, your focus is on double plays with runners on first base, first and second base, or the bases loaded, and a ground ball hit to the infield. The skills that you will work on for this double play are the sidearm throw, shortstop's drag step and inside pivot techniques, and the second baseman's crossover and rocker-pivot techniques.

The double play is important because the defense can get two players out on one pitch. Not only is the baserunner already on base put out as a lead runner, but the batter-baserunner is also put out as part of the continuous play.

In game play, the successful execution of a double-play can deal a psychological blow to the offensive team and at the same time motivate the team that has successfully executed it. Thus, the momentum in a game often changes hands as a result of a successful double play.

How to Execute the Double Play

Double plays on ground balls are typically initiated by a throw from an infielder to second base, third base, or home plate. The infielder playing the base to which the initial throw was made then throws the ball to first base. The first out is made on the lead runner, who is forced; the second out is made on the batter-baserunner at first base, also a force-out. In fast-pitch softball, where runners can lead off the base on the pitch, the only hope of getting the second out is to make that play on the batter-baserunner. Even in slow-pitch, the batter will be at least a step behind the other baserunners because of completing the swing and shifting gears to get out of the batter's box. The right-handed batter, in particular, has a greater distance to run than any other runner because she is on the side of home plate farther away from first base. The recommendation for both fast- and slow-pitch play is to get the second out of the double play at first base.

You have already had experience executing portions of the double play—namely, throwing, both overhand and sidearm; catching; and footwork for a force play. The sidearm throw is used by the shortstop when executing the *feed* (throw) to the second or third baseman for the first out of the double play, and by the second baseman when making the feed to the shortstop at second base for the *front end* (first out) of the double play. You use the overhand throw, which you can execute well by this point, when the throw is fairly long for either of the outs in the double play.

When executing the double play, you need to make only slight additions to the footwork technique you have already practiced for force-outs at home and third. To make a strong throw for the second out of the double play, you need to take a step toward first base as you throw the ball. Thus, for the force-out at third or home for the first out of the double play, do not stretch out as far as you would to catch the ball on a regular force-out. You need to be in balance to take the step toward first base on your throw for the second out. Stretching to catch the ball for the first out of the double play puts your body in an unbalanced position. You will consequently be slower and less powerful in your throw to first base. On the other hand, if you're the first baseman, you must stretch as far as possible in order to shorten the length of the throw for the second out. You try to cut down the time it takes for the ball to arrive at first base, because in the double play the play there is usually very close.

You have not had experience to date with the footwork involved in making the first out of the double play at second base. This footwork is much different from the footwork done at third or home when that is the location of the first out. In your practice as both shortstop and as second baseman, you have learned how to make a force play at second base, but not a force play that must be followed by a throw to first base. The footwork for the double play at second base is called a *pivot*. Basically, your pivot must position you to make the force-out on the runner at the base, let you move into position to make a strong throw to first base for the second out, and get you out of the way of the runner.

In order to be in a position for a strong throw to first base, you must be out of the path of the oncoming runner, and you must also be able to step in the direction of first base on the throw. In softball, unlike baseball, the first out of the double play at second base is almost always made with the runner close to the base. Therefore, the need to get out of the path of the runner is ever present for the fielder making the pivot at second base. You do not want to be knocked down by the runner, because then you cannot make the throw to first. In addition, you must have a clear path for the ball to travel to first base; the path must not be blocked by the runner. The runner has no option but to go to the base. You, therefore, must be the one to move away from the base in order to find the clear path needed for your throw. The following sections provide the techniques used by the shortstop and the second baseman when making the pivot on the double play at second base and the throw to the pivot player. Use the double-play drills on pages 142-145 to practice all of the pivots used by infielders when making the double play. You then will be able to experience the excitement of "turning the double play" in a real softball game.

Note: Descriptions of techniques for executing the first out of the double play at second base, as used by the shortstop (and, later, the second baseman), are for a right-handed player. A left-handed player would have great difficulty getting into position to receive the throw at the base for the force-out, and then to get out of the way of the runner, still leaving the left side of second base unobstructed for the throw to first base. For this and other reasons, left-handers do not usually play shortstop or second base.

How to Execute the Shortstop's Drag Step

The *drag step* is used by the shortstop to make contact with second base while catching the ball for the force-out and positioning the body for the throw to first base for the second out. This technique gets the shortstop out of the baseline so that the runner cannot in any way be in the line of the throw. The drag step is used when the feed for the play is thrown by the second or first baseman from the outfield side of the baseline between first base and second base.

When a ground ball is hit to the first-base side of the infield in a double-play situation, you, the shortstop, move from your initial fielding position to just behind second base. You straddle the back corner of the base (the corner pointing to center field) with the inside of your right foot contacting the very corner of the base and your shoulders parallel with an imaginary line between first and third base. If there is not time to get to the base and stop in the straddle position over the back corner, move through that position without stopping. As you catch the ball to make the force-out, step toward the right outfield grass with your left foot (see figure 8.4a), dragging the toes of your right foot across the back corner of the base (see figure 8.4b). Still moving, step to close your right foot to your left (see figure 8.4b), then step left again and throw to first base for the second out (see figure 8.4c). To accomplish these objectives without the runner's interference, the direction of your movement past the base must be toward the right outfield area, *not* down the baseline toward first base!

How to Execute the Shortstop's Inside Pivot

In Step 6, you learned that the shortstop is responsible for covering second base on a double play when the ball is hit to the catcher or to the pitcher. The reason for this coverage is that the shortstop has easier skills to execute than the second baseman does when making the play at second base. The shortstop, when moving toward second base from the regular fielding position, is already going in the general direction of first base. Thus, the whole flow of the play is in the direction of the throw for the second out of the double play. The movement of the second baseman going to cover second base, on the other hand, is away from first base and, therefore, away from the direction of the throw for the second out.

Similar principles apply to covering a base for a double-play force-out, as for any force play. As you know, when the feed for the force play is coming from the infield side of the baselines, the covering position is at the inside corner of the base. In a double-play situation, when the ball is hit up the middle to either the pitcher or the catcher, the shortstop covers second on the inside corner and uses an *inside*

FIGURE 8.4 KEYS TO SUCCESS

SHORTSTOP'S DRAG STEP

Approaching the Base

1. Straddle back corner ___
2. Weight on right foot ___
3. Face thrower ___
4. Focus on ball ___

Footing the Base

1. Catch ball ___
2. Step past base with left foot ___
3. Drag right foot across back corner ___
4. Close right foot to left ___

Leaving the Base

1. Step with left foot ___
2. Ball to throwing position ___
3. Throw to first base ___
4. Weight on glove-side foot ___
5. Knees bent ___
6. Throwing arm horizontal ___
7. Glove arm back ___

pivot to make the force-out and complete the throw to first base for the double play. On the other hand, if the ball is clearly hit to the first-base or third-base side and is played from the infield side of the base lines, the regular guidelines for base coverage apply (grounder to first-base side, shortstop covers second base; third-base side, second baseman covers).

When the ball is hit up the middle, you, the shortstop, come to the inside corner of second base, step on the inside corner of the base with your left foot, and face the player making the feed (see figure 8.5a). As you make the catch for the force-out, bend your knees, take the weight fully on your left foot, and spring away from the base (off your left foot) toward the pitching rubber, landing on your right foot well clear of the base runner (see figure 8.5b). Step toward first base with your left foot, and make the throw for the second out of the double play (see figure 8.5c).

FIGURE 8.5 **KEYS TO SUCCESS**

SHORTSTOP'S INSIDE PIVOT

Approaching the Base

1. Step on inside corner with left foot ___
2. Hips square to thrower ___
3. Focus on ball ___

Footing the Base

1. Catch ball ___
2. Take full weight on left foot ___
3. Bend knees ___
4. Spring from base off left foot ___
5. Land on right foot ___
6. Step onto left foot ___
7. Ball to throwing position ___
8. Throw to first base ___

Leaving the Base

1. Weight forward ___
2. Knees bent ___
3. Throwing arm horizontal ___
4. Throwing shoulder forward ___

How to Execute the Second Baseman's Crossover Pivot

For the second baseman, turning the double play at second base involves a true pivot, or change of direction. The second baseman must clear the base after making the force-out, stop the momentum of the body going away from first base, and step back toward first on the throw. The second baseman uses the *crossover pivot* when the feed is coming from the infield side of the baseline between second and third, or when timing demands shortening the distance the feed has to travel (that is, on any throw from the third baseman or a long throw from the shortstop). As the second baseman, you should move to cover second base from your regular fielding position so that you can cross the base in a direct line toward the person feeding you the ball. If time allows, move to a position just short of the base, facing the direction of the incoming throw (see figure 8.6a). As the thrown ball approaches, step on the base with your left foot, move over the base, and catch the ball on the far side of the base (third-base side) while still in contact with the base with your left foot for the force-out (see figure 8.6b).

FIGURE 8.6 **KEYS TO SUCCESS**

SECOND BASEMAN'S CROSSOVER PIVOT

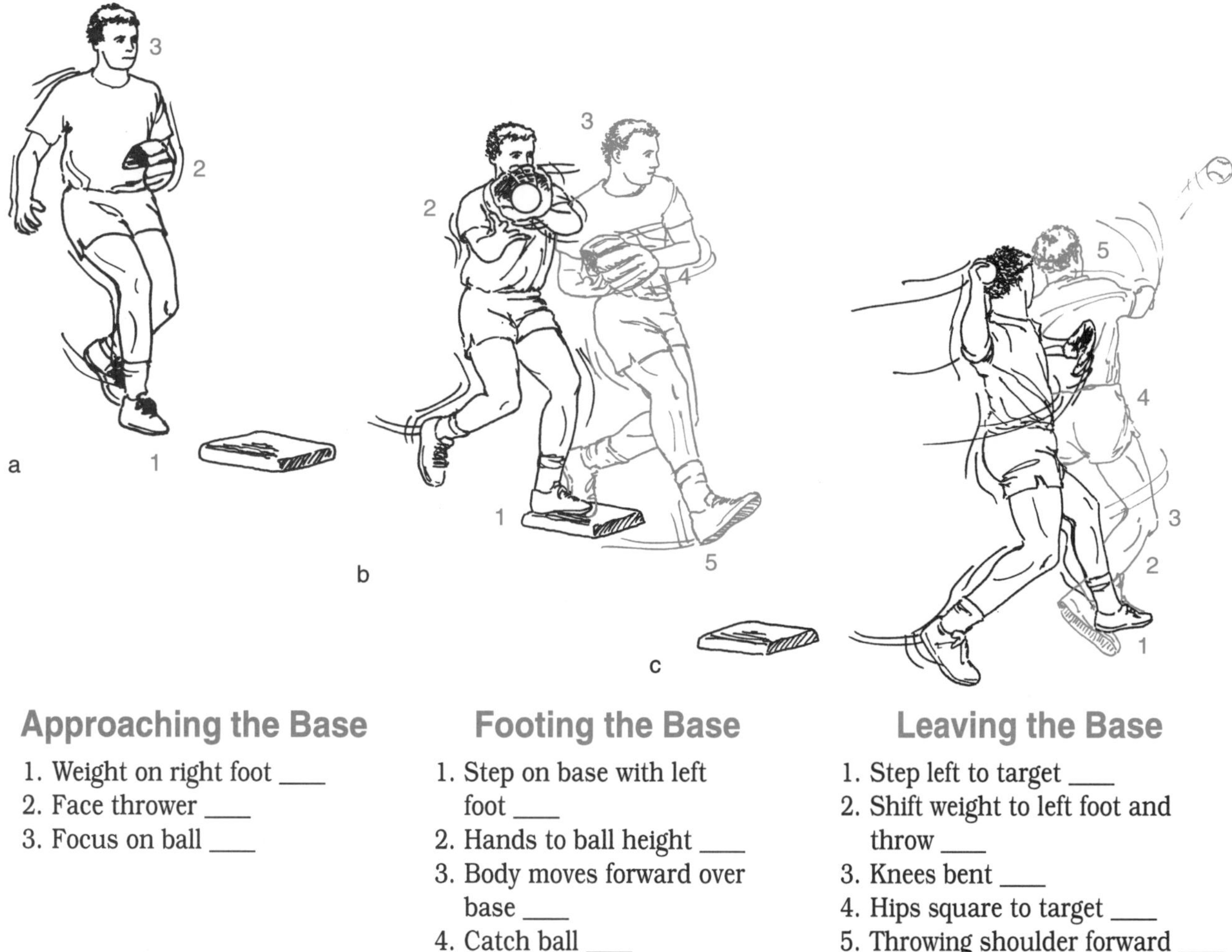

Approaching the Base

1. Weight on right foot ___
2. Face thrower ___
3. Focus on ball ___

Footing the Base

1. Step on base with left foot ___
2. Hands to ball height ___
3. Body moves forward over base ___
4. Catch ball ___
5. Block with right foot ___

Leaving the Base

1. Step left to target ___
2. Shift weight to left foot and throw ___
3. Knees bent ___
4. Hips square to target ___
5. Throwing shoulder forward ___

Immediately block your forward momentum by landing on your right foot and bending your right knee. This step onto your right foot should carry you well clear of the base in order to get out of the path of the runner. Shift your weight to the left side. Step left and throw the ball to first base (see figure 8.6c).

The major-league style of play in which the second baseman leaps straight up into the air over second base to avoid the incoming runner, spins in the air, and—while suspended in midair—makes the throw to first base is technique above and beyond our expectations of you in this book!

How to Execute the Second Baseman's Rocker Pivot

The *rocker pivot* is used by the second baseman when the feed from the shortstop is initiated very close to second base. As second baseman, you move to the base and place the toes of your right foot in contact with the outfield side of the base. With your weight on your left foot, catch the ball (making the force-out), step back onto your right foot, step left toward first base, and throw the ball. Stepping back with the right foot in this way, called the *deep drop*, gets you out of the path of the runner. Another rocker technique involves standing with your weight on your *right* foot, kicking the base with your *left* foot for the force-out, and stepping left to throw. This move, the *short drop*, is quicker by one step, but leaves you in the base line. Base your choice of footwork technique on the position of the runner at the time of the play at the base: use the deep drop if the runner is close, and the short drop if the runner is farther away. Figure 8.7a-c shows how to execute both the deep- and short-drop rocker pivots.

FIGURE 8.7 KEYS TO SUCCESS

SECOND BASEMAN'S ROCKER PIVOT

a

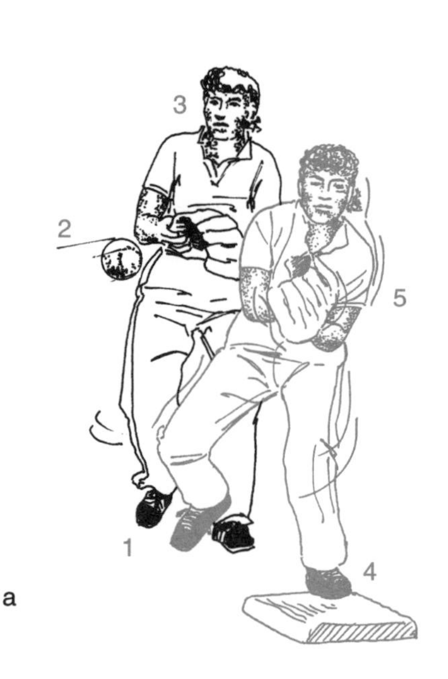

a

Preparation

Deep Drop

1. Approach base, weight on left foot ___
2. Hands to ball height ___
3. Focus on ball ___
4. Right foot contacts base ___
5. Catch ball ___

Short Drop

1. Approach base, weight on right foot ___
2. Hands to ball height ___
3. Focus on ball ___
4. Left foot contacts base ___
5. Catch ball ___

Execution

Deep Drop

1. Weight on left foot ___
2. Step back on right foot ___
3. Ball to throwing shoulder ___
4. Step left toward target ___
5. Right hip drives forward ___
6. Left elbow points toward target, throw to first base ___

Short Drop

1. Weight on right foot ___
2. Step left toward target ___
3. Ball to throwing shoulder ___
4. Weight to left side ___
5. Right hip drives forward ___
6. Left elbow points toward target, throw to first base ___

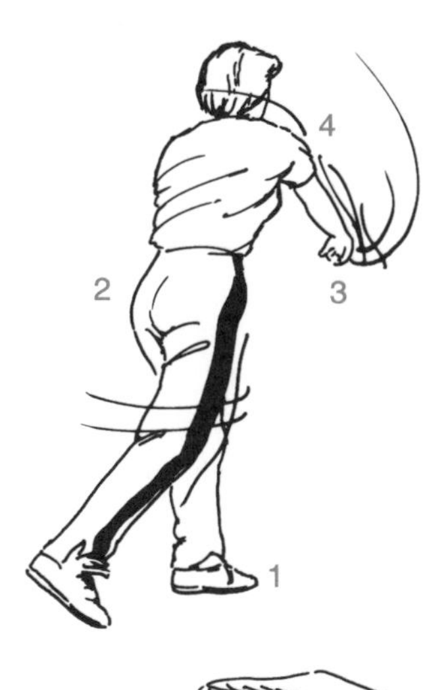

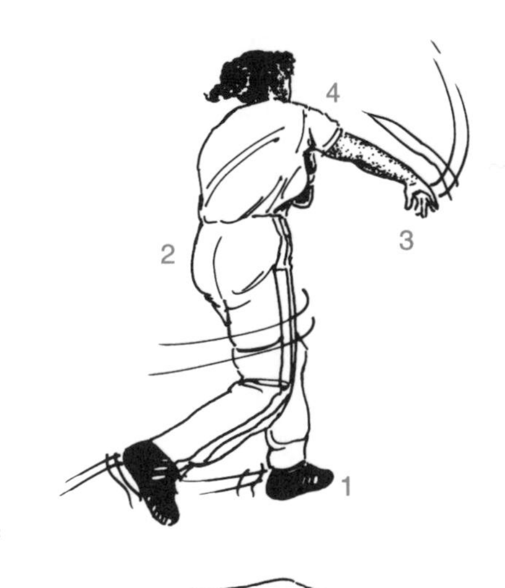

Follow-Through

Deep Drop ***Short Drop***

1. Weight on glove-side foot ___
2. Hips square to target ___
3. Throwing hand low ___
4. Throwing shoulder forward ___

Why Is the Sacrifice-Bunt Defense Important?

In fast-pitch softball, the offensive game situations with a runner on first base and runners on first and second base just described as double-play situations for the defense could also call for the offensive team to use the sacrifice bunt explained in the previous step. Successfully carrying out the sacrifice bunt not only puts the runners in scoring position, but also takes them out of a forced double-play situation.

As stated in Step 7, scoring runs in elite-level fast-pitch softball is very difficult. At any level, when pitching dominates the hitting game, offensive teams have to resort to bunts, slap hits, and taking advantage of defensive mistakes (including walks by the pitcher) in order to score runs.

If the first and third basemen in fast-pitch played at the same depth as their counterparts in slow-pitch, any bunt put on the ground down either foul line would be a hit most of the time. That is why bunting is not allowed in slow-pitch. Hitting in slow-pitch is so strong that the first and third basemen would be in serious jeopardy from a hit ball if they had to play closer to home plate to protect against the bunt.

In a sacrifice-bunt situation, the resolve of the defense is to deny the sacrifice and get the lead runner out. When one run can mean victory, the defense needs to keep runners out of scoring position. Aggressive bunt defense is a necessity for a successful advanced-level fast-pitch softball team.

How to Execute the Sacrifice-Bunt Defense

The specific tactics that the defense will use in a sacrifice-bunt situation depend on several factors. First, the game situation—is the potential run represented by the lead runner important? Second, the position of the runners on base dictates where the play on the lead runner will be. With a runner on first base only, the play on the lead runner will be to second base. The play will be to third when there are runners on first and second. Therefore, in addition to covering first base, the defense needs to cover the base to which the lead runner is going. Although the intent is to get the lead runner, if that play is not likely to be successful, the batter-baserunner must be put out at first base. Third, the skills of the players involved in the bunt defense and the skills of the offensive players will help determine the defensive coverage scheme. Do the first and third basemen have good reaction time? Can they react quickly to a slap bunt after charging home plate? Is the pitcher quick enough off the pitching rubber to be able to field a bunt on the first- or third-base side if those fielders stay back to cover their respective bases? How fast is the lead runner? The batter-baserunner? What are the tendencies of the offensive team? Do they use a run-and-bunt, or do they use a safety sacrifice in which the runner, after taking a good lead on the pitch, must see the ball go down toward the ground before going to the next base? Can the batter be influenced not to bunt by a hard-charging defense at the corners? On the other hand, is the batter a good slap or push bunter? These are some of the questions that must be answered as a team prepares its bunt defensive scheme for an opponent. For each of the following sacrifice situations, potential options are presented.

Sacrifice Bunt: Runner on First Base

The following is the defensive play used by the majority of teams and therefore is the only option presented for this situation. Teams might make some adjustments only to try to cover some individuals' defensive weaknesses.

Prior to the pitch, the first and third basemen move to a position approximately halfway to home. The second baseman shifts slightly toward first base and the shortstop shifts slightly toward second base, their respective cover responsibilities. As the batter squares around to bunt, the first and third basemen charge the plate and stop in a low fielding position approximately 15 feet from the batter. The second baseman and the shortstop move toward the bases they are to cover—however, they must watch the batter and be ready to react to a slap or a slash hit toward their vacated position. The center fielder moves toward a back-up position at second base. The left fielder moves to a position to cover a slap bunt or hit to the regular shortstop position. If the ball is bunted, the left fielder runs from the slap-coverage position to cover third base in case the third baseman fields the bunt, the play is made to first base, and the runner attempts to go all the way to third base. The right fielder moves to cover the hole left by the second baseman's movement toward first. The pitcher assumes a fielding position at the front edge of the 8-foot (radius) circle. The catcher prepares to field a ball that falls directly in front of the plate, and also—of greater importance—directs the play by calling the base to which the play should be made. The catcher is the only defensive player facing the field of play who can see the relative positions of the runner, batter-baserunner, and the other defensive players. If the third baseman does not field the bunt, he returns to cover third base and the left fielder backs up the base on any play made there.

Sacrifice Bunt: Runners on Second and First Base

Option 1: The coverage is the same as with the runner only on first base, with the following exceptions:

a. The shortstop covers third base and leaves second base uncovered. Chances are, the play is either going to be made on the lead runner going to third base or the batter-baserunner going to first base.
b. The left fielder covers for a possible slap hit into the shortstop hole as before, but on the bunt moves to back up a throw to third.

Option 2: The coverage is the same as with a runner only on first base, with the following exceptions:

a. The third baseman stays back to cover third base.
b. The pitcher covers a bunt to the third-base side.
c. The left fielder backs up the throw to third after covering for the slap hit.

Many of the drills in previous steps can be modified to practice the defensive skills involved in the sacrifice-bunt defense. You have already had the opportunity to practice making a force play at first, second, and third base in Step 6. Modify these drills so that the throws come from the home plate area, where a bunt would be made, and travel the regulation distance to first, second, or third base. Throws should be made by fielders in the positions of first and third basemen, pitcher, and catcher—the players normally fielding a bunt.

Because sacrifice-bunt defense requires the entire defensive team to react to an offensive situation, it is best practiced in a modified game situation. In the following step, Situation Ball is a modified game with set situations for teams to practice in a controlled environment. The offensive scenarios calling for a sacrifice bunt could be used in this game. Scrub and One-Pitch (also in Step 9) are modified games that offer a less controlled, more gamelike setting to practice the various offensive and defensive situations described in Steps 7 and 8 as they arise in the game.

Why Are the Relay and Cutoff Plays Important?

You have now had opportunities to work on some skills and game concepts used in intermediate-level game play. Two new defensive skills, the *relay* and the *cutoff*, are not necessarily intermediate-level skills in terms of difficulty. However, the relay (especially) and the cutoff (in some instances) require the ability to make strong, accurate overhand throws, as well as good catching skills. By now you should have had enough practice time to develop sufficient throwing and catching skills so that you will have success executing both the relay and cutoff.

Both of these plays increase the defense's chance of making an out on a hit ball. The *relay*, as its name might imply, uses more than one player to get the ball to its destination. It is used when the throwing distance is too great for one player to execute a fast, accurate throw. The *cutoff*, interrupting the flight of a throw, is used when one baserunner cannot be thrown out but another baserunner is *in jeopardy*, in a position to be put out. Without the use of these two plays in the situations described, all runners might be safe.

How to Execute the Relay

The relay is typically executed by the shortstop or the second baseman. When a hit ball goes past the outfielders in left and center fields, or when these fielders retrieve a hit ball and the throwing distance is beyond their capabilities, the shortstop goes out to receive the throw and relay it to its ultimate destination. Similarly, when a ball is hit to right field in this manner, the second baseman is the relay person. Another option in the slow-pitch game is to use the short fielder as a relay person, if he is covering the area between the other three outfielders and the infield and is in a good position to take the outfielder's throw. When the short fielder is the fourth outfielder and all are equidistant from home plate, the shortstop and second baseman must assume the relay responsibility.

The player executing the relay faces the outfielder with the ball and raises her arms to make a big target. The throw from the outfielder should arrive chest-high to the relay person. The relayer catches the ball, pivots by turning to the glove side, and throws the ball to the intended destination (see figure 8.8a-c).

FIGURE 8.8 **KEYS TO SUCCESS**

RELAY

Preparation

1. Face outfielder with ball ___
2. Identify yourself as relay person ___
3. Raise arms to increase your size as target ___
4. Focus on ball ___
5. Extend hands to prepare to catch ___
6. Begin pivot by stepping toward target with glove-side foot ___
7. Catch ball ___

a

b

c

Execution

1. Complete pivot ___
2. Begin crow-hop step ___
3. Weight on throwing-side foot ___
4. Glove side toward target ___
5. Step toward target with glove-side foot ___
6. Throw the ball using two-finger grip ___

Follow-Through

1. Weight on glove-side foot ___
2. Throwing-side shoulder forward ___
3. Throwing hand pointed at target ___

How to Execute the Cutoff Play

In slow-pitch softball, the cutoff play on a throw to home plate is executed by the first baseman (see figure 8.9) when the throw is from right or center field, and by the third baseman (see figure 8.10) when the throw is from left field.

Because in fast-pitch the first baseman plays in front of the base line, much closer to home, the first baseman is the cutoff player on *all* throws from the outfield to home and the base coverage responsibilities shift accordingly (see positions in color in figure 8.10). On throws to third base from right and center field (see figure 8.11), the shortstop is the cutoff person in both slow- and fast-pitch softball.

As the cutoff person, you assume a position about 35 feet from the original target base, facing the thrower. Stand with the glove side of your body aligned with the line of flight of the ball, so that you do not block the covering player's view of the ball. Because the play on the baserunner will be a tag play, the throw from the fielder should arrive at the covering player about knee-high. The throw should thus be passing you, the cutoff person, at about head or shoulder height.

Cutoff plays require strong communication between the intended fielder and the cutoff person. The covering player directs the cutoff play. If there is still a play to be made on the incoming baserunner and the throw is on-target, the covering player says nothing—and as the cutoff person, you allow the throw to go through to him. On the other hand, if the incoming runner is already safe or the throw is off-target, the covering player calls "cut" and further indicates to you by a verbal signal where (if at all) to play the ball. "Cut second" or "cut two" indicates that you should cut off the incoming throw and then throw to second base, making a play on the batter-baserunner trying to advance. On an off-target throw to home, "cut home" or "cut four" tells you to cut off the throw and relay the ball to home plate because there is still a play on the incoming runner. "Cut" with no further direction tells you to cut off the throw and simply hold it.

As with the relay person, any pivot toward home by the cutoff player is done to the glove side. Pivoting to your glove side puts your body in direct throwing position with only a quarter-turn change of direction. Drills for practicing the relay and cutoff begin on page 145.

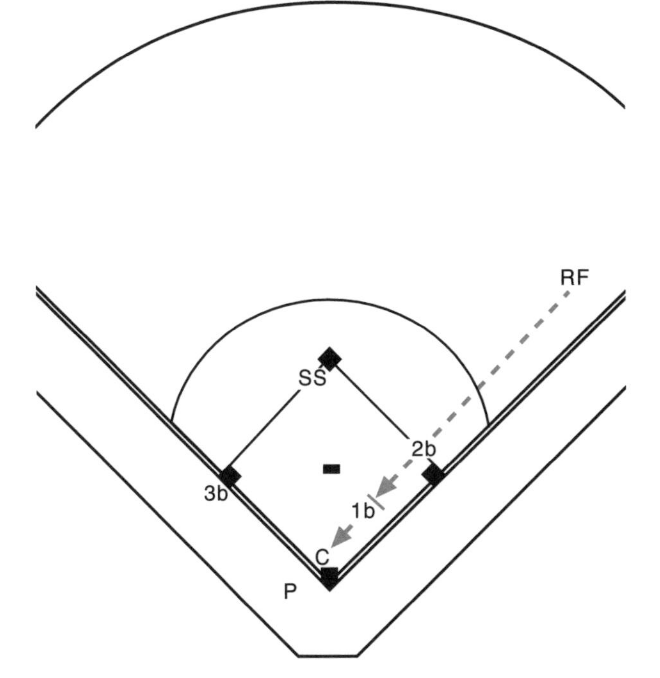

Figure 8.9 Cutoff play on throw from right or center field to home (slow- or fast-pitch softball).

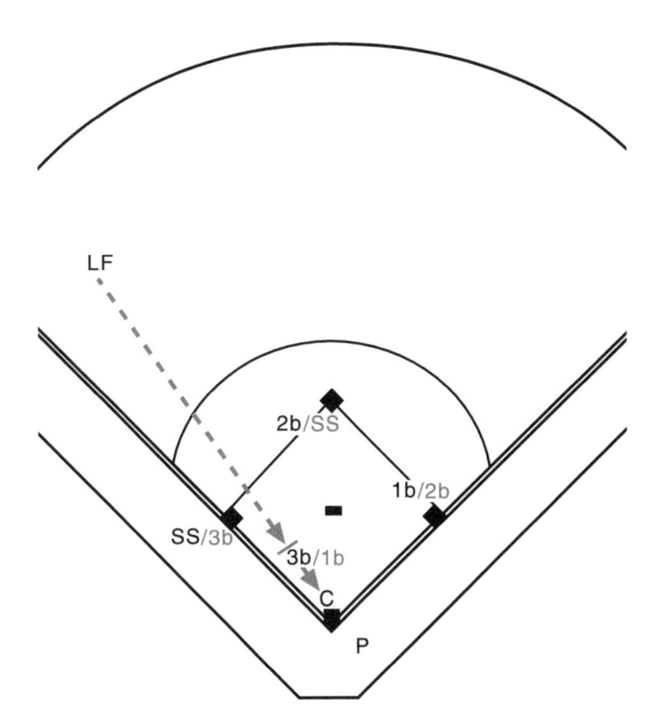

Figure 8.10 Cutoff play on throw from left field to home (positions in color indicate fast-pitch cutoff and base coverage responsibilities).

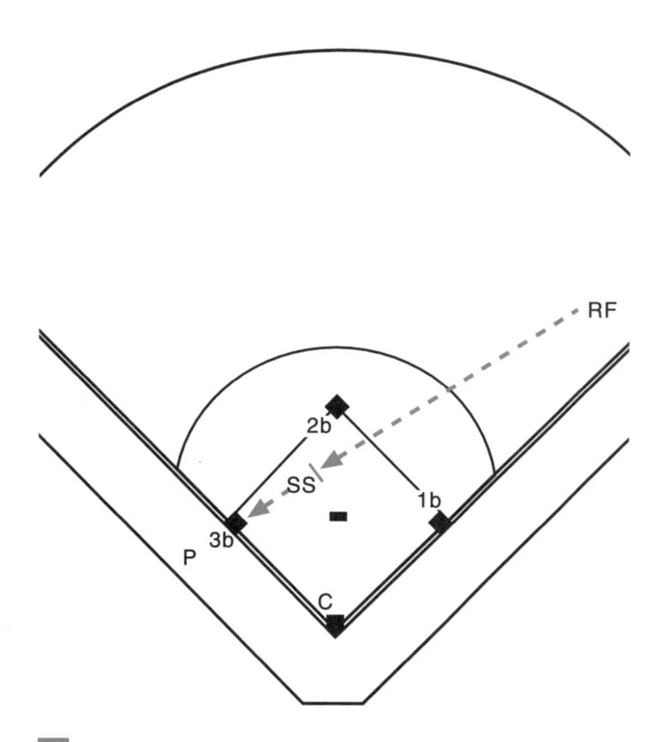

Figure 8.11 Cutoff play on throw from right or center field to third base (slow- or fast-pitch softball).

Why Is the Rundown Important?

The final defensive situation you will deal with in this step is the *rundown*. Rundowns occur when a runner is caught between bases by the defense. Remember, you may freely overrun first base and home plate, but not second or third base; also, if you go toward second base after overrunning first, the defense can make a play on you. Anytime you are off a base and not free to return to that base, and the defense tries to pick you off (catch you between bases) by throwing the ball to a covering fielder, you are in a rundown.

On defense, you want to take advantage of any mistake made by a baserunner and get an out. The challenge is always there for the defensive players and for the baserunner. As a baserunner, however, you do not want to be caught in a rundown unless a run can score on the play. If there is no opportunity for a run to score, it means that you were not concentrating and got caught between bases. As defensive players, you want to be alert to the fact that a runner caught in a rundown when another runner is on third base may be trying to distract you to allow the run to score. Be sure that you keep an eye on the runner at third base.

Planned and practiced techniques are necessary to ensure that a runner caught off-base will be tagged out. If no set play were used, the runner could more easily escape the situation and reach a base safely.

How the Defense Executes the Rundown

The rundown is more effectively executed when the defensive players have back-up help in case the runner gets past one of the original chasers. The defensive players closest to the bases between which the runner is caught, the original chasers, are called *primary fielders* for the play. The players next closest to the two bases involved back up those original chasers and are called the *back-up fielders* for the play. A back-up fielder takes an initial position in front of the base she is responsible for. As the rundown play develops, the back-up fielder should stay at least 10 feet behind the primary fielder unless the play has moved close to the base (see figure 8.12). The chart below identifies the fielders and their responsibilities in rundown plays.

Runner caught between	Primary fielders	Back-up fielders
First and second	First baseman Second baseman	Pitcher Shortstop
Second and third	Shortstop Third baseman	Second baseman Pitcher
Third and home	Third baseman Catcher	Shortstop Pitcher

Figure 8.12 Rundown between second base and third base.

The primary fielders can execute the rundown alone unless one is passed by the baserunner. When passed, the primary fielder steps aside to allow the back-up fielder to move up to receive the throw. The original primary fielder rotates back behind the now-active back-up fielder and assumes the back-up role. The original back-up fielder has now moved up to assume the new primary role. Rotation in this manner continues each time a primary fielder is passed by the baserunner. Of course, this rotation should not be necessary if the runner is put out with no throws or one throw! All persons involved in the rundown must maintain positions in front of the bases. The back-up fielder, particularly, must not line up behind the base, because a runner passing a primary fielder could then get to a base safely before encountering the back-up fielder.

There are several possible rotation methods for executing the rundown play in addition to the one just described. However, certain principles apply to any rundown situation, regardless of the method used to get the runner out:

1. Try to get the runner out with the least possible number of throws. The ideal is no throw at all; one is good, two is all right, and more than two is too many.
2. The person with the ball (not necessarily one of the primary or back-up fielders) initiates the play by holding the ball and running at (directly toward) the runner until he commits to moving toward one base or the other. This person can actually make the tag if he is close enough before the baserunner gets to the base. If the tag is not made by the initiator, the ball is thrown to the fielder toward whom the runner is going.
3. Keep the runner away from the bases, but closer to the base last touched than the one not yet reached.
4. Throw the ball back and forth beside the runner, not over the head of the runner. Hold the ball at head height in your throwing hand close to your throwing shoulder. Use a short snap throw (with a motion like throwing a dart) from this position to get the ball to the covering fielder.
5. When making the tag, grip the ball with your bare hand and hold the ball and hand securely in your glove. Tag the runner with the back of your glove.

Use the drills on pages 149 and 150 to practice the offensive and defensive techniques in the rundown.

How the Offense Executes the Rundown

As the runner, you must watch the person with the ball. Once the initial throw is made, you must decide whether to run at full speed toward the base away from the throw or to stay in the rundown situation. If the throw is a long throw and you are fairly close to the person throwing the ball, your chances of making it to the base are good. If a preceding runner has a chance to score while the defense has you in the rundown, stay in the rundown and try to avoid being tagged out until the run scores.

COMBINATION FIELDING DRILLS

1. Direct Grounders

In groups of three, set up so that one person is the hitter, one the catcher, and one the fielder. The hitter and the catcher assume positions at home plate; hitter in the batter's box, catcher in the catching position. The fielder stands at one of the infield positions and assumes the infielder's ready position (preparation phase for fielding).

The hitter fungo hits a ground ball directly to the fielder. The fielder fields the ball and, using an overhand throw, throws the ball to the catcher. The catcher moves from the catching position into the position to cover home to receive the throw for a force or tag play. The catcher then tosses the ball to the hitter and returns to the catching position. As the ball is hit, the fielder tracks the ball and moves into position directly in front of the ball to execute the fielding skill. The catcher covering home plate gives the fielder a target with the glove.

To extend the distance of the fielder's overhand throw, do this drill with the fielder in one of the outfield positions. The fielder stands 130 to 160 feet from the hitter and catcher (the approximate distance from a regular outfield position to home plate). The distance can be adjusted to the throwing ability of the fielder. If a ground ball should get by an infielder in a game, an outfielder would have to field the grounder and throw it to the appropriate person.

For this variation, with the exception of the position of the fielder, set up and execute the drill as in the initial description. The fielder assumes the outfielder's ready position—knees slightly bent, hands about waist-high, weight on the balls of the feet, and eyes focusing on the hitter. If you are the fielder, as the ball is hit, track the ball and move into position directly in front of the ball. If possible, move in the direction of the catcher if you must field the ball on the move. As you bring the ball to the throwing position, take a crow-hop step (step with the glove-side foot toward the target, hop on the throwing-side foot while bringing the ball to throwing position) and make a strong overhand throw to the catcher, remembering to take a step toward the target with the glove-side foot as you throw. If you cannot throw the ball in the air without an arc all the way to the catcher, execute a one-bounce throw; aim your throw to hit the ground 10 to 15 feet in front of the catcher. The throw to that landing point should travel in a straight line.

After 10 repetitions, rotate roles. A successful fielding and throwing combination requires that the ball is fielded and thrown so that the catcher can catch the ball without moving more than one step from the covering position.

Success Goal = 25 successful combinations out of 30 total attempts:

8 fielding and throwing combinations out of 10 attempts ___

8 hits out of 10 attempts ___

9 catches at home out of 10 attempts ___

Success Check

Fielder:

- Move into position directly in front of the ball ___
- Field and throw ball in continuous motion ___
- Make an accurate throw to the catcher ___
- As an outfielder, use the crow-hop step when throwing to the catcher ___

Hitter:

- Make the ball contact the ground at least 30 feet in front of the fielder ___
- Hit the ball directly at the fielder ___

Catcher:

- Move quickly into position to cover home plate from catching position ___
- Catch the ball with two hands ___

To Increase Difficulty

- Batter hits the ball with greater force.
- Batter hits the ball so that the fielder has to move to field it (see next drill).
- Fielder moves to glove side, fielder moves to throwing side, or fielder moves to glove side and throwing side alternately.
- Batter hits the ball so that the fielder does not know the direction it will go or the speed at which it will travel (see next drill).
- Fielder charges the ball as it is coming.
- Catcher gives different targets for the throw.

To Decrease Difficulty

- Batter hits the ball with less force.
- Reduce the distance of the throw.
- Use a softer ball, such as a Rag Ball or Incrediball.

2. Moving to the Ball

Use the same three-player setup as in the previous drill. The fungo hitter now directs the 10 grounders to the fielder's glove side—five hits at a moderate speed, and five that are faster. The fielder fields the ball and uses an overhand throw to return the ball to the catcher. Rotate roles after 10 hits.

Next the fungo hitter directs grounders to the throwing-hand side, five moderate and five faster. The fielder uses an overhand throw to return the balls to the catcher. Rotate roles. Finally, the fungo hitter hits 10 grounders, randomly hitting to the glove side, the throwing side, and directly at the fielder. The hitter should vary the speed of the ground balls. Rotate roles.

For a variation of this drill for the more experienced player, follow the suggestions listed under "To Increase Difficulty" at the end of this drill. The fielder will not know in advance the direction or the speed of the grounder. You will practice reading the ball's direction and speed as it leaves the fungo hitter's bat. This variation represents a gamelike situation for the fielder.

Success Goal = 23 successful fielding plays and on-target throws out of 30 total attempts:

8 out of 10 attempts, glove side ___
8 out of 10 attempts, throwing side ___
7 out of 10 attempts, mixed sides ___
8 out of 10 attempts, target hits for each situation ___
9 out of 10 attempts, catches at home for each situation ___

Success Check

Fielder:

- Move into a fielding position directly in line with the ball ___
- Field the ball in front of the body with both hands ___

Hitter:

- Hit the grounder to extend the range of the fielder ___
- Direct the grounder without telegraphing its direction ___

Catcher:

- Receive the throw with *soft hands* ___
- Catch the ball with two hands ___

To Increase Difficulty

- Hitter randomly varies the speed and the direction of each hit.
- Extend the fielder's range to the maximum without hitting the ball past the fielder.
- Catcher varies the target from chest to knee height as for force- or tag-outs.

To Decrease Difficulty

- Reduce the speed of the grounder.
- Reduce the range expected of the fielder.

3. Triangle Drill

Two pairs of partners take part: one pair, the hitter (H) and catcher (C), positioned at home plate; the other pair, fielders (F), positioned at first base and third base.

The hitter hits ground balls to each of the two fielders, alternating between them. The person fielding the ball uses the overhand throw and makes the throw to the other fielder. The second fielder then throws the ball to the catcher covering home for a force or tag play, who tosses the ball to the hitter.

After five grounders to each fielder, the hitter and catcher exchange roles, and the two fielders exchange positions. After the next set of five grounders to each fielder, the fielders exchange roles with hitter and catcher. Keep repeating the sequence.

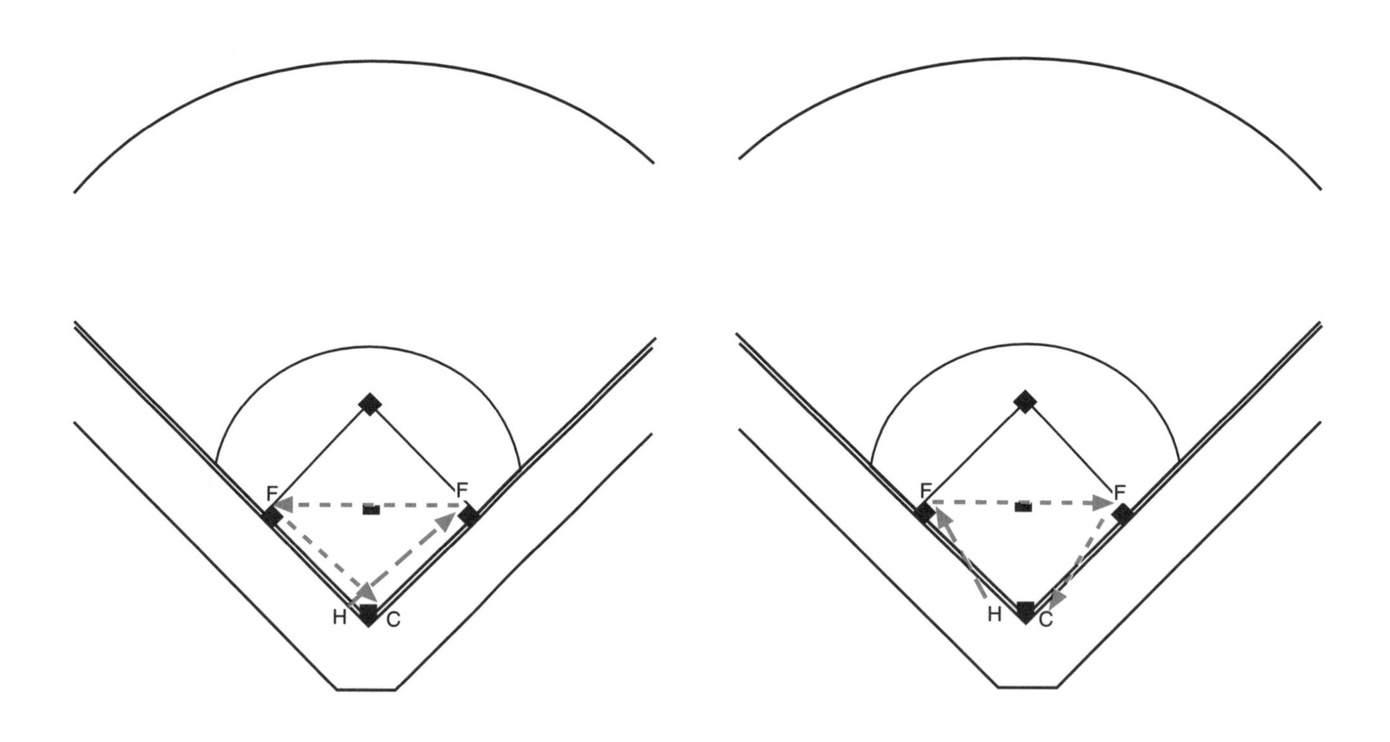

Success Goal =

Number of error-free plays ___

Fielder at first base:

4 fielding plays at first-base side out of 5 attempts ___

3 throws from first-base side out of 5 attempts ___

Fielder at third base:

4 fielding plays at third-base side out of 5 attempts ___

4 throws from third-base side out of 5 attempts ___

Hitter:

8 hits out of 10 attempts ___

Catcher:

9 catches at home out of 10 attempts ___

Success Check

Fielder at first base:

- Field the ball with two hands ___
- If right-handed, field the ball, pivot so glove side is toward third base, step toward third to throw ___

Fielder at third base:

- Field the ball with two hands ___
- Step in the direction of first base and throw the ball overhand ___

Hitter:

- Hit the grounder so that it first contacts the ground within 10 feet of home plate ___
- Match the difficulty of the hit with the experience level of the fielder ___

Catcher:

- Catch the ball with two hands ___
- Watch the ball into the glove ___

To Increase Difficulty

- Hitter varies the force of the hit.
- Hitter varies the direction of the ground ball (glove side, throwing side, alternate sides).
- Hitter hits a random mixture of direct, glove-side, and throwing-side grounders.
- Hitter varies both the direction and the force of the hit.
- Fielder charges the ball to field it earlier.

To Decrease Difficulty

- Hitter uses the batting tee.
- Fielder plays a rolled ball.
- Use a softer ball.
- Decrease the distance of the throw from the fielder to the base.
- Lengthen the distance from the hitter to the fielder.

4. Get One Out

This drill is called Get One Out because in a real softball game, once you field a ground ball you throw it to get a baserunner out. Outs are made one at a time in a game, and only if you cleanly field the ball and make the throw to the base accurately and on time. For this drill, set up in two sets of partners as in the previous drill. The fielders are positioned at first base and shortstop. The hitter and the catcher are positioned at home.

The hitter grounds the ball to the fielder at the shortstop position, who in one motion fields the ball and makes an overhand throw to the fielder at first base. The ball is then thrown to the catcher, who tosses it to the hitter for the next hit.

The hitter should vary the placement of the grounders—that is, to the glove side, to the throwing side, and directly at the fielder. The hitter should also vary the speed of the grounders—both hitting hard, and hitting softly so the fielder must come in on the ball to make the play. All players should work on overhand throws only.

After 10 hits, the fielders exchange positions, and the hitter and catcher exchange roles. After the next set of 10, the fielders exchange roles with hitter and catcher. Keep repeating the sequence.

Success Goal = 41 error-free plays out of 50 total attempts:

8 error-free fielding and overhand throwing combinations out of 10 attempts ___
8 catches at first base out of 10 attempts ___
8 error-free overhand throws to catcher out of 10 attempts ___
9 catches at home out of 10 attempts ___
8 fungo hits to intended direction out of 10 attempts ___

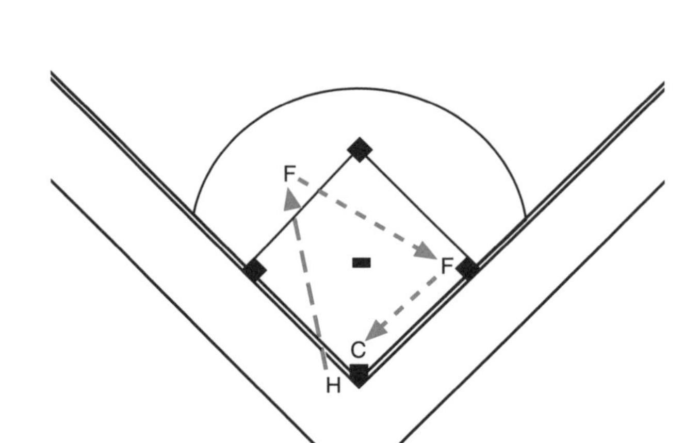

Success Check

Fielders:

- All fielders: Get in front of the ball prior to fielding it ___
- Shortstop: Field and throw the ball in one continuous motion ___
- First baseman: Make an accurate throw to the catcher ___

Hitter:

- Make the ball contact the ground at least 30 feet in front of the shortstop ___
- Vary the placement of the grounders ___

Catcher:

- Move quickly into position to cover home plate from your catching position ___
- Catch the ball with two hands and mimic a tag- or force-out ___

To Increase Difficulty

- Batter hits the ball so that the fielder does not know the direction it will go or the speed at which it will travel (see next drill).
- Fielder charges the ball as it is coming.
- Catcher gives different targets for the throw.
- Batter varies the force of the hit grounder.

To Decrease Difficulty

- Batter hits the ball with less force.
- Reduce the distance of the throw.
- Use a softer ball, such as a Rag Ball or Incrediball.

5. Rapid Fire

This drill is for more experienced players only. It should be done on a regulation infield with bases in position and foul lines marked.

Set up in two groups of three; one trio consists of a hitter standing on the third-base foul line about 10 feet from third base down the line toward home, a third baseman, and a second baseman. The other group has a hitter standing on the first-base foul line about 10 feet from first base down the line toward home, a shortstop, and a first baseman. The hitter on the third-base side hits ground balls to the second baseman, who makes an overhand throw to the third baseman. The third baseman tosses the ball to the hitter for the next hit.

The hitter on the first-base side hits ground balls to the shortstop, who makes an overhand throw to the first baseman. The first baseman tosses the ball to the hitter for a repeat play. The ground balls are hit simultaneously and therefore are crossing in the infield area. You must hit the balls *directly* at the fielders. The fielders must stay *behind* the baseline to field the ball.

Fielders, do not charge a poorly hit ball, and work on good fielding and quick release on the throws. Use of two balls in play by each hitter increases the challenge of this drill.

After 10 repetitions, the players rotate within the group of three. After each player has had a turn at each of the three positions, groups switch locations.

Success Goal =

Number of error-free plays ___

Fielders:

8 combined fields and on-target throws by each second baseman out of 10 attempts ___

8 combined fields and on-target throws by each shortstop out of 10 attempts ___

8 catches at first base out of 10 attempts ___

8 catches at third base out of 10 attempts ___

Hitter:

8 fungo hits directly to each fielder out of 10 attempts ___

Success Check

Fielders:

- Field the ground ball behind the base line between first and second, or second and third ___
- Do not charge in on the ground ball ___
- At the base, use proper footwork to catch an off-target throw ___

Hitter:

- Hit the ball hard ___
- Hit the grounder directly at the fielder ___

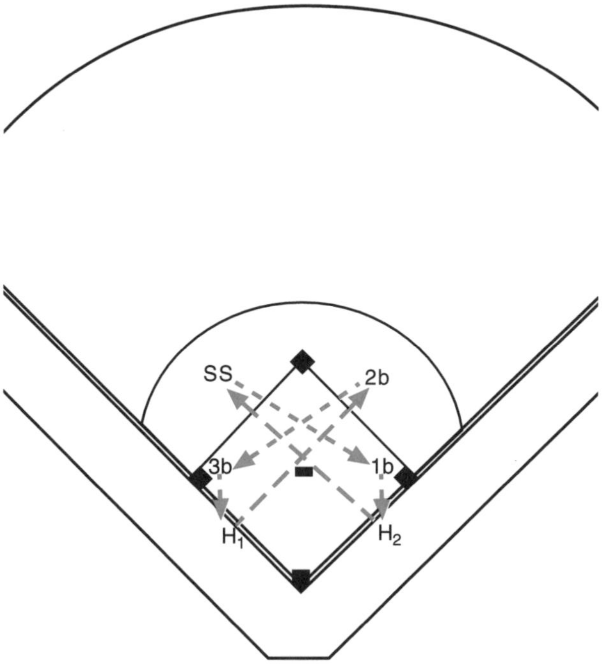

To Increase Difficulty

- Hitter speeds up the drill by barely waiting before hitting the next ground ball.
- Hitter moves the fielders to their right and left (no more than 4 feet) to field the ball.
- Fielder makes a target at chest height, then at knee height.
- Use two balls so that as soon as the fielder has thrown the ball to the other fielder, the hitter hits a second ball to the first fielder. If this is done, it may be helpful to have an additional catcher with the hitter so that she can toss the extra ball to the hitter, then receive the toss from the base fielder.

To Decrease Difficulty

- Hitters hit in sequence rather than at the same time.
- Hitter slows the series by pausing between hits to the fielder.

6. Lateral Fly Ball

This drill allows you to work on moving in different directions to get under the fly balls in order to make the catches. It requires two pairs of partners. One pair consists of the hitter and the catcher, positioned at home plate. The other pair has fielders positioned together in center field.

The hitter hits a fly ball so that one fielder must run laterally a minimum of 60 feet to field the ball. After the fielder makes the catch, he comes to a stop, steps toward the catcher, and makes an overhand throw to the catcher. The catcher yells "Home, home" to simulate the calls made in a game situation. The fielders should make an overhand throw to the catcher after each fielding attempt, whether a catch is made or not. When you are the fielder, be sure to concentrate on stopping your lateral movement and getting your body moving in the direction of the throw. This will add both force and accuracy to your throw. The first fielder moves out of the way for the next fielder to come over and make the same play. The hitter repeats the task for the next fielder. Both fielders should remain at their new locations on the field.

For the next sequence, the hitter sends fly balls back toward center field, where the fielders started. The first fielder runs back in the other direction, fields the fly ball, stops, and throws overhand to the catcher. The second fielder does the same. After four hits to each fielder (two to the left and two to the right for each fielder), the hitter and catcher change roles; the fielders continue in their roles. After the next set of four hits, the fielding pair changes roles with the pair at home.

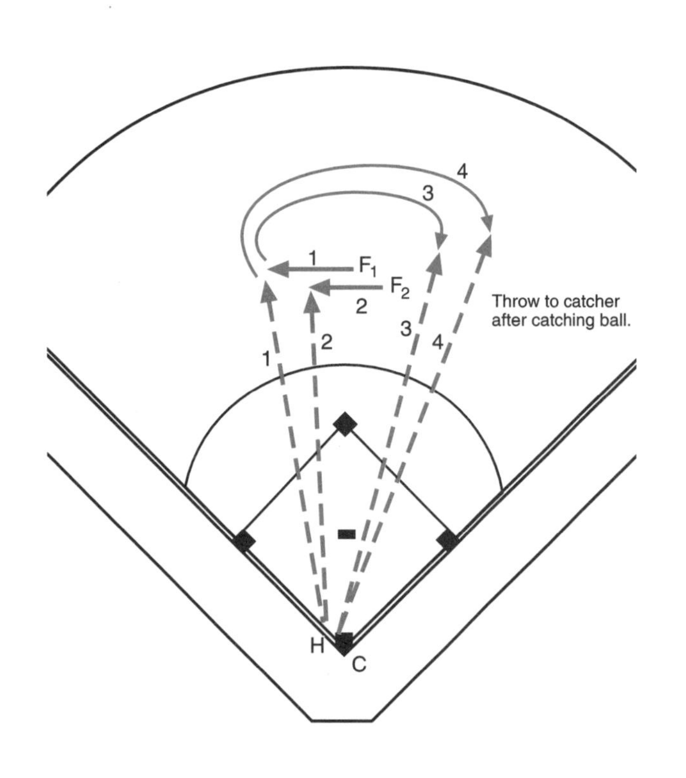

Success Goal =

Number of error-free plays ___
5 on-target hits out of 8 attempts ___
5 fielding and throwing combinations out of 8 attempts ___
6 catches at home out of 8 attempts ___

Success Check

Fielders:

- React to the ball off the bat, start running as soon as the ball is hit ___
- After the catch, stop lateral movement, step or crow-hop toward the catcher to throw ___

Hitter:

- Low-to-high swings resulting in fly balls hit for fielders ___
- Hit fly balls that make the fielder run at least 60 feet to make the catch ___

Catcher:

- Call out "Home, home!" as the fielder is catching the ball ___
- Make a big, clear target with your body and glove at which the fielder can throw ___

To Increase Difficulty

- Increase the distance the fielder has to run to catch the ball.
- Increase the distance the fielder has to throw the ball.
- Vary the distance the fielder has to run to catch the ball.
- Vary the distance the fielder has to throw the ball.

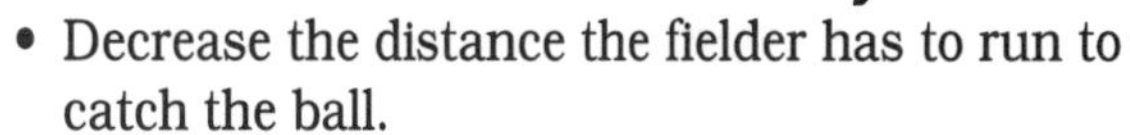

To Decrease Difficulty

- Decrease the distance the fielder has to run to catch the ball.
- Decrease the distance the fielder has to throw the ball.
- Decrease the distance the hitter has to hit the ball.
- Use any type of softer ball.

Now, just for fun, combine the numbers that you and your partner achieved in each of the previous Success Goals. Compare that score with the combined score of the other pair. If there are differences, see if you can determine whether the largest scores were achieved in hitting, fielding and throwing, or catching at home plate. Do those scores indicate to you that you need more practice on any of the skills?

7. I've Got It

This drill also requires two pairs of partners, and it gives you the chance to practice with a teammate who is trying to make the same catch as you. One pair consists of the hitter and catcher, positioned at home. The other pair is comprised of fielders positioned in center field and left field (one in each field position).

The hitter hits a fly ball between the two fielders. Remember, the ball is being hit into the *interaction* area where both fielders share coverage responsibility. Therefore, both fielders go for the ball. The fielder who gets under the ball first yells, "I've got it!" and catches the ball. The other fielder drops behind to back up the fielder making the play. An overhand, one-bounce throw is made to the catcher.

The fielders exchange starting positions after every sequence. After 10 hits, the hitter and the catcher exchange roles. After the next set of 10, the fielders exchange roles with the players at home.

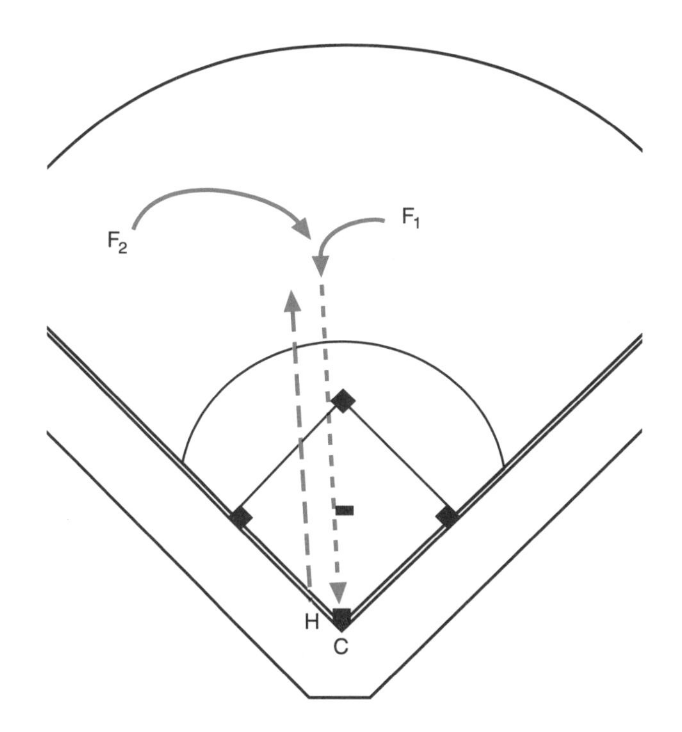

Success Goal =

Number of error-free plays ___
8 on-target hits (between fielders) out of 10 attempts ___
8 fielding and throwing combinations out of 10 attempts ___
10 well-done backing-up plays ___
8 catches at home out of 10 attempts ___

Success Check

Fielders:

- Move on the hit ___
- Call for the ball ___

Hitter:

- Fungo hit *high* fly balls ___
- Hit fly balls between fielders ___

Catcher:

- Give a big target ___
- See the ball bounce ___

To Increase Difficulty

- Increase the distance between the fielders.
- Use three outfielders and vary the ball placement.

To Decrease Difficulty

- Decrease the distance between the fielders.
- Throw the fly ball.
- Predetermine the catching fielder and the back-up fielder.

8. In the Air

Two pairs of partners are needed. One pair consists of a hitter and a catcher, positioned at home. The other pair is made up of fielders, one positioned in center field and the other at second base.

A fly ball is hit to the fielder in center field. This fielder catches the ball and makes a throw in the air (no bounces) to the partner at second base. The fielder at second then throws the ball to the catcher. These throws are relatively short and should not be bounced; they should still be thrown overhand.

After 10 sequences, one partner changes roles with the other. After the next set of 10, the fielders exchange roles with the hitter and catcher.

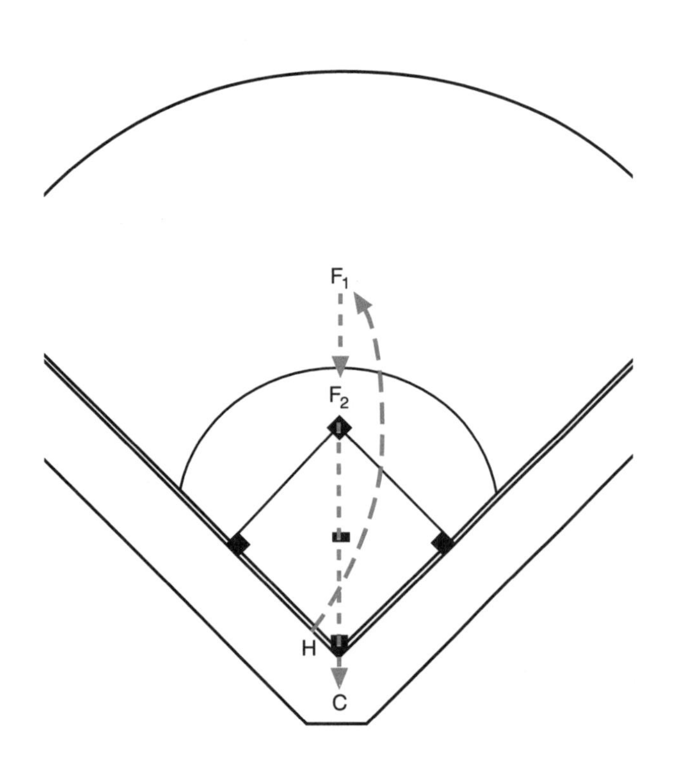

Success Goal =

Number of error-free plays ___
8 on-target hits out of 10 attempts ___
8 fielding and throwing combinations in the outfield out of 10 attempts ___
9 catching and throwing combinations at second base out of 10 attempts ___
9 catches at home out of 10 attempts ___

Success Check

Outfielder:

- Get behind ball and catch while moving toward second baseman ___
- Shoulder-high throw to second baseman ___

Second baseman:

- Give shoulder-high target with glove ___
- Pivot to glove side to throw to home ___

Hitter:

- Hit high fly balls ___
- Hit fly balls directly at the fielder ___

Catcher:

- Call "home" as ball is thrown to second baseman ___
- Move to front of home plate to receive ball ___

To Increase Difficulty

- Lengthen the distance between the outfielder and the second baseman.
- Hitter varies the distance of the fly balls so that the outfielder has to move to the ball and throw different distances to second base.
- Hitter varies the direction of the fly ball so that the outfielder has to move to get into position to make the throw and must throw to second base from various locations.
- Hitter randomly varies the direction and distance of the fly ball so that the outfielder has to react to the ball off the bat, then adjust the throw to second base according to direction and distance.

To Decrease Difficulty

- Use any type of softer ball.
- Change the distance of the throw to second base so that it is easy for the outfielder to make a throw on the fly to the second baseman.

9. Back to the Fence

Set up with a hitter, a catcher, and a fielder. The hitter and catcher stand about 130 feet from the outfield fence. The fielder stands 30 feet from the fence, facing the hitter.

The hitter hits a fly ball so that it comes down in the vicinity of the fence. The fielder, using the drop step, retreats toward the fence and fields the ball, then makes an overhand throw to the catcher. If the ball is very close to the fence, the fielder should visually locate the fence and then slow her run in order to go right up to the fence. After locating the fence, the fielder should then field the ball and make the throw. After 10 sequences, rotate roles.

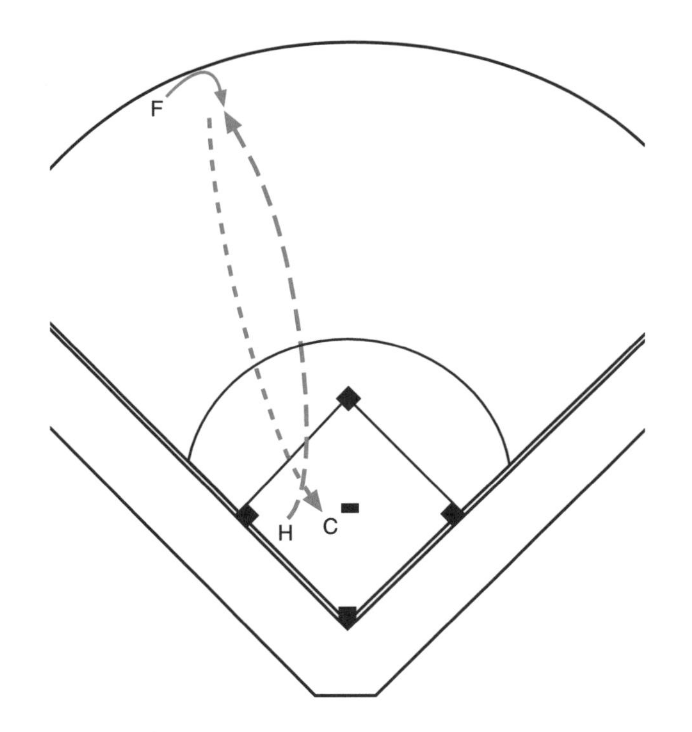

Success Goal =

Number of successful plays ___
7 hits to the fence out of 10 attempts ___
7 fielding and throwing combinations out of 10 attempts ___
9 catches back near the hitter out of 10 attempts ___

Success Check

Outfielder:

- Use the correct footwork for the drop step ___
- Unless right at the fence, make the catch moving toward the catcher ___
- Make an overhand throw on one bounce or straight in the air to the catcher ___

Hitter:

- Hit high fly balls ___
- Hit the ball close to the fence ___

Catcher:

- Make a big target with your body and glove ___
- Catch the ball with two hands ___

To Increase Difficulty

- Hit the ball so that the fielder moves laterally as well as back.

To Decrease Difficulty

- Increase the distance of the hit ball from the fence.
- Throw the ball rather than fungo hit.

SIDEARM THROWING DRILLS

The next three drills can be done inside or outside, using a wall or fence, respectively, for the throwing target. Because the ball will not rebound off a fence and come back to you, use a partner with a bucket of balls to roll a ball to you from a short distance when you're practicing outside. If no partner is available, take 10 balls and place them one foot apart in a straight line in front of you, going away from you. Move up to field each ball and make the sidearm throw to the fence. Remember, these are not accuracy drills; your target is simply the wall or the fence. If your sidearm throwing skills are good and you want to work on accuracy, make small targets on the wall or fence and throw to hit those targets.

10. Wall Practice to the Glove Side

This drill is best done in a gymnasium. Stand in a corner of a gym facing one wall, with the other wall to your glove side. Position yourself 30 feet from each wall.

Throw the ball against the front wall so that a ground ball rebounds to you, then field the ball and make a sidearm throw to the wall on your glove side using the techniques described in the Keys to Success for the sidearm throw (see figure 8.3). Turn to the wall on your glove side, field the rebounding ball, and move it directly into throwing position. Do not immediately throw the ball; instead, resume your starting position and repeat the sequence.

The major purpose of this drill is for you to practice the sidearm throw. However, take the opportunity to work on your ground ball fielding skills also!

Success Goal = 10 consecutive error-free sequences ___

Success Check

- Stay low, flexed at waist, back flat ___
- Step toward target ___
- Throwing arm stays parallel to the ground ___

To Increase Difficulty

- Have a partner roll or bounce the ball to you with varying speed.
- Have a partner roll or bounce the ball so you must move laterally.
- Use a target.
- Have a partner fungo hit the ball from various directions with different speeds.

To Decrease Difficulty

- Start with the ball stationary on the ground or floor.
- Use a softer ball for a slower rebound.

11. Wall Practice to the Throwing Side

Stand as in the previous drill, except that what was the side wall is now the front wall, and the side wall is now on your throwing-arm side. Throw the ball to the front wall so that the rebound is a ground ball. Field the ball, pivot to your throwing side, and sidearm throw the ball to that wall. Field the rebound and return to your starting position.

Success Goal = 6 consecutive error-free sequences ___

Success Check

- Stay flexed at waist and keep back flat throughout pivot and throw ___
- Weight is on throwing-side foot as you start to pivot ___
- Complete pivot so glove side is to target ___
- Step toward target ___
- Throwing arm moves horizontally to target ___

To Increase Difficulty

- Use a target.
- Have a partner roll the ball in the opposite direction of the throw so that the pivot to make the throw is more difficult.
- Have a partner fungo hit the ball from various directions with different speeds.

To Decrease Difficulty

- Have a partner roll the ball more toward the wall or fence so you are already moving in the direction of the pivot.
- If using a target, make it larger.

12. Four-Player

Now you will practice fielding and throwing the ball to a partner. One important consideration in this drill is that your short sidearm throw be "sympathetic" in force, so that it can be caught.

This drill requires four people. Whether inside or outside, set up this drill as if you are on a field. You, the primary fielder, play in the position of shortstop. A partner with a bucket of 10 balls fungo hits ground balls to you from home plate. Another partner plays second base, and the last plays third base.

The hitter hits 10 ground balls to you at varying speeds and varying directions (to either your glove side or throwing side). In one smooth motion, field each ball and throw sidearm to the base on the side of your body that the ground ball came to. Field 10 balls and throw sidearm to the proper base. Focus first on clean fielding, then on the throw. Be sure that your throw does not overpower the base player. The base player catches the ball and rolls it back to the hitting station.

Count the number of good fielding plays and sidearm throws. After your 10 practice attempts, rotate positions and repeat the drill. Continue until each partner has completed 10 attempts at fielding and throwing sidearm to a base player. Were you more successful throwing to your glove-side base or your throwing-side base? Were your throws at a force that was catchable? Work on those areas that gave you problems so that you can perform the sidearm throws consistently.

Success Goal = 6 good fielding plays and sidearm throws out of 10 attempts ___

Success Check

Third baseman:

- Assume the force-play cover position on the ball-side corner of the base ___

Second baseman:

- Assume the force-play cover position on the ball-side corner of the base ___

Shortstop:

- Get in front of the ball to field it ___
- Stay low with back flat throughout the fielding and throwing sequence ___
- Arm travels horizontally throughout the throw ___
- Field the ball, pivot, and sidearm throw in one fluid motion when making the play to third base ___

Hitter:

- Successfully hit the ball so the fielder can make at least 4 throws to each base ___

Because this is a game-situation drill there is no need to increase or decrease difficulty—those adaptations occurred in the previous drills. The double-play drills that follow will provide several combination drills in which you will have an opportunity to further practice the sidearm throw.

DOUBLE-PLAY DRILLS

13. Mimetic Footwork

You and a partner are positioned at the regular shortstop and second-base fielding positions. Without using a ball, you and your partner practice the footwork for the double play. First, the shortstop moves to second base and executes the correct footwork for the drag step. That player goes back to the shortstop position and repeats the drill for a total of five times. Then the shortstop practices the inside pivot.

The partner in the second baseman's position then executes the rocker pivot. Be sure to go back to regular fielding position between repetitions. After completing five rocker pivots, the second-base player practices the crossover pivot. After each player practices both pivots in their initial fielding position, switch positions and practice the other pivots.

Success Goal = 20 correctly executed pivots:

5 shortstop drag steps ___
5 shortstop inside pivots ___
5 second-baseman crossover pivots ___
5 second-baseman rocker pivots ___

To Increase Difficulty

- Mimic the catch and throw of the ball in addition to the footwork for the full double-play action.

To Decrease Difficulty

- Walk through the sequence.

Success Check

Shortstop:

- Face home plate while dragging right foot across base ___
- Spring off the base to get out of the base line on inside pivot ___

Second baseman:

- On deep drop, step back on right foot ___
- On short drop, contact base with left foot and step to first with left foot ___
- On crossover, step on base with left foot, block with right, and step to first with left foot ___

14. Simulated Hit

This drill requires three pairs of partners: a feeder and a pivot player (shortstop and second baseman); the first-base cover player and a "hitter;" and a catcher and a pitcher/third baseman (this person plays either position, according to the chart on page 143). This drill may also be practiced for fast-pitch. See page 3 for proper fast-pitch positioning.

All fielders take regular-depth fielding positions. The hitter stands with a bucket of five balls 20 feet from the feed player. The catcher should have an empty bucket.

The hitter rolls a ground ball to the feed player (1). The feed player, using a sidearm throw, throws to the pivot player covering second base (2). This player, after using correct footwork to tag the base, throws overhand to first base for the completion of the double play (3). The first baseman throws the ball to the catcher (4).

Repeat the sequence five times for each of the variations on the chart. After completing the six variations, exchange positions within the pairs. When both partners have completed the double-play variations, the pairs rotate. The hitter and first baseman become the shortstop and the second baseman. The catcher and pitcher/third baseman become the hitter and first baseman. The shortstop and second baseman become the catcher and the pitcher/third baseman.

If you and the others in your group are more experienced players, you can add complexity to the drill by having a baserunner run from first to second base on each play. If you do, be sure the baserunner wears a batting helmet to protect against errant throws.

Feeder, pivot player, and first-base coverage variations:

Feeder	Pivot player	First-base coverage
Variation a: Second baseman	Shortstop	First baseman
Variation b: First baseman	Shortstop	Second or first baseman
Variation c: Catcher	Shortstop	First baseman
Variation d: Pitcher	Shortstop	First baseman
Variation e: Shortstop	Second baseman	First baseman
Variation f: Third baseman	Second baseman	First baseman

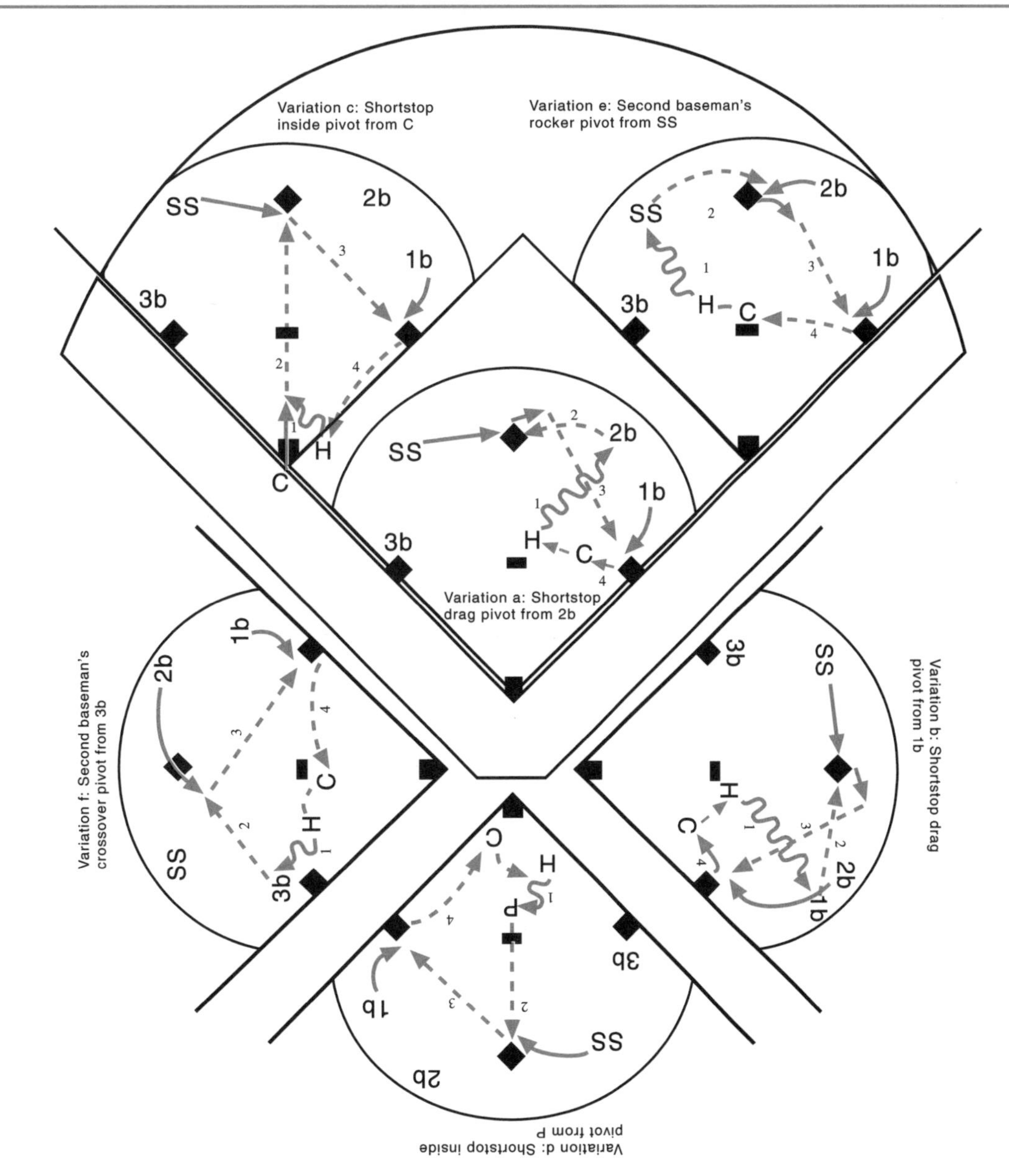

Success Goal = 4 successful executions of each variation out of 5 attempts (24 out of 30 attempts) required as feeder and pivot player ___

Success Check

- Use correct footwork ___
- Use sidearm throw or underhand toss for close feeds ___
- Use overhand throw for long feeds ___
- Stretch to catch the ball at first base ___

To Increase Difficulty

- Vary the force of the "hit" ball.
- Vary the direction of the "hit" ball.

To Decrease Difficulty

- Practice only one variation per practice session.
- Call out the footwork cues as the person is doing the steps.
- Covering player moves closer to the base in the starting position.

15. Fungo Double Play

This drill is practiced like the previous drill, except there is a defensive player (feeder) at each of the infield positions, including a pitcher, and a fungo hitter at home. The hitter fungo hits ground balls from home plate to the feed players. The feed player makes the throw to the pivot player at second base, who in turn completes the double play by throwing to the first-base cover player, who returns the ball to the catcher. The catcher should hold a second ball and toss it to the hitter after the first ball is hit. In addition, a fourth pair of players serve as runners.

This drill is more gamelike than the previous one because you execute the double play off a hit ball. Furthermore, on the last three practices of the five sequences of each play variation (see drill 14), the baserunners are added. One runner goes from home to first on the ground ball, while the other runs from first to second. Baserunners, *be sure you wear batting helmets*.

Success Goal = 4 successful executions of each variation out of 5 attempts (24 out of 30 attempts) required as feeder and pivot player ___

Success Check

- Feeder has good, clean field before throw ___
- Pivot player avoids the baserunner ___
- First-base cover player makes good stretch for the ball ___

To Increase Difficulty

- Vary the speed and direction of the ground ball.

To Decrease Difficulty

- Hit the ball slowly, directly at the feeder.

16. Home-to-First Double Plays

By now you should be proficient as both the pivot player and as the feeder for all of the double-play combinations from second to first base. The following variations are possible combinations for home-to-first double plays:

Feeder	Pivot player	First-base coverage
Third baseman	Catcher	First baseman
Shortstop	Catcher	First baseman
Second baseman	Catcher	First baseman
Pitcher	Catcher	First baseman
First baseman	Catcher	Second baseman

All of the previous drills can be set up for practicing the double play when the first out occurs at third or home. The coverage at third is by the third baseman, except when the ball is hit to the third baseman, in which case the shortstop covers third for the first out of the double play. The coverage at home is by the catcher, and the coverage at first is by the first baseman.

Set up with a catcher, a first baseman, a runner at third, a runner at home, a hitter, and a fielder who moves around to play each of the various feed positions. The hitter hits five balls to the fielder at each different infield position to give the fielder good practice making feeds (overhand throws) to the catcher. The catcher practices positioning to receive throws from the various infield positions to make the force-out at home while at the same time getting out of the way of the runner and making the throw to first base.

Success Goal = 20 successful double plays as feeder out of 25 attempts ___
20 successful double plays as pivot player out of 25 attempts ___
20 successful covers at first base out of 25 attempts ___

To Increase Difficulty
- Fielder charges the ball.

To Decrease Difficulty
- Eliminate use of runners.

Success Check

Feeder:
- Set up in "infield in" starting position ___
- Charge a slowly hit ball ___
- Clean field, strong throw ___

Catcher:
- Start in regular catching position ___
- When ball is hit, move up to the front of the plate ___
- Clean catch, step, and strong throw to first ___

Hitter:
- Get out of way after hit ___

RELAY AND CUTOFF DRILLS

17. Mimetic Pivot

You and a partner are in a "boss-worker" setup, with the boss calling directions and the worker executing the pivots and pretending to throw to the intended target. Both of you, the boss and the worker, should use mental imagery as you participate in this drill.

At the command "hit the relay," the worker as an outfielder turns and runs a few steps after an imaginary ball. He picks it up from the ground, pivots to the glove side, and makes an overhand throw to an imaginary relay person about 100 feet away.

At the command "relay home" or "relay four," the worker as the relay person catches an imaginary throw from an outfielder at chest height. She pivots to the glove side and makes an overhand throw to home plate.

At "cut second, third, or home" or "cut two, three, or four," the worker as the cutoff person assumes a starting position as the first or the third baseman. From this position, he moves to the cutoff position for an imaginary throw to home. The worker follows the call of the boss by mimicking the cutoff, pivoting, and making the imaginary throw to the base called. When first practicing this drill, the boss should call the bases in order, starting with "cut two." Do five combinations in each role. The boss and worker change roles after practice at each position.

Success Goal = 4 performances executed with correct form and technique at each position out of 5 attempts ___

Success Check

- Relay and cutoff players face the outfielder who has the ball ___
- Catch and pivot to the glove side ___

To Increase Difficulty

- Infielder mimics catching the ball for the relay while moving slightly toward home, then steps and throws to home plate.
- "Worker" cuts off the ball, uses the proper footwork, and mimics the overhand throw to second or to third on the random call of the "boss."

To Decrease Difficulty

- Practice either the relay or the cutoff play (not both) to a specific base.
- Do the catch, pivot, and throw in slow motion.

18. Relay Pivot and Accuracy Using a Wall

On a wall, mark a 2-foot-square target 5 feet from the floor. Take a position 80 to 100 feet from the wall.

a. With your back to the target, slowly roll a ball away from you, run to retrieve it, pivot to your glove side, and make an overhand throw to the target. Field the rebounding ball and repeat the sequence. If a wall is not available, use a fence or a net, and a bucket of 10 balls.

b. Now repeat the drill, but this time roll the ball away from you toward your glove side. Run to retrieve it, pivot to your glove side, and make an overhand throw to the target. Field the rebounding ball and repeat the sequence for a total of 10 throws. Next, do the same thing, except roll the ball to your throwing side.

Success Goal =

a. 8 on-target throws out of 10 attempts ___

b. 8 on-target throws out of 10 attempts, glove-side roll ___
8 on-target throws out of 10 attempts, throwing-side roll ___

Success Check

Ball to front and to glove side:

- Two-hand pick-up, use glove to stop ball ___
- Pivot to glove side ___
- Look to target ___

Ball to throwing side:

- Two-hand pick-up, throwing hand stops ball ___
- Pivot to glove side ___
- Focus on target ___

To Increase Difficulty

- Roll the ball faster.
- Relay person moves farther from the target.
- Partner rolls the ball and varies the direction of the roll.

To Decrease Difficulty

- Decrease the number of on-target throws for success.
- Roll the ball more slowly.
- Fielder runs to stationary ball.
- Make the target larger.
- Relay person moves closer to the target.

19. Three-Person Relay

Three of you stand 100 feet apart from each other in a straight line. One end person acts as an outfielder and the other as the catcher; the middle player is the relay person. The relayer and the outfielder are facing the catcher.

The catcher throws a ball past the outfielder (using a fence or wall to stop the ball facilitates the drill). The outfielder turns, retrieves the ball, pivots to the glove side, and throws to the relay person, who has turned to face the outfielder. The relay person at this point has her back to the catcher and cannot see the straight-line relationship needed for an efficient relay play, that being the shortest distance between the outfielder and the catcher. Therefore, the catcher lines up the relay person between the moving outfielder and the catcher by giving verbal directions of "right" or "left." The relay person catches the ball, pivots to the glove side, and throws to the catcher.

After 10 sequences, rotate positions. Score a successful catch and throw combination as 1 point. A point is scored when the outfielder fields the ball and makes an on-target throw to the relayer, and when the relayer catches the outfielder's throw and makes an on-target throw to the catcher. There are 2 points possible on each relay sequence. Accumulate points for *consecutive* error-free throws by the outfielder and the relay person. Because your goal is consistency in performance, you must begin scoring again at 1 after any error in execution.

You will be attaining points when you are in the outfielder's position and when you are in the relayer's position. Add the points you get in each position to establish a total score. The object of this drill is for each of the three of you to come within 2 points of each other in total score.

Success Goal = 30 total points in two sets of 10 sequences, one set at outfielder and one set at relayer position:

15 points at outfielder position ___
15 points at relayer position ___

Success Check

Outfielder:

- Two-hand scoop pick-up, glove in front of the ball ___
- Pivot to the glove side ___
- Focus on relayer as target ___
- Strong overhand on-target throw ___

Relayer:

- Hands and arms up, make a large target ___
- Focus on ball, begin pivot as you catch the ball ___
- Pivot to the glove side, crow-hop step, and make an on-target throw ___

Catcher:

- Give loud verbal line-up directions to relayer ___
- Focus on ball as it is released ___
- Watch ball into glove, two-hand catch ___

To Increase Difficulty

- Catcher throws the ball forcefully past the outfielder.
- Catcher throws the ball past the outfielder to the right and the left so that the relayer must move some distance to get into position.
- Catcher throws the ball past the outfielder at random speeds and in random directions.
- Add a baserunner to the play. The baserunner (who must wear a batting helmet) should start jogging toward home plate as the outfielder throws the ball to the relay person.

To Decrease Difficulty

- Catcher throws the ball less forcefully past the outfielder.
- Relay person makes a shorter throw to home plate.
- Catcher throws the ball at consistent speed and with consistent accuracy so that the outfielder won't need to move right or left, and the relay person will already be in proper lateral position.

20. Cut Two, Cut Three, Cut Four

On a regulation field, position an outfielder, a cutoff person, a base cover player, and a catcher to practice cutoff plays for each of the following simulated (no actual runners or hitters) gamelike situations:

1. "Runner" on second, ball "hit" to the left fielder
   - cut two
   - cut three
   - cut home
   - no call, let the ball go through to home
2. Repeat the drill with the "hit" going to the center fielder.
3. Repeat the drill with the "hit" going to the right fielder.

For each of the gamelike situations, players will take the appropriate positions. As an example, on the play from left field for the "cut second" variation, the outfielder takes the position of the left fielder, the covering player is the second baseman, the cutoff person is either the third baseman (slow-pitch) or first baseman (fast-pitch), and the catcher is at home plate. The catcher throws a ground ball to the left fielder, who fields the ball and makes the throw toward home plate. The appropriate cutoff person moves into position from her regular starting position. The second baseman moves into the covering position at second base. The catcher lines up the cutoff person on a straight line between the outfielder and home plate. The catcher calls "cut second," then the cutoff person cuts the ball and makes the throw to the second baseman covering second. After an agreed-upon number of repetitions, players rotate positions and the drill is repeated, or the drill could be repeated for the "cut third" variation with the covering player changing his covering responsibility (shortstop for slow-pitch or third baseman for fast-pitch).

Success Goal = 3 error-free cutoff plays out of 5 attempts ___

Success Check

- Outfielder's throw is on-target and chest-high to the cutoff person ___
- Cutoff person moves quickly into position, arriving prior to the ball ___
- Catcher lines up the cutoff person and makes a timely call of "cut" ___
- Covering player arrives in the appropriate covering position prior to the cut call ___

To Increase Difficulty

- Add a relay person to the drill.
- Cause the outfielder to move laterally to field the ball.
- Add baserunners.

To Decrease Difficulty

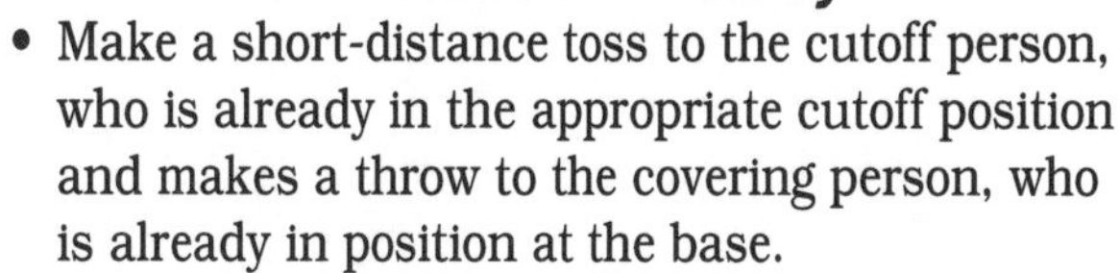

- Make a short-distance toss to the cutoff person, who is already in the appropriate cutoff position and makes a throw to the covering person, who is already in position at the base.

RUNDOWN PLAY DRILLS

21. Rotation

This drill requires four players positioned between two bases—two in primary roles and two in back-up roles. No runner is used.

One primary fielder with a ball starts the drill by throwing the ball to the other primary fielder. After each throw, the assumption is made that the imaginary runner passes the thrower. Therefore, the thrower in the primary role rotates back, and the person in the back-up role moves up to receive the next throw.

Success Goal = 30 seconds of continuous error-free rundown play (throwing, catching, and rotation movement) ___

Success Check

- Give glove target outside of glove-side shoulder, not in front of your body ___
- Throw ball beside "runner," hit glove target ___
- Primary fielder rotates back to back-up position after every throw ___

22. Full Rundown Play 1

Use the same setup as in the previous drill, except a runner is used and rotation occurs only when the runner actually passes a primary fielder. The baserunner must wear a batting helmet.

Success Goal =

As runner, reach base safely or stay in the rundown for 30 seconds without being tagged ___

As defense, tag the runner out in less than 30 seconds, with no more than two throws ___

Success Check

- Try not to exceed two throws in getting runner out ___
- Throw beside runner ___
- Rotate back to back-up after each throw ___

23. Full Rundown Play 2

Three pairs of partners are set up with both a back-up fielder and primary fielder in front of two bases, and the third pair acting as the runner and the "initiator."

The initiator, with the ball, stands 20 feet from the runner (remember to wear a helmet), who is in the base line midway between the bases. The initiator starts the drill by running toward the runner. Once the runner commits to run to a base, the initiator throws the ball to the primary fielder at that base. From that point, the drill proceeds as in the previous drill.

After three 20-second rundown bouts, rotate roles within each set of partners. After the next set of three 20-second bouts, pairs of partners rotate roles: The Base 1 pair becomes runner and initiator; the runner and initiator pair becomes Base 2 fielders; and Base 2 fielders move to Base 1. Continue the drill until the rotation has gone full circle.

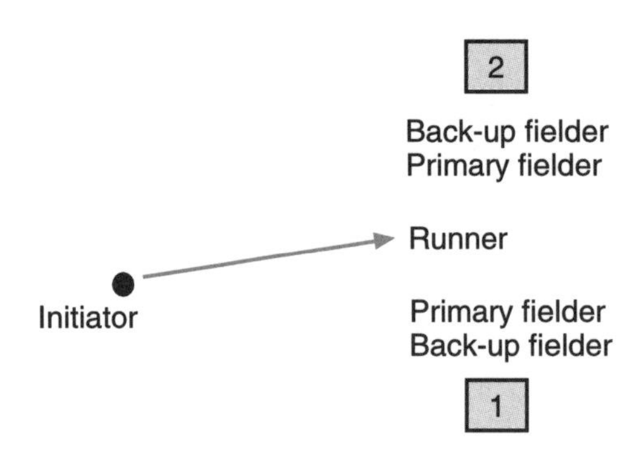

Success Goal =

As runner, reach base safely or stay in rundown for 20 seconds ___

As initiator, tag the runner out yourself, or make a throw so that the runner stays in the rundown for the time being ___

As defense, tag the runner out in less than 20 seconds, with no more than two throws ___

Success Check

- Initiator tags runner out ___
- Primary fielders get runner out with one throw or less ___

DEFENSIVE SITUATIONAL PLAY SUCCESS SUMMARY

Defensive skills such as fielding ground balls and fly balls and throwing are performed by individuals. However, the very important concept of softball team defense usually requires several players to effectively perform individual defensive skills in combinations and in specific sequences in order to put out one or more baserunners. In order to appropriately react to a particular situation as a defensive player, you must know your positional responsibilities, and you must be able to adjust your on-the-spot decision-making to a continuously changing situation (such as runners moving around the bases or getting caught off-base). In softball games, however, certain situational plays tend to repeat themselves when the situation is the same. With a runner on first base and less than two outs, there is usually a double-play possibility if the ball is hit on the ground in the infield. In fast-pitch softball, the preceding situation could also call for a sacrifice bunt. Ask your coach or a teammate to observe you in gamelike drills or game situations, using the checklists in figures 8.3 through 8.8 to evaluate your ability to execute the skills needed in specific game situations and to give you feedback to help you improve your performance.

STEP 9 MODIFIED GAMES

The purpose of participating in modified games is twofold. First, you have the opportunity to see how well you can execute various skills under simulated game conditions. As an infielder in a real game, you get only one chance to cleanly field the ball and make an accurate throw if the batter hits the ball to you. In a real game, you never know when the ball will come to you until it is hit. Modified games give you the opportunity to see just how proficient you are at reading, reacting, and executing in real game situations. Second, modified games provide you with the opportunity to better develop your understanding of, and ability to execute, techniques of position play and game strategy.

Grounders-Only T-Ball

Modified games focus your practice on specific skills, sometimes to the exclusion of other skills. As the name might imply, Grounders-Only T-Ball is intended to give you practice in fielding ground balls that have been hit off a batting tee. Using the tee is not gamelike. It does, however, ensure that the ball is hit on every swing, thereby providing opportunities for a great number of fielding plays in a relatively short period of time. Despite the fact that this is not the same as hitting off a pitcher, this modified game gives you the opportunity to work on your hitting technique without having to wait for the pitcher to make good pitches. Also, you get a chance to practice baserunning. The major purpose of this game, though, is to work on fielding ground balls and throwing runners out.

Game Skills

During the game, you are asked to focus on both your skill execution and your application of knowledge. To be a successful softball player, you must not only have good skill techniques, but also know how and when to execute those skills in a game. The "good 4 o'clock hitter" is a hitter who hits the ball out of the park during warm-up, but doesn't get a base hit during a game.

On defense, knowing how to make the force-out is important, but being able to make the play with the runner coming at you in a game is the mark of a good softball player. Participation in this modified game will help you become a better game player *if* you practice the following skills. The coaching tips in italics after each skill will help you focus on the key elements of each one. In addition, they are included to help coaches and teachers focus on the key elements in order to cue the performance of less experienced players and give feedback on performance to more experienced players.

1. Basic skills
   - Hitting off the batting tee
     - *Emphasize the high-to-low swing to produce a ground ball.*
     - *Keep head down—focus on the ball.*
     - *Adjust position at the tee to place-hit the ball to different locations in the infield. Focus defensive players' attention on these same points so that they can work on the anticipation skills of reading and reacting.*
   - Fielding ground balls
     - *Emphasize moving into position to field the ball in front of the body.*
     - *Stress keeping the head down and watching the ball go into the glove.*
     - *Reinforce the importance of the smooth transition from fielding to throwing.*
   - Overhand throws of various distances used in infield play
     - *Stress the overhand delivery and moving the body in the direction of the throw.*

- *Discourage the sidearm throw except where appropriate, such as from the second baseman to first or a feed at second for a double play.*
- Catching a ball
  - *Focus on the ball.*
  - *Give with the ball using "soft hands."*
- Baserunning
  - *Reinforce the necessity of running full speed over first base, turning to the left toward the field of play, and returning directly to the base.*
  - *Review what constitutes making an attempt to go to second base after overrunning first base.*
  - *Reinforce the spooning technique of rounding a base when there is the possibility of advancing more than one base.*
  - *Remind the base coaches of their responsibilities and the use of both verbal and visual signals to assist the baserunners.*

2. Infield position-play techniques
   - Area coverage
     - *Help your players define position coverage areas and interaction areas.*
     - *Remind them about calling for the fly ball, even if a certain hit ball is an automatic out.*
   - Covering and back-up responsibilities
     - *Go over covering and back-up responsibilities; review the general principles applying to ground balls hit to the right side and left side; discuss the specifics of base coverage based on the situations that could develop.*
     - *Verbally cue the more experienced teams just before the batter hits the ball—however, stop play and set the situation for the less experienced teams if they appear confused.*
3. Defensive and offensive tactics
   - Force plays
     - *Review all base-coverage responsibilities.*
     - *Emphasize the importance of the fielder moving to the ball side of the base to receive the throw from the fielder (cut down on the distance of the throw).*
     - *Review footing the base and stretching for both on- and off-target throws.*
     - *With the less experienced teams, work on getting the lead runner.*
     - *With the more experienced teams, work on the double play.*
   - Tag plays
     - *Work on footwork of the player moving from the fielding position to a covering position at the base.*
     - *Review how positioning at the base is based on the path of the runner and the direction of the incoming thrown ball.*
     - *Stress the concept of the fielder placing the ball in the glove at the base so that the runner coming into the base tags herself out, and then sweeping the glove and ball out of the way to avoid getting the ball dislodged from the glove.*
   - Baserunning
     - *Review the concept of being forced or not forced to advance to the next base.*
     - *Remind players about taking a few steps off the base on a pop-up to the infield, as well as the necessity of tagging up if the ball is caught or advancing if the ball is dropped and the runner is forced to go to the next base.*
     - *Remind the players to watch the base coaches for signals.*
   - Place-hitting
     - *Discuss the concept of hitting behind the runner.*
     - *Emphasize reading the defense and taking advantage of open spaces into which to hit (only in the infield area in this game).*

Game Rules

Specific rules of the game and method of play include the following:

1. The infield area, both fair and nearby foul territory, is the only area where the ball is in play. The outfield is out of play.
2. When hitting the ball off the tee, the batter *must* hit a ground ball (a hit that makes initial contact with the ground within the infield).
   - Any ball that first lands in the outfield or is touched by a player in the outfield is an automatic out for the batting team. The ball is dead, and baserunners cannot advance.

- Any fly ball or pop-up is an automatic out. A pop-up in the infield area need not be caught to be an out. The ball is in play, and baserunners advance at their own risk.
- Any line drive caught by an infielder is an out.
- Any ball (other than a fly ball or pop-up) that is misplayed by an infielder standing in the infield is a legally hit ball. If the misplayed ball goes into the outfield, the ball is out of play. However, the batter takes first base on an *error* credited to the infielder misplaying the ball, and all other baserunners advance only one base. If the misplayed ball stays in the infield area (including nearby foul territory), the ball stays in play and play continues.
- Any ball that is not touched by a fielder but first lands in the infield area and goes into the outfield is a base hit. The ball is out of play, the batter takes first base with a single, and all other baserunners advance only one base.

3. There are six players per team: a pitcher, a catcher, and one player for each infield position.
4. Each team gets six outs per turn at bat. These six outs constitute a half-inning. Teams change offensive and defensive roles after each half-inning.
5. Use a batting tee. The pitcher plays at the defensive position of pitcher, but does not pitch the ball to the batter.
6. The batting order follows order of position number: 1 through 6, or pitcher through shortstop.
7. A baserunner cannot leave a base until the ball is hit.
8. All other situations are governed by the official softball rules (such as those found in the *NAGWS Softball Guide* or the *ASA Official Rules of Softball*).
9. Method of scoring:
   - For every offensive and defensive play you execute correctly, 1 point is credited to your team. For every error you commit, 1 point is subtracted from your team's score. The team with more points at the end of an equal number of half-innings of play is the winner. *Note*: The purpose of the game is to work on game concepts and the execution of skills during gamelike conditions. Therefore, performance points, not runs scored, determine which team does better.
   - Look over the Player Scoresheet (page 154) to see the kinds of actions that typically occur in this game, actions for which you can both earn and lose points. Use the Player Scoresheet to keep track of the points you contribute to your team's score. A Team Scoresheet is also provided so that each player's points can be tallied into the total team score.
   - When you are out in the field playing defense, you need to remember the plays you make and whether they were correctly executed. Then, when your team goes on offense, you should write down those defensive plays on the Player Scoresheet. When your team is at bat, you can easily keep a record of your offensive tallies.

Success Goal =

Your team scores more performance points than the other team ___

Make as few physical and mental errors as possible ___

Your score =

(#) ___ your score

(#) ___ team score

Grounders-Only T-Ball

Player Scoresheet

Name ______________________ **Position** ______________

Skill/concept	*Plus performance points*	*Minus performance points*
	(Score 1 point each occurrence)	
Offensive skills		
Hitting using the tee		
ground ball	______	______
fly ball	______	______
Baserunning		
overruns first base	______	______
rounds a base	______ ______	______
Defensive skills		
Fielding a ground ball	______	______
Overhand throw (not toss)	______	______
Catching a thrown ball	______	______
Game concepts		
Area coverage		
covers base	______	______
covers area	______	______
backs up play	______	______
Force play	______	______
Tag play	______	______
Baserunning	______	______

Grounders-Only T-Ball

Team Scoresheet

Position	**Player**	**Offense points**		**Defense points**		**Game concept points**		**Total team points**
		Plus	*Minus*	*Plus*	*Minus*	*Plus*	*Minus*	*(Plus-Minus)*
1.	______	___	___	___	___	___	___	______
2.	______	___	___	___	___	___	___	______
3.	______	___	___	___	___	___	___	______
4.	______	___	___	___	___	___	___	______
5.	______	___	___	___	___	___	___	______
6.	______	___	___	___	___	___	___	______
							Team score	______

Position-Play Half-Field Games

The next two modified games use the skills of position play, ground ball and fly ball fielding, fungo hitting (or soft-toss hitting), and baserunning. These games will require you to analyze each situation, anticipate the action of the other team, react as the play develops, and apply the teamwork skills you have acquired. This is where the real fun begins—putting together skills and strategy.

These modified games are for the purpose of practicing anticipation and reaction in as many different situations as possible. Play a different position every new inning of these modified games.

Try to "keep yourself in the game" for every play. Remember, no one is perfect. You can expect to make an occasional physical error, but you must forget it and concentrate on the next play. Mental errors also occur, and these are the errors you should overcome (not just brush off) quickly. Figure out why you made the error so that you won't make it again. Then get ready for the next pitch.

Warm-Up Before the Game Drills

Before beginning the warm-up drills, you should review the Position Play Keys to Success Checklist for covering and back-up responsibilities found in Step 6 (pages 89-90). These drills are good not only before regulation games, but also between "innings" of the games that follow in this step. You will be in a different position each inning; the drills give you practice at the throws, force plays, and tag plays that occur at each new position.

For these drills, you need 10 players if practicing for fast-pitch and 11 players for slow-pitch. Players start at every defensive position, including short fielder for slow-pitch. The extra player is a fungo hitter at home plate. Have a bucket of at least six balls near home plate (but out of the field of play).

Outfield Portion of Warm-Up

The fungo hitter begins by hitting three fly balls (unintentional grounders count) for each of the fielding situations given in the Outfield Warm-up Chart. The outfielder fields the ball and makes an overhand

Outfield Warm-up Chart

Fielder	Throws to	Covered by
Left fielder	Second base	Second baseman
Center fielder	Second base	Second baseman
Short fielder (in left center)	Second base	Second baseman
Right fielder	Second base	Shortstop
Short fielder (in right center)	Second base	Shortstop
Short fielder (in right center)	First base	First baseman
Right fielder	First base	First baseman
Center fielder	Third base	Third baseman
Short fielder (in left center)	Third base	Third baseman
Right fielder	Third base	Third baseman
Short fielder (in right center)	Third base	Third baseman
Left fielder	Home plate	Catcher
Short fielder	Home plate	Catcher
Center fielder	Home plate	Catcher
Right fielder	Home plate	Catcher

throw to the designated infielder and base. The covering infielder gets into position out of the baseline but in a direct line with the throw. The infielder responsible for back-up must move into position behind the covering infielder and directly in line with the throw.

After completing this warm-up, only the outfielders will practice a combination drill of soft-toss hitting (or in the case of fast-pitch, fungo hitting) and fielding. Two outfielders (as tosser and hitter) or a single fungo hitter position themselves on the left-field foul line with a bat and a bucket of 10 balls. The other two outfielders position themselves in center field, facing the hitter and tosser, with an empty bucket for fielded balls.

The hitter either fungo hits or hits the tosser's soft toss to the outfielders. The outfielders alternate fielding the balls, the second outfielder backing up the play.

After five hits, the tosser and the hitter switch roles. After 10 hits, the tosser and hitter exchange roles with the outfielders. When there are only three people in the drill, one of the outfielders comes in to exchange places with the fungo hitter. The outfielder(s) brings the bucket with the 10 balls to the hitting location; the hitter and tosser or fungo hitter take the empty bucket to the outfield. The outfielders repeat the drill until the infield portion of the warm-up drill (following) is completed.

Infield Portion of Warm-Up

The fungo hitter now hits two consecutive ground balls for each of the situations in the Infield Warm-up Chart. The fielding infielder delivers the ball overhand to the infielder covering the base, who should be positioned on the side of the base from which the

Infield Warm-up Chart

Fielder	Throws to	Covering infielder
Third baseman	First base	First baseman
Shortstop	First base	First baseman
Second baseman	First base	First baseman
Pitcher	First base	First baseman
Catcher (ball rolled not far from HP)	First base	First baseman
First baseman (ball hit close to 1b)	First base	First baseman (runs to base)
First baseman (short hit)	First base	Second baseman
Third baseman	Second base	Second baseman
Shortstop	Second base	Second baseman
Second baseman	Second base	Shortstop
First baseman	Second base	Shortstop
Pitcher	Second base	Shortstop
Catcher (rolled ball)	Second base	Shortstop
Third baseman (ball hit close to 3b)	Third base	Third baseman (runs to base)
Third baseman (short hit)	Third base	Shortstop
Shortstop	Third base	Third baseman
Second baseman	Third base	Third baseman
First baseman	Third base	Third baseman
Pitcher	Third base	Third baseman

(continued)

Fielder	Throws to	Covering infielder
Catcher (rolled ball)	Third base	Third baseman
Third baseman	Home plate	Catcher
Shortstop	Home plate	Catcher
Second baseman	Home plate	Catcher
First baseman	Home plate	Catcher
Pitcher	Home plate	Catcher

throw is coming, and out of the base line. The baseman returns the ball to the catcher.

Before primary throws to home plate, the infielders assume the infield in position (see Step 6). This position is used in real games when the bases are loaded with less than two outs, or when the score of the game is close and a runner is on third base.

The fungo hitter goes through the chart two times, thus hitting a total of four ground balls for each situation. The first time through (two ground balls), the covering infielder should be positioned for a force-out; the second time through (two more), for a tag play.

Infield Warm-Up Return Throws

The fungo hitter now hits two consecutive balls for each situation in the Infield Warm-up Return Throws Chart. The infielder throws the ball to the first baseman, who immediately throws the ball to the catcher. The catcher then throws back to the infielder who originally fielded the fungo hit and who has moved into tag-play position on the base she is responsible for covering. The covering baseman immediately throws back to the catcher for a tag play at home plate. As the covering player, be in position to receive the ball at the base without being in the base line.

Infield Warm-up Return Throws Chart

Fielder	Throws to	Throws to	Throws to	Throws to
Third baseman (playing deep in slow-pitch, or in fast-pitch)	First baseman	Catcher	Third baseman	Catcher
Shortstop	First baseman	Catcher	Shortstop (covering 2b)	Catcher
Second baseman	First baseman	Catcher	Second baseman (covering 2b)	Catcher
First baseman (playing deep in slow-pitch)	Pitcher (covering 1b)	Catcher	First baseman (covering 1b)	Catcher
First baseman (playing in fast-pitch)	Second baseman (covering 1b)	Catcher	First baseman (covering 1b)	Catcher
Catcher	First baseman	Catcher		

These warm-up drills probably offer the best practice of position play and throwing to the bases for both force plays and for tag plays; in the future, you can add double plays just prior to the return-throw portion. It will profit you greatly to alternate infield and outfield positions on successive practices with this drill, making yourself a more versatile and proficient player.

Half-Field Games

There are two games in this section, one using the left side of the playing field (from the second baseman's fielding position to the left-field foul line), and the other using the right side (from the shortstop fielding position to the right-field foul line). Each game requires nine players, organized into three groups of three. In an inning, each of the three groups has a turn to score, and each turn is comprised of three outs. Thus an inning has three "half-innings" for a total of nine outs. Several rules are common to both games:

- A caught fly ball is an out.
- A person can be put out at a base by a force play or a tag play.
- Only the team running the bases can score. You must keep track of your group score.
- If the covering player blocks the base when a runner is approaching, the runner is safe, no matter what happens.
- A hit to the "wrong" side of the field (to right field in the left-side game, and to left field in the right-side game) is an automatic out.

Left Side of Field

Fair territory for this game is the area bounded by the left-field foul line and a line that extends from home plate to the outfield fence, passing through the second baseman's regular fielding position. One group of three players consists of a catcher, a fungo hitter, and a third baseman. A second group contains a center fielder, a left fielder, and a second baseman. The third group includes baserunners starting lined up at first base, with one person on the base and the others just outside the coaching box.

The game begins with one baserunner on first base. The fungo hitter, though belonging to a different team, is in the role of teammate of the baserunners. He hits the ball (either fly or grounder) to any place on the field of play (remember that this game uses only the left side of the field). When you are the fungo hitter, think about where to place the ball to help the lead runner advance. (*Hint:* Hit the ball away from the base to which the lead runner wants to advance. Also, try to hit a line drive so that an infielder cannot get to the ball.)

The runner runs to second base on a grounder or tags up on a fly ball. The runner must decide whether to try to advance on a fly ball. The defensive players can make a play on the baserunner.

In any case, if the baserunner is forced or tagged out, it is an out on the running team. If the baserunner makes it safely to second base (or farther), the ball goes to the catcher at home. A second runner moves to first base. Play continues with the fungo hitter again hitting the ball and the fielders making plays on the lead and following runner.

The object of the game is for the baserunners to score as many runs as possible (get all the way to home plate safely) before there are three outs. The defense (infielders, outfielders, and catcher) work together to get three outs on the baserunners as quickly as possible.

After three outs, the baserunners rotate to the outfield and second-base positions. The outfielders and second baseman rotate to the hitter, catcher, and third-baseman positions. The hitter, catcher, and third baseman become the baserunners. Every inning, rotate roles within your group so that by the end of the game you will have played every position. In doing so, you will play at least a three-inning game (27 outs).

Success Goal =

Your group scores more runs than either of the other groups ___

Make as few physical and mental errors as possible ___

Your score =

Team	Runs, inning			Final score	Problems and noticeable improvements
	1	2	3		

Right Side of Field

Fair territory for this game is the area bounded by the right-field foul line, and a line extending from home plate to the outfield fence that passes through the shortstop's regular fielding position. There are three groups of three players. One group is comprised of a fungo hitter, third baseman, and first baseman. A second group is set up as shortstop, center fielder, and right fielder. The third group is the baserunning group, now located at home plate.

The game begins with a runner at first base and one at home plate. The fungo hitter hits the ball anywhere on the modified playing field. When the ball is hit, the runner at home plate runs to first base as the batter-baserunner. If the hit is a caught fly ball, the batter-baserunner is out and returns to home plate and goes to the end of the baserunner line.

The runner on first base, meanwhile, runs to second base on a grounder or tags up on a fly ball. The defensive players attempt to make a play on the lead runner. Once an out is made or play has stopped (the baserunners are safe at their bases), the ball is rolled back to the fungo hitter. Play then continues with the fungo hitter hitting another ball.

The object of this game is for the baserunners to score a "run" by advancing to third base (not home). The object of the game for the defensive players, again, is to get three outs on the baserunners as quickly as possible. Rotation is similar to the left-side game, and this game is also three innings long.

Another offensive strategy that can be practiced in this game is called *hitting behind the runner.* With a runner on first base only and less than two outs, the hitter tries to hit a line drive to right field. The baserunner rounds second base and tries to get to third base on the hit to right field.

Success Goal =

Your group scores more runs than either of the other groups ___

Make as few physical and mental errors as possible ___

Your score =

Team	Runs, inning			Final score	Problems and noticeable improvements
	1	2	3		

Situation Ball

The modified game Situation Ball requires you to make judgments about *how* and *when* to use the various skill responses and game concepts you have developed to date. Because the game play will be more controlled than in a regulation game, you will have more time to prepare yourself both physically and mentally for each of the situations.

Be confident on both defense and offense. As a defensive player, always concentrate on each situation, focus on the roles you may play, and anticipate what your responses should be, especially regarding covering and backing up. The Keys to Success Checklist for reading a defensive situation (see page 162) suggests factors that you should quickly run through in your mind before each pitch in every situation. Your answers to these questions will provide the basis for you to decide which responses you could use in a given situation. The response you actually use when the ball is hit will be a matter of instantaneously selecting the *best* option, based on your on-the-spot judgment about the exact nature of the hit ball and the unfolding of the baserunning.

You also need to concentrate and plan ahead as a batter. Before you step into the batter's box, you must evaluate the situation and anticipate what you are going to try to do as the hitter. The Keys to Success Checklist for reading an offensive situation (see page 163) lists factors to think about to make informed decisions in any situation. Your initial decision is to determine the major objective of the situation: to get on base, to advance a runner, or to score a runner. Your next step is just like the defensive player's: Determine the options you have for accomplishing the major objective. Next, read the positioning of the defense to determine your *best* possible option.

Although the batter figures out what to do even before stepping up to the plate, both baserunners and defensive players must wait until the ball is hit to make their *final* decisions on plans of action. This is why anticipation is so important for these players. As a baserunner, you usually do not have too many options. If you are in a force situation, you must run on a grounder; if you cannot be forced, you need to make judgments based on all the things listed in the Keys to Success Checklist for reading an offensive situation. Be aware of applicable rules, anticipate, read the defense, and think of your potential responses. Once the ball is hit, there is only enough time to select the *best* action to take. Hopefully, your prior analysis of the situation and of your options provides you with a successful response.

What to Practice

In a regulation softball game, it may be very difficult to get experience with a specific situation, because that situation may never present itself in the game! For example, say you and the other outfielders on your team feel that you all need work on throwing out a runner tagging up and trying to score on a fly ball. However, if your opponents never have a runner on third base with less than two outs (or, if they do, the batter doesn't hit a fly ball), you won't get a chance to practice that type of throw. With Situation Ball, though, you can set almost any situation to practice. If you'd like, the offensive team must try to hit a sacrifice fly.

Look over the following list of game components that you can select to work on in Situation Ball.

1. Basic skills
   - Pitching
   - Hitting the pitched ball
   - Fielding ground balls
   - Fielding fly balls
   - Throwing overhand
   - Catching the ball
   - Baserunning
2. Game concepts
   - Position-play area coverage
   - Position-play covering and backing-up responsibilities
   - The force play
   - The tag play
   - Baserunning
   - Advancing a runner via base hit, place-hitting, error, fielder's choice, base on balls (walk), sacrifice fly, tag after a caught fly ball (fair and foul)
3. Knowledge of rules
   - Fair ball and foul ball
   - Pitching regulations
   - Batting regulations
   - Ways a batter may be put out
   - Ways a baserunner may be put out
   - In play, out of play

- Infield fly
- Regulation game, innings
4. Safety concerns
   - Use of equipment
   - The playing area

How to Play

The following rules and method of playing the game have been established to both facilitate play and ensure that opportunities are presented to work on specific offensive and defensive situations under gamelike conditions. Prior to the start of the game, members of each team should get together and decide on a specified number of offensive and defensive situations the teams want to work on. (The number of situations specified will depend on the anticipated number of innings to be played.) Determine the order for selection of situations to be practiced (for example, Team A selects the situation for the odd-number innings and Team B selects for the even-number innings). Teams should check with each other to see that similar situations are not repeated. Examples of situations you can practice include the following.

- Runner on first base, no outs, 1 out, 2 outs
- Runner on second base, no outs, 1 out, 2 outs
- Runner on third base, no outs, 1 out, 2 outs
- Runners on first and second base, no outs, 1 out, 2 outs
- Runners on first and third base, no outs, 1 out, 2 outs
- Runners on second and third base, no outs, 1 out, 2 outs
- Bases loaded, no outs, 1 out, 2 outs

Until you get familiar with the Keys to Success Checklist for reading the offensive and defensive situations, it would be helpful to put them on an index card to keep in your pocket and review from time to time. During Situation Ball, new game situations will undoubtedly arise as plays unfold. Keep a list of those different game situations so that you will remember to practice them another day. It also helps you develop your anticipation and reaction skills to note the situations that continue to give you trouble. Mentally practice these situations to acquire an edge the next time you play Situation Ball or a regulation game.

Specific rules of the game and method of playing the game are listed here:

1. Use the regulation field of play. You must establish ground rules for out-of-play areas.
2. Teams are either slow-pitch teams with 10 players or fast-pitch teams with 9 players, one at each official position for the game being played.
3. The batting order will follow position numbers 1 through 9 (10). In other words, starting with the pitcher (position 1) as the first batter, progress to the right fielder in fast-pitch (position 9), or to the short fielder in slow-pitch (position 10) as last batter. The player(s) who made the last out(s) in an inning serves as baserunner(s) for the situation setup in the next inning.
4. Both teams' half-innings of a single inning start with the same specified situation setup. For example, the first inning for each team starts with the last batter (9 or 10) as a runner on first base. The team that is first up in the inning stays at bat until three outs have been made. The team that started the inning on defense then comes to bat and sets up the same situation, and plays until making three outs. At the start of the second inning, a new situation is established. Because each team has the opportunity to play through the same situation as the other, it is important that complete innings are played.
5. All play is governed by the official softball rules for either slow-pitch or fast-pitch once the situation to start the half-inning has been established.

READING A SITUATION KEYS TO SUCCESS CHECKLISTS

The Keys to Success Checklists outline aspects of both the defensive and offensive situations that you as a player need to mentally check off before each pitch. At first glance, the lists look long. However, as you work with this mental exercise in a modified game, you will find the task easier than it looks. For example, when you take the field as a defensive player, you know the inning and the score of the game before you get to your position. You answer the questions about the batter before the batter gets into the box. Determine the number of outs, position of runners on base, and the ball-and-strike count on the batter during the inning. The answers to those questions *must* run through your mind before every pitch. As the batter, you answer most of the check items before you step into the batter's box. The same is true if you are a baserunner.

Reading a Defensive Situation

1. What inning is it?	1 ___ 2 ___ 3 ___ 4 ___ 5 ___ 6 ___ 7 ___ ___ ___		
2. What is the score of the game?	Visitor ___	Home ___	
3. How many outs are there?	0 outs ___	1 out ___	2 outs ___
4. Runners on what bases?	First ___	Second ___	Third ___
5. Speed of the runners on base?	Fast ___	Slow ___	at first
	Fast ___	Slow ___	at second
	Fast ___	Slow ___	at third
6. Who is the batter?			
a. right- or left-handed hitter?	Right ___	Left ___	
b. running speed?	Fast ___	Slow ___	
c. strong pull hitter?	Yes ___	No ___	
d. line-drive hitter?	Yes ___	No ___	
e. longball hitter?	Yes ___	No ___	
f. contact hitter?	Yes ___	No ___	
g. can hit to opposite field?	Yes ___	No ___	
h. can hit with power to opposite field?	Yes ___	No ___	
i. good bunter (FP)?	Yes ___	No ___	
7. What is the ball-and-strike count?	Balls ___	Strikes ___	
8. How does pitcher like to pitch to the batter?	Inside ___	Outside ___	
	High ___	Low ___	

Reading an Offensive Situation

1. What inning is it?	1 ___ 2 ___ 3 ___ 4 ___ 5 ___ 6 ___ 7 ___ ___ ___
2. What is the score of the game?	Visitor ____ Home ____
3. How many outs are there?	0 outs ____ 1 out ____ 2 outs ____
4. Runners on what bases?	First ____ Second ____ Third ____
5. Speed of the runners on base?	Fast ____ Slow ____ at first
	Fast ____ Slow ____ at second
	Fast ____ Slow ____ at third
6. Major objective for batter?	Get on base ____
	Sacrifice bunt (FP) ____
	Advance the runner(s) ____
	Score runner(s) ____
	Sacrifice fly ____
7. What is the ball-and-strike count?	____ Balls ____ Strikes
8. Positioning of the outfield defense?	Playing straightaway ____
	Shifted to left ____
	Shifted to right ____
	SF aligned with LF, CF, and RF (SP) ____
	SF in front of LF, CF, and RF in
	L ____ C ____ R ____ area (SP)
	Largest gap(s) at
	LF foul line ____
	left center ____
	right center ____
	RF foul line ____
	Strongest arm at
	LF ____ CF ____ RF ____ SF ____
	Weakest arm at
	LF ____ CF ____ RF ____ SF ____
9. Positioning of the infield defense?	Regular depth ____
	Infield in ____
	Double-play depth ____
	Bunt defense: first and third in ____ (FP)
	Bunt defense: first in, third back ____ (FP)
	Bunt defense: first back, third in ____ (FP)

(continued)

9. Positioning of the infield defense? *(continued)*	3b shifted toward SS ____ third ____
	deep ____ shallow ____
	SS shifted toward second ____ third ____
	deep ____ shallow ____
	2b shifted toward second ____ first ____
	deep ____ shallow ____
	1b shifted toward second ____ first ____
	deep ____ shallow ____
	Strongest arm at
	P ____ C ____ 1b ____ 2b ____ 3b ____ SS ____
	Weakest arm at
	P ____ C ____ 1b ____ 2b ____ 3b ____ SS ____

Scrub and One-Pitch Modified Games

The preceding modified game play provided you with opportunities to respond to predetermined game situations in controlled settings. They were designed to give you specific offensive and defensive situations to work on in gamelike conditions. You had the advantage of knowing in advance the particular strategy or technique that you would be called upon to use. The rules were designed to increase the number of opportunities you had during the game to execute a particular technique.

The modified games of Scrub and One-Pitch are less controlled and more like a regulation game. The situations that come up in each of these games result naturally from your play and the play of the others participating in the game. Thus, if no one gets on first base with fewer than two outs, you will not be able to work on the second-to-first double play. You now must recognize situations as they spontaneously occur and be able to effectively respond both mentally and physically.

These final two games are modified to only a limited extent, primarily to increase participation. In Scrub, the rules of regulation softball are modified in order to allow you to play different defensive positions. One-Pitch is played like a regulation game, with the exception of some new pitching rules that speed up the game so that you can be more active. The official rules govern the remainder of the play situations in both games. Thus, you can continue to develop your knowledge and understanding of the rules of the game. Also, review and use the defensive and offensive checklists from Situation Ball to enhance your softball game sense as you participate in these games.

You may play a game for a variety of reasons. Having fun, enjoying the company of others, and soaking up the rays are all legitimate reasons for playing softball. However, playing a game can also be looked upon as a test of sorts. Although we may not always think of tests in a positive light, a softball game can be a fun test. It is a chance for you to see what you can do with the skills and knowledge you have learned. The game skills of hitting a ball, running the bases, fielding ground balls, making a force-out on a baserunner, and so forth can provide challenges for you to self-test.

As you play the modified games, list the skills you know and execute with ease and success. Also, list the skills with which you have difficulty. The problem areas should become your focal points as you play additional innings in these games and as you play future games. Your weak areas can become your strengths. To make this happen, however, you need to recognize your problem skills and concepts, and then work hard to master them. A complete softball player executes the skills proficiently and knows what every game situation calls for (review the game components previously outlined in Situation Ball).

Scrub

Scrub is a good game to play when you do not have enough players for two full teams. It is also a good game for increasing your understanding of the total game, because it requires you to play all of the defensive positions.

Rules of Scrub and Method of Play

The following rules govern the method of play.

1. Use the regulation field of play. You must establish ground rules (that apply only to a given field and game) for out-of-play areas.
2. The participating group should number between 13 (FP) or 14 (SP) and 15 (FP) or 16 (SP). A full defensive team starts in the field, and the remainder start as the team at bat.
3. A player remains in the group at bat until she makes an out. A player hitting a ball that is caught in the air by a fielder (a fly ball, pop-up, or line drive) exchanges places with *that* fielder before play continues. The fielder comes in to join the group at bat and hits at the end of the batting order. A player (either batter or baserunner) making an out on any other kind of play goes out into right field in fast-pitch or short field in slow-pitch. All fielders then rotate to the next lower numbered position—10 to 9, 9 to 8, and so on. Remember, shortstop is 6, so the left fielder (7) rotates into the infield there, not to third base (5). The shortstop (6) rotates to third base (5), not around the infield to second base (4). The pitcher (1) moves in to the end of the batting order of the group at bat.
4. After three outs have been made, clear the bases of runners and start a new half-inning. Remember, players remain on the team at bat until making an out.

Scoring

There can actually be no team score in Scrub. Scoring, if desired, must be oriented toward the individual player. For example, keep track of the offensive statistics of each person: the number of times at bat; the number of base hits (singles, doubles, triples, and home runs); the number of walks; and the number of runs scored. At the end of a predetermined amount of time, winners are declared in each category. Use the Offensive Player Scorecard to record your score for this game.

Offensive Player Scorecard

Name ____________________

Times at bat	_____	×	1	point	=	_____	points
Walks	_____	×	1	point	=	_____	points
Runs scored	_____	×	2	points	=	_____	points
Base hits							
Singles	_____	×	2	points	=	_____	points
Doubles	_____	×	3	points	=	_____	points
Triples	_____	×	4	points	=	_____	points
Home runs	_____	×	5	points	=	_____	points
				Total	=	_____	points

If you wish to keep track of your individual defensive play, you can make a scorecard of defensive skills and concepts, such as the Defensive Player Scorecard. You know best just what you want to work on, so adapt your scorecard to reflect this.

Defensive Player Scorecard

Name ____

Number of fielding attempts

ground balls	(#) ____ attempts	(#) ____ successes	×	2	=	____	points
fly balls	(#) ____ attempts	(#) ____ successes	×	1	=	____	points

Number of throwing plays

(#) ____	attempts					
(#) ____	on-target	×	1	=	____	points
(#) ____	to proper position	×	2	=	____	points

Number of covering and backing-up plays

(#) ____	correct covers	×	2	=	____	points
(#) ____	correct back-ups	×	2	=	____	points
(#) ____	incorrect covers or back-ups	×	-1	=	____	points

Number of pitches thrown (if 50 percent of pitches are strikes, add 2 points)

(#) ____ balls	(#) ____ strikes	×	1	=	____	points
			Total	=	____	points

You can use these scorecards in Scrub and in all softball games that you play. If you analyze the scorecards after you play, they can indicate your physical and mental levels of play. If you see areas in which scores are not satisfactory, challenge yourself to work harder on those areas next time you play.

One-Pitch

One-Pitch is played exactly like a regulation game, except that the batter is allowed only one pitch per time at bat: if the pitch is a ball, the batter walks; if the pitch is a strike, the batter must swing. This pitching-rule modification speeds up the game.

One-Pitch provides you with opportunities for practicing all softball skills and game concepts. You might review the scorecards you used in Scrub. If there are any particular skills or concepts in which you are weak, concentrate on them when relevant situations occur in the game. Anticipate the actions that might be called for by each situation; then your reaction is likely to be appropriate.

It will help you become more versatile if you play different positions during the game. Do not be afraid to change positions. In fact, you can become very skillful and knowledgeable by practicing *all* the infield and outfield positions, and don't forget the pitcher and catcher positions. You know the old saying, "Try it, you'll like it!"

Rules of One-Pitch and Method of Play

The following rules govern the method of play.

1. Use the regulation field of play. You must establish ground rules for out-of-play areas.
2. Use official teams in terms of the number of people on a team and the positions played.
3. Official rules govern play, except that the pitcher delivers one pitch per batter, with the following results:
   - If the pitch is a ball and the batter does not swing at it, the batter gets a walk (base on balls).
   - If the pitch is a strike and the batter does not swing, the batter is out on a strikeout.
   - If the batter fouls off the pitch, the batter is out.
   - If the batter hits the pitched ball fair, the hit ball is played out.

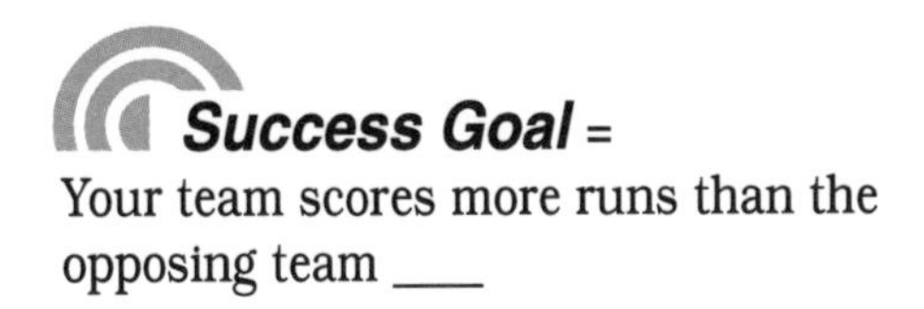

Success Goal =
Your team scores more runs than the opposing team ___

Your score =
(#) ___ your team's score
(#) ___ opposing team's score

MODIFIED GAMES SUCCESS SUMMARY

These modified games have given you the opportunity to execute all of the skills and strategies used in the game of softball under both controlled and real game conditions. The various charts have outlined for you the game concepts and the responsibilities that various players have in given situations. The cognitive aspect is probably the most difficult part of the game of softball to master, and it can only be practiced in game or modified game settings. Your participation in these modified games is a means for you to increase your ability to read and react spontaneously to game situations. By now you have mastered some skills and know the areas of weakness that demand your continued practice. The only experience left for you now is to become a member of a team and play in an "official" competitive game; that is, of course, if you have not already done so! Pair up with another player, and use the Offensive and Defensive Scorecards to evaluate each others' play in either a modified or real game. Continue to play and enjoy the satisfaction that comes from getting a hit, making a throw to the proper base, and sliding into home with the winning run!

STEP 10 COED SLOW-PITCH GAME

Because this book has been designed both for your individual use and for use in instructional settings, this final step presents, for your participation and enjoyment, one of the official games that is particularly appropriate for class use. Most classes today are coeducational, with females and males learning and participating together. To facilitate play in coed settings, specific rules have been developed for coed slow-pitch softball. However, only the basic rules are presented here. You will need to refer to an official rulebook for a description of the complete set of rules.

Why Is Coed Slow-Pitch Softball Important?

Participation in coed softball takes place in a setting that is reflective of society. Males and females working together toward a common goal is an everyday occurrence in the workplace and in the family, but usually not so in sport, especially team sports. Softball is one of the few team sports (volleyball being another) that has an official game designed specifically for coed play. Coed softball thus provides class and recreational play opportunities in which women and men can learn to work together and develop respect for one another's abilities. In 1981, the ASA added a coed slow-pitch tournament to its offerings of national championships. Currently, the coed game is one of the fastest-growing versions of the game of softball. Whether you have aspirations of playing in a national championship or playing with friends in a local league, opportunities abound for young and not-so-young adults to participate in the game of coed slow-pitch softball.

The prerequisites for playing coed slow-pitch include skill proficiency, decision-making ability in the strategies of game play, and the ability to participate in accordance with the rules of play. Most of the skills and knowledge that you have worked so hard to develop over the past nine steps (remember, no stealing or bunting in slow-pitch) are now put to use in an official game between two teams. There are no special rules to ensure that you have ample opportunity to practice a particular skill or utilize a specific game concept. This game is for real! It can be a part of a tournament, or, as the students in the class, you can direct the focus of the game each day to be playing with friends, playing for "fun," or even working on certain aspects of the game.

As you undoubtedly noticed before you were far along on your climb up the Steps to Success staircase, softball is not a game that can be played alone. It isn't even very easy to practice the individual skills alone. You can play catch with yourself using a wall, hit a ball off a tee, or run around the bases all by yourself, but only for a short time. Others had to join you on your climb up the staircase if, indeed, you were to make much progress in your quest to become a skillful softball player. Softball is a team sport, and the ultimate in enjoyment occurs when two teams take the field together and challenge one another's skill and knowledge in game situations.

Rules and Method of Play

Uniforms and a freshly lined field are not a prerequisite for your enjoyment of a class version of coed softball, but teams made up of five females and five males are a must. Most of the rules that you have learned for slow-pitch softball are applicable to the coed game. Some of the rules that specifically apply to the coed game follow.

1. Use a regulation field of play. You must establish ground rules for out-of-play areas.
   - Baseline distances: 65 feet for adults, and girls and boys (youths) 13 to 18 years old; 60 feet

for youths 11 and 12 years old; 55 feet for youths 10 years and younger.

- Pitching distances: 50 feet for adults and youths 13 to 18 years old; 40 feet for youths 11 and 12 years old; and 35 feet for youths 10 years and younger.

2. Defensive positioning must include five females and five males.
   - Outfield: two females and two males in any of the four positions.
   - Infield: two females and two males in any of the four positions.
   - Pitcher and catcher: one female and one male in either position.
3. Adhere to the batting rules.
   - Batting order alternates between the genders.
   - Walk (base on balls) to a male batter: the batter is awarded two bases, and, if there are two outs, the next batter (a female) may choose between an automatic walk or hitting before stepping into the batter's box. *Note*: this is the official rule, which could be modified (or even not used) in an unofficial class game, if desired. The official rule's purpose is to prevent the pitcher from intentionally walking the male batters in order to have to pitch only to female batters.
4. Keep score.
   - Official rules concerning scoring runs and deciding the winner apply. The team with the most runs wins the game.

Enjoy the game!

RATING YOUR PROGRESS

Throughout this book you have been working on developing both the physical skills needed for softball and the psychological preparation for play. The following self-rating inventory is provided so that you can rate your overall progress. Read the statements carefully and respond to them thoughtfully.

Physical Skills

The first general success goal is to acquire the physical skills needed to practice and to play the game of softball. How would you rate yourself on these skills?

	Very Good	Good	Okay	Poor
Catching	______	______	______	______
Throwing overhand	______	______	______	______
Fielding ground balls	______	______	______	______
Hitting using the batting tee	______	______	______	______
Fungo hitting ground balls	______	______	______	______
Pitching	______	______	______	______
Baserunning	______	______	______	______
Overrunning the base	______	______	______	______
Rounding the base	______	______	______	______
Fielding fly balls	______	______	______	______
Hitting a soft toss	______	______	______	______
Tossing for soft toss	______	______	______	______
Fungo hitting fly balls	______	______	______	______
Hitting a pitched ball	______	______	______	______
Sidearm throwing	______	______	______	______
Detecting your errors	______	______	______	______
Correcting your errors	______	______	______	______
Detecting your partner's errors	______	______	______	______
Helping your partner correct errors	______	______	______	______

Game Concept Skills

The second general success goal is utilizing your game-concept skills to improve your game play. How would you rate your physical and mental abilities to utilize the following to your advantage?

	Physical	Mental	Physical	Mental	Physical	Mental	Physical	Mental
Position play as an infielder								
Covering								
Backing up								
Position play as an outfielder								
Covering								
Backing up								
Force play								
Tag play								
Double plays								
Shortstop drag step								
Shortstop inside pivot								
Second-baseman crossover								
Second-baseman rocker								
Third to first								
Home to first								
Relays								
Cutoffs								
Rundowns (defensive)								
Rundowns (offensive)								
Rules of play								
Do you know the rules?								
Do you play by them?								

Overall Softball Progress

Considering all the factors you rated above, how would you rate your softball progress?

____ Very successful

____ Successful

____ Barely successful

____ Unsuccessful

Are you pleased with your progress?

____ Very pleased

____ Pleased

____ Somewhat pleased

____ Not pleased

Additional Comments and Questions

Look back over your self-ratings. What are your strengths and weaknesses? Are you willing to spend time to improve your game? Where do you want to go from here?

If you have made some improvement and feel comfortable in at least some aspects of the game, you should feel good about those accomplishments. The real rewards for becoming skillful do not always come in the form of trophies or plaques, but rather in the way you feel about yourself. That is what this game (or any game) is really all about. Helping you develop some skill and knowledge—so that you can have fun, meet some new and interesting people, and enjoy yourself when playing softball—is the goal of this book.

GLOSSARY

ball—A pitch that does not enter the strike zone.

base on balls—A batter gains first base when four pitches judged to be balls are delivered to the batter during a turn at bat; also called a *walk.*

base path—An area 6 feet wide running between the bases, the center of which is a direct line from base to base.

baserunner—A player on the offensive team who has reached first base safely.

batter-baserunner—A player who has finished her turn at bat and has not yet reached first base.

bunt—A ball intentionally tapped with the bat and meant to go a short distance within the infield. (Legal in fast-pitch softball only.)

catch—A ball caught by a fielder in the bare hand or the glove.

chopped ball—An illegal hitting technique in slow-pitch softball; the batter hits the ball with a short downward swing.

coed softball—An official game of softball played by teams made up of five men and five women, positioned so that two men and two women are in the outfield, two men and two women are in the infield, and one man and one woman pitch and catch.

defensive team—The team in the field.

double—A two-base hit.

double play—A play by the defense in which two offensive players are put out by continuous action.

fair ball—A batted ball that is touched or comes to rest in fair territory in the infield; that touches first, second, or third bases; that is touched or first lands on or over fair territory in the outfield (beyond first, second, or third base).

fair territory—That part of the playing field between the first- and third-base foul lines, including home plate.

fast-pitch softball—An official game of softball, played by teams of nine players, in which the underhand pitch is delivered to the batter with considerable speed.

fly ball—A batted ball that goes into the air.

foul ball—A batted ball that is touched or comes to rest in foul territory in the infield; that is touched or first lands on or over foul territory in the outfield (beyond first or third base).

foul territory—That part of the playing field between the first- and third-base foul lines and the out-of-play area surrounding the field.

foul tip—A batted ball that goes no higher than the batter's head, directly back to (and is caught by) the catcher.

ground ball—A batted ball that is hit directly onto the ground; a *grounder.*

ground rule—A rule of play typically established to identify the boundaries of a field (especially out-of-play areas) for a playing field that is not an enclosed ballpark.

ground-rule double—A base hit that, because of going into an out-of-play area, limits the batter to two bases.

home team—The team upon whose field the game is played.

infield—That area of the playing field in fair territory typically covered by infielders for most softball fields; it is the area of the playing field that is dirt, or "skinned."

inning—That portion of a game in which each team has three outs while on offense and three on defense; a softball game is seven innings long.

line drive—A fly ball that travels into the playing field relatively parallel to the ground.

middle line of knuckles—The batting-grip knuckle alignment in which the second knuckles of the fingers of both hands are lined up one over the other in a straight line.

offensive team—The team at bat.

outfield—That area of the playing field in fair territory beyond the infield.

overthrow—A thrown ball that goes beyond the intended receiver; in rules terminology, it is a thrown ball that goes into foul territory or out of play.

pop fly—A fly ball hit in the infield area; a *pop-up.*

runner—A term used synonymously with *baserunner* and *batter-baserunner.*

slow-pitch softball—An official game of softball played by teams of 10 players, in which the pitch must be delivered underhand and must traverse an arc between 6 and 12 feet.

strikeout—Occurs when the batter swings at and misses, or fails to swing at, a third strike.

strike zone—In fast-pitch, that area over home plate between the batter's armpits and the top of the knees; in slow-pitch, that area over home plate between the batter's highest shoulder and the knees.

ABOUT THE AUTHORS

Diane L. Potter

Gretchen A. Brockmeyer

Diane L. Potter, EdD, is professor of physical education at Springfield College in Springfield, Massachusetts. A teacher with over 40 years of experience in physical education, Dr. Potter also coached the Springfield College softball team for 21 years. In addition, she was a player for 15 years in Amateur Softball Association (ASA) Class A Fast-Pitch.

Potter has been an international clinician in softball, conducting clinics in Italy and The Netherlands and taking teams to The Netherlands in 1971, 1975, and 1982. In 1982, she was awarded the Silver Medallion by the Koninklijke Nederlandse Baseball en Softball Bond (the Royal Dutch Baseball and Softball Association); she is the only woman so honored.

Dr. Potter is an outstanding leader in women's sport; she has served as a member of the AIAW Ethics and Eligibility Committee and was inducted into the National Association of Collegiate Directors of Athletics Hall of Fame in 1986.

Gretchen A. Brockmeyer, EdD, is Vice President for Academic Affairs at Springfield College. She has been a teacher-educator for over 20 years, with primary responsibility for secondary physical education methods and supervision of field-based teaching.

An inductee to the Luther College Athletic Hall of Fame, Brockmeyer has applied her coaching talents to many sports beyond softball, including swimming, basketball, field hockey, and tennis. In 1990, she was named the College Level Teacher of the Year by the Eastern District Association for Health, Physical Education, Recreation and Dance.

Brockmeyer served as assistant coach for the Springfield College softball team for seven years. She is committed to helping her students become physical educators who possess the skills and the professional commitment necessary to provide meaningful learning opportunities for those they teach.